I SANK THE BISMARCK

www.**rbooks**.co.uk

I SANK THE BISMARCK

John Moffat

with Mike Rossiter

BANTAM PRESS

LONDON • TORONTO • SYDNEY • AUCKLAND • JOHANNESBURG

TRANSWORLD PUBLISHERS
61–63 Uxbridge Road, London W5 5SA
A Random House Group Company
www.rbooks.co.uk

First published in Great Britain
in 2009 by Bantam Press
an imprint of Transworld Publishers

A CIP catalogue record for this book
is available from the British Library.

ISBN 9780593063521 (cased)
9780593063514 (tpb)

Addresses for Random House Group Ltd companies outside the UK
can be found at: www.randomhouse.co.uk
The Random House Group Ltd Reg. No. 954009

The Random House Group Limited supports The Forest Stewardship
Council (FSC), the leading international forest-certification organization. All our
titles that are printed on Greenpeace-approved FSC-certified paper carry the FSC logo.
Our paper procurement policy can be found at
www.rbooks.co.uk/environment

Typeset in 11.75/15pt Sabon by
Falcon Oast Graphic Art Ltd.
Printed and bound in Great Britain by
CPI Mackays, Chatham, ME5 8TD

2 4 6 8 10 9 7 5 3 1

Mixed Sources
Product group from well-managed
forests and other controlled sources
www.fsc.org Cert no. TT-COC-2139
FSC © 1996 Forest Stewardship Council

John Moffat would like to dedicate this book to the memory of his lovely wife Marjorie, who shared his life for 58 years; their two daughters Pat and Jan, who encouraged him to write about his life; and his four grandchildren, Nicole, Amanda, Ian and Valerie.

Mike Rossiter would like to thank the Headmaster of Kelso High School, and the former crew members of HMS *Ark Royal* for their help in researching this book. Also the assistance of his agent Luigi Bonomi, editor Simon Thorogood, and copy-editor Brenda Updegraff are gratefully acknowledged.

Contents

Contents

Introduction

I slid the canopy of my Grumman single-engined aeroplane shut and tightened my safety harness, then pushed the yoke forward so that I could turn to the passenger seat to see if Ian needed any help to strap himself in properly. He was a smart lad, but he was just nine years old. I wanted to make sure he was safe.

'Are you OK, lad?' I asked him.

'Yes, Grandad, I'm fine.'

It was a lovely September evening in the year 2000. I was eighty-one years old and had brought up two daughters, but now I had a grandson, and I loved him. It was funny how life turned out. He had just started playing rugby at school and I had given him a few tips that his mother thought were more suited to the adult game than to a prep-school team, but he was coming on a treat.

I looked through the windscreen: some slight cloud cover, with a south-westerly wind of about 5 knots. We were on a small grass airfield on the Isle of Bute, with a runway length of 1,300 feet. We were about 1,730lb in weight and should be able to take off in about 800 feet, giving us plenty of room.

I made sure the handbrake was on, then pressed the starter

motor. The Lycoming engine turned over, once, twice, three times, then it fired up. The twin-bladed propeller became a blur in front of the engine cowling and I waited for the temperature and the oil pressure to stabilize. Everything looked fine. I released the handbrake, eased a touch on the throttle, and the plane moved forward, trundling over the grass to the end of the strip.

I was going to make what is called a performance take-off, which I think is the safest option. You hold the plane on the brakes until the engine is running at full power, then you release the brakes and take off in half the recommended distance. Grumman's handbook for the AA-5 suggests taking off with no flap – the sections at the rear of the wing that, if moved down, provide more lift – but you can get a higher rate of climb with 10 degrees of flap and so I selected this with the flap lever, then with the handbrake on again increased the revs to full power. The orange windsock hung loosely, barely extended in the light breeze. Everything was clear above and behind. I patted Ian on the knee and released the handbrake. We were lightly loaded, and the air-speed indicator quickly started rising.

We had rolled for about half our take-off distance when the engine started misfiring. The r.p.m. needle was bouncing up and down, and there were more misfires. We were travelling more slowly than we needed to be at this stage of the take-off, but we still had some distance left on the runway. I could keep going and hope that the engine would give us enough power to take off, but then I could be faced with having to crash straight ahead if it cut while we were struggling for height. I quickly decided that I was not going to risk it.

'Oh Christ, this would happen,' I thought. I cut the engine and tried to put on the brakes, but we were still moving at close to our lift-off speed. There was a hump in the grass strip at the end of the runway: we hit it, bounced up from it and rose into the air. Then we dropped again as the undercarriage hit the hedge.

'Hang on!' I shouted and put out my arm to protect Ian. Then, as clods of earth and grass hit the windows, we banged and scraped along, and finally smashed into a deep ditch.

The silence as we came to a halt was eerie. I was desperate to get Ian out in case we caught fire. The poor lad was sitting there, trying to gather himself together, and I undid his straps. The canopy still opened, thank God, so I slid it back and told him to get out and run to the edge of the field. Once he had gone, I slowly undid my own straps and climbed out. I couldn't move as fast as I would have liked, and I had been shaken about by the impact. Ian was looking at me anxiously, so I walked over to him and said as reassuringly as I could, 'Not to worry, son – we're fine.'

I didn't feel fine. I was shaken up and I knew that actually we were lucky not to have been hurt. The plane, which I co-owned, was damaged – how badly I didn't know at the time, and probably wouldn't until an engineer had had a good look at it. It might be a write-off. I didn't yet know why the engine had failed. As far as I was aware, there was no water in either the tank or the lines. There were bound to be gentle hints that maybe a man of my age should hang up his flying helmet, and similar talk.

All this was going through my mind – but, thank God, Ian was safe.

A couple of men came running from the airstrip, one of them carrying a fire extinguisher, and told me that they had called the Royal Naval Air Station (RNAS) rescue helicopter from the mainland and it should be here in a few minutes. It was too late to protest that we were really not hurt at all.

Sure enough, ten minutes later a Sea King helicopter swooped over us, its turbines whining and its rotors clattering. This would be a flight that Ian hadn't bargained for, and

I hoped it would be exciting enough to lessen the shock of our crash. The young winchman got out, looked us over, and said that he would take us to hospital for a check-up as a precaution. He lifted Ian in, then helped me up the steps into the cabin.

We lifted off, the young man sitting opposite us in his polished black flying boots and green flight overalls, a whippersnapper probably still in his twenties. While he talked to the pilot over his intercom, he was also looking at me slightly quizzically. I imagined he was probably thinking, 'What's an old crock like this doing trying to fly?' but then he said, 'I think you and I have met before, sir.'

I must say I couldn't place him, but ten minutes later he said, 'I know – we met when you were guest of honour at HMS Gannet for our Taranto Night dinner, sir.' HMS Gannet is the Fleet Air Arm air-sea rescue base at Prestwick airport. They, like other Fleet Air Arm bases, celebrate the attack on the Italian fleet moored in Taranto harbour on 11 November 1940, when twenty-one Fairey Swordfish torpedo bombers flew in and sank several Italian warships, inflicting as much damage as they might have suffered in a major sea battle. By the year 2000 very few of the thirty or so who had flown on that historic mission were still alive. I had not taken part in the raid on Taranto, but I had flown Swordfish aircraft in the Second World War, against the Italians in the Mediterranean and the Germans in the Atlantic, and as someone who knew what it was like, I was often asked to attend these annual celebrations.

'I certainly recognize you, sir,' the young man continued. 'You were one of those who hit the *Bismarck*.'

My hesitation must have shown, because he went on, 'You must remember, sir – that was the night that we set light to the piano.'

The wardroom had become rather raucous after the toasts

and, typically, someone had sat down at the piano and started playing tunes from the *Fleet Air Arm Song Book*, and we had sung away to our hearts' content. Some of the men had poured rum into the top of the piano and set light to it, and, as it was wheeled outside burning vigorously, others were pushing the pianist along with it and he was still playing away. It took me back to the days when, as a young sub-lieutenant, I was roused from my bunk to hammer out some tunes on the wardroom piano – but pianos were not easy to replace at sea during a war, so we refrained from setting light to ours. I enjoyed myself so much that night at HMS Gannet that I offered to help them pay for a new piano, but they wouldn't hear of it. 'We never spend much on a wardroom piano,' I was assured.

Our companion and I talked a bit about the dinner, then we landed at the hospital. The pilot and co-pilot also wanted to shake my hand and wish me luck, and then they were off.

Feeling my grandson's hand in mine, I looked down at him. 'Grandad,' he said, 'why were you at their dinner, and why did they set light to the piano?'

Where to start?

1
The Beginning

Looking back over eighty or more years to when I was a young child, younger even than my grandson when we crashed on the Isle of Bute, I cannot help but think that I grew up in another world entirely, one that has now completely vanished. It was slower, much quieter, it seemed infinitely safer, and of course the sun was always shining. This seems unlikely, I know, but there you are!

I spent my childhood in a part of the country known as the Scottish Borders – that bit of Scotland to the south of Edinburgh, close to Northumberland, along the northern border of England. My parents moved from town to town as my father's business dictated, with one brief stay among the 'Sassenachs' in County Durham.

Although I seemed to get into all sorts of scrapes, I enjoyed life; I remember the fun and excitement of various incidents rather than the tears that followed. At all events, two of the most important influences in my life were triggered by things that I first saw and experienced as a child growing up in southern Scotland.

I was born in a small village called Swinton, but my parents moved fairly soon, when I was still just a baby, to Earlston, where my father opened the town's first garage. It was here that I spent the extremely happy, by and large carefree, first years of my life.

My father, Peter, had served in the First World War, joining up in 1914 to qualify as an air engineer for the Royal Naval Air Service and then serving in No. 2 Wing RNAS under Commander Charles Sampson, who in 1912 had become the first man to fly a plane off a ship. My father saw part of the war in Belgium, then was posted to the seaplane carrier *Ark Royal*, which sailed for Gallipoli, the site of the bloody attempt to land forces in the Dardanelles. I gather that my father not only served on *Ark Royal*, but was part of a detachment that went ashore to build an airfield at Mudros on the island of Lemnos. He left the service in 1917 and married my mother Mary a year later. It might seem obvious that, with my father's background, I would also join the navy, but this was not the case. My father, like most men at the time, rarely if ever talked about his wartime experiences, and I found out only a little about them much later in my life. No, I was left to make my own way, and my own mistakes.

Earlston, like many towns in the Borders, was built round a large open square. Here each year they held the 'Hirings', to which farmworkers from the surrounding countryside would come hoping to find new employment for the next twelve months. It was a giant annual labour exchange and needless to say it could be a desperate time for people. There was little in the way of a welfare state for those who were too old or too ill to work. Rural areas saw a great deal of poverty in those times.

The square in Earlston was also the site of a yearly summer fair, and then it would be filled with all sorts of sideshows and entertainers, fire-eaters, jugglers and boxing booths. The arrival of the fair always caused great excitement.

Steam-driven traction engines would haul wagons into the square, then would be set up to drive roundabouts and steam organs.

Entertainment was by and large a communal affair. One local custom I loved to watch was a wedding. The groom would have purchased a rugby ball from the local saddler, and after the ceremony the newly married couple would go to the saddler's and the groom would kick the ball as hard and as high as he could into the town. This was a signal for all the men to rush after it and try to grab it, with the idea that one of them would secure it and hang on to it. There was no prize for this – gaining the ball was an end in itself. The struggle for possession would often go on until dark; it was taken very seriously. Naturally the whole town enjoyed it, so a wedding was a major event.

When I was about four years old my parents gave me a pet, a terrier that I named Wiggy. I wandered far and wide with Wiggy, securing him with a length of rope for a lead. Roaming away from home must have given my parents several anxious moments, but looking back I can only marvel at the freedom I had and the adventurous habits I developed. My favourite walk was to go to see the grounds of a large house called Cowdenknowes. I was always welcome at the gardener's cottage on the estate, where there was always something to eat – a piece of cake fresh from the oven or an apple out of the orchard.

I also used to wander off to the railway station to watch the steam trains come and go. The porter there was also called Moffat, although we had no family connection of which I was aware. After I had been making regular visits for a while, the train drivers and firemen on the local route all got to know me. Naturally, as a young boy I found the steam engines absolutely enthralling, belching steam and smoke, shrieking and clanking as they pulled to a halt and then heaving away gathering speed. It didn't take long before the crews were willing to let me on the footplate, and then it became a regular occurrence for me to travel on the engine to St Boswells, a town about 4 miles away down the line. It was enormously exciting, with the heat from the firebox, the gleaming brass levers and dials, the smell of hot oil and smoke, and me in the company of the overalled men in charge of this monster. When we got to St Boswells I would hop off and the driver would ensure that I was safely ensconced on another engine making the return journey. When I got back my parents would chastise me for running off without a by your leave, but what little boy would be able to resist such an amazing opportunity? I certainly couldn't.

I became extremely adventurous, and absolutely fearless, feeling that I could go anywhere I chose without coming to any harm. One day I got it into my head to visit a good friend of my grandfather, a man called Mr Deans who was the landlord of a pub, the Black Bull, in the town of Lauder, which was about 6 miles north of Earlston. I hopped on to a local bus and hid beneath a seat, but someone must have seen me and told my parents. My father clearly thought this was the last straw. He telephoned the local constable in Lauder and this fine fellow was waiting for me when the bus pulled in. I can still see him, with his blue cape, his helmet and his fierce waxed moustache, like a typical sergeant major. Towering over me, he grabbed me by the ear and none too gently marched me off to the police station, up the iron steps to the front door. There I was led to the cells and put in the first one on the left. They were in the centre of the village, and they are still there now, to remind me whenever I pass by. Naturally I was not very happy and I am sure that my distress took the edge off my father's anger when he arrived to take me home. Mr Deans at the Black Bull was incensed at the constable's treatment of me and before he was calmed down by my father he threatened to take his shotgun to the man. This was a very unpleasant experience all round, but I cannot say that it made me curb my wanderlust.

Even wandering around the town offered plenty of opportunity for mischief. There was almost no motor traffic, so I could walk about with Wiggy without any fear of being run over, but there were other hazards. My father's garage was located next to the church, and then on the other side of that was the local baker's, and then the public house next to that. For a young boy the baker's was an enormously attractive place, with its iced buns and doughnuts in the window. The baker was always very friendly towards me and I was allowed to go down to the cellar where the dough was being mixed in large tubs, then cut up into portions to be baked into rolls and loaves. Even then I felt that there was something extremely satisfying and wholesome about the smell of flour and yeast and new-baked bread.

In those days the roads around Earlston were covered by layers of stone chippings spread over hot tar and the council roadworkers came every few years to renew the surface. Piles of grit were brought by lorry and left by the side of the road, along with barrels of tar ready to be used. I can't imagine how I did it, but I managed to get into one of those barrels and started shouting for help. My father rescued me and dragged me into the garage, where he cleaned me off with paraffin. Ever since, the smell of paraffin or tar has brought back that experience, taking me back to my earliest days. So too does the smell of whisky. One day I was walking past the public house, and I must have been without my constant companion Wiggy because the landlord's terrier bounded out and bit me on the upper arm. I was very upset, and so of course was the landlord. He rushed me into the pub, sat me on the bar and cleaned the wound with neat whisky. Another alarming experience for a young lad – but I have to say that it has never stopped me from enjoying a dram.

My father's business prospered in Earlston. The garage was usually busy, as cars and buses were starting to replace horse-drawn vehicles. I enjoyed loitering in the area, watching the workmen, and I became fascinated by engines and anything mechanical, although things were still fairly primitive by modern standards. My father bought a chassis from Albion, the lorry manufacturer in Glasgow, and had the local joiner build what was known as a charabanc body on it. It was the first bus to operate in Earlston and was often hired to take local clubs and church groups on excursions or picnics. The wheels still had wooden spokes and wheel rims, like the old wooden horse-drawn carts. On very hot days in summer the wood would dry out and shrink, so the driver always had to make sure that a bucket of water was available to keep the wood wet to prevent the wheels from collapsing.

My father also started to sell cars, and in about 1925 he sold the local doctor, Dr Young, a new Model T Ford. This led to my first ever crash. These cars had been in production for some years, but the prices had started to fall, so doctors and other professional people had now started to buy them. Ford kept on improving them and the car bought by Dr Young had been fitted with what was then a very modern innovation, an electric starter, as an alternative to cranking the engine over by hand with a starting handle. This electric starter was operated by a large button mounted on the floor beside the driver. Shortly after the car had been proudly handed over by my father, the doctor used it to visit a patient who lived above the big grocer's shop that fronted on to the main square. The pristine Ford, black of course, was left next to the shop. Motor cars were still a novelty in those days and I was particularly intrigued by this concept of the electric starter. Seeing the car parked, I took the opportunity to clamber up into it. I was five years old and fascinated by the shiny new button sticking out of the floor. I pressed firmly on it with both my hands, as hard as I could. To my utter surprise, the car leapt forward over the cobbles and smashed into the plate-glass window of the grocer's shop. There was utter chaos. The assistants were screaming inside the shop, people all round the square rushed out to see what had caused the sound of shattering glass; all this accompanied by my cries of shock, and my tears at the realization of the trouble I was in. It didn't take long before first the doctor and then my father added to the tumult. I was correct about the trouble I was in, for my father treated me very sternly. I was forbidden all sorts of treats and was told I must stay indoors, but I think it is hard for people to remain angry at small children for long. Soon I found myself wandering my favourite haunts again and running over the fields with Wiggy.

When I was around six or seven we moved to Low Fell, a coal-mining district of County Durham close to Gateshead, where we lived in a flat above my father's car showroom. It was not a time that I enjoyed very much. I was growing up and beginning to be affected by events in the wider world. We had moved from Earlston, comparatively quite a rural town, to an area dominated by coal mining. We lived at first in a very poor part of town and I was singled out in the local school as being Scottish and slightly more well-to-do than most of the children. Also, 1926 saw the General Strike, when the transport workers and dockers came out on strike in support of the coalminers, who were refusing to take a pay cut. The streets were full off striking miners, with police and the army guarding the entrances to the pits and escorting food lorries driven by volunteers. Families had no money, there was an air of desperation and violence, and I think my father's business was badly affected by the strike.

The only enjoyable memory I have of our time in County

Durham was when my mother took me to the Empire Theatre to see the famous singer Al Jolson, who performed made up as a black minstrel. It would not be accepted now, but he was truly an amazing performer, holding the audience spellbound when he sang his most famous song, 'Sonny Boy'. It was a real tear-jerker.

We stayed in England for a couple of years, with things slowly improving, then my father decided to move once more and we headed back across the border to Scotland, to the lovely town of Kelso, a few miles east of Earlston.

Kelso is built round a big cobbled square, apparently the largest in Scotland, with four main roads leading into it; many people say that it is similar to a French provincial town. It is where the Tweed and Teviot rivers meet and, as both are good salmon rivers, Kelso is well known for its game fishing. It has a fine National Hunt racecourse and a high school, which, at that time, had an excellent reputation for rugby. At the end of Roxburgh Street a horseshoe was embedded in the pavement, and the local legend says that it was thrown by Bonnie Prince Charlie's horse back in 1745. There was also a big ring set in the cobbles in the middle of the square where bulls were tied up on market days.

We lived in and around Kelso for the next few years, and I first went to school at the Abbey public school in Wark. For some of that time we lived in a small village on the outskirts of a town called Carham and from there I walked to the school, which had only one classroom and one lady teacher. My parents then moved into Kelso, but I was occasionally sent to my grandparents at Waskerly and then had to walk about a mile and a half to school on my own. The walk was fine in summer, but pretty tough going in winter, when it seemed to be dark when I left home in the morning and dark again on the journey back. On the way home I had to pass a solitary building called the Moor Lock Inn and I was once attacked there by a very angry gander, which flew at me and knocked me down. He would not leave me alone, but luckily somebody heard my shouts and came and beat him off with a stick. I gave the building a very wide berth after that, which added to the unpleasantness of the journey.

This area of country was often used for motor-bike trials and a checkpoint for the riders was set up nearby. I remember seeing a well-known woman motorcyclist, Marjorie Cottle, there, riding an extremely impressive bike called a Red Indian. I had heard a lot about her, as she was one of the few women motorcyclists in those days, and she was very successful in races and time trials. The fact that she was competing in a sport dominated by men was controversial – after all, women had only been given the vote in 1928 – and she was often the subject of articles in newspapers and magazines. She had blonde hair and, even with her riding gear on, she was quite glamorous. She left a great impression on me. I must have been growing up!

I had not had a very pleasant time in the schools I had been attending so far, because of the behaviour of the other children towards me and the arduous journeys. By the time I was eleven I was determined to go to Kelso High School, where the pupils wore very impressive red-and-white-striped jerseys and the building was in the centre of town. I was very pleased when I passed my entrance exams and was accepted. The school was marvellous compared to what I had had to put up with in County Durham and at the school in Wark. The headmaster, Mr Shepherd, was one of those characters who was both imposing and charismatic. When he entered a classroom the pupils just ate out of his hand, he was so respected. At Kelso High School I started to excel at rugby and I eventually made it to the school's first team. I continued to enjoy playing rugby long after my schooldays, and still today think it is a marvellous game.

Before I qualified for the High School I used to walk past Kelso Abbey to the Abbey school and was fascinated by a stone obelisk in the Abbey grounds. It bore a rather ominous inscription: REMEMBER MAN AS YOU PASS BY, AS YOU ARE NOW, SO ONCE WAS I, AS I AM NOW SO MUST YOU BE, PREPARE FOR DEATH AND FOLLOW ME. I had no way of knowing then, but there were to be times in my life when I had to confront the prospect of death rather urgently, as did many of my friends. I often remembered that inscription, though I cannot say that it helped, or offered any way out of a dreadful situation.

There was a very active social life in the town, as there was in those days in most towns around the country. There were two annual gatherings in the big square, when the townsfolk all made an appearance. One was every Hogmanay – New Year's Eve – and the other was in the summer for the start of the annual trip to Spittal, a seaside town on the coast across the estuary from Berwick-upon-Tweed, where everybody was transported free by bus or train for a day at the beach.

My parents took an active part in some of the town's clubs. The Kelso Swimming Club was formed while I was at school. A hut was built on the riverbank near the Duke of Roxburghe's estate boundary, and the Pirelli company, a manufacturer of electricity cables, which was putting up pylons to bring mains electricity to the town, was persuaded to build a diving board with 10-foot and 20-foot platforms for the club's use. My father was one of the first to dive off the top, but I'm afraid I never managed it.

My mother, who was very musical, had a good voice and was a keen amateur singer. She was active in the local Operatic Society, which was extremely well supported and attracted talent from other towns around Kelso. Their repertoire ranged from Gilbert and Sullivan's *Pirates of Penzance* to the operetta *Goodnight Vienna*. I was always recruited for the chorus. My mother also encouraged me to take up a musical instrument and eventually I started to perform with a band.

The ability to play the piano and violin served me in good stead later on. Amateur musical performances were extremely important for all of us during the war, and my experience with them started at the age of ten or eleven, when my friends and I took part in a custom that was very popular back then but now seems to have died out altogether. It was carried out at Halloween, but instead of going round asking for trick or treats we did something called 'Guising'. A group of us lads would go to the front door of a house we thought might be welcoming and politely ask if we could come in and perform.

Our particular playlet was suggested by my father; it was one he had performed when he was a lad, although whether there was any deeper tradition behind the verses we recited I cannot say. We were all dressed up in costumes, with one boy dressed as a king with a cardboard crown on his head. Once all were in the house most of us would cluster behind the sitting-room door, then the first boy would enter the room on his own and say, 'Red up sticks and red up stools here comes in a pack of fools, a pack of fools behind that door. Step in King George and clear the floor.'

The boy with the crown on his head would enter and recite, 'King George is my name, sword and pistol by my side, I hope to win the game.'

The first boy would answer, 'The game, sir, the game, sir, is not within your power. I will slash you and slay you within half an hour.' These two boys would then have a duel with toy swords and the first boy would drop down as though dead, at which the king would kneel down and say, 'Is there a doctor in the town?' A small boy with a little attaché case would then pop out from behind the door saying, 'My name is Doctor Brown, the best little doctor in the town. A little to his nose and a little to his bum, now rise up, jock, and sing a song.'

It was an absurd little sketch, but we used to get showered with pieces of cake and home-made toffees and fudge, and we would pass from house to house performing the same sketch. Even now I can recall the words perfectly.

I also started to enjoy horse riding, which did not go down very well with my parents. My grandfather had been a keen gambler and had lost a considerable sum of money over the years on the horses. For understandable reasons, my father didn't approve of gambling; he also took the view that anything to do with horse racing or riding was dangerous and would inevitably lead to ruin. However, I became fascinated by the meetings of the local hunt, where I would turn up in shorts, rugby jersey and running shoes, and try to keep up with the hounds.

Naturally I was told off by my father, and the school also took a dim view of it. But I soon found that opening the odd gate to allow some of the less adventurous riders through would be rewarded with a sixpence and, as I became more familiar, riders would encourage me to hang on to a stirrup to help me along. Soon I started to learn to ride at the local stables with the help of the stable boys. I enjoyed it and found that I was good at it. Whether it was my years of running around with just my dog Wiggy for company I don't know, but I felt easy with horses and they felt easy with me. Even now, as I look out of my window and observe some of the pupils at a riding school in the nearby fields, I have to resist the urge to rush out and tell them to relax, loosen the reins a little and encourage the horse to feel that he is working with them, not against them.

I got on very well with one particular horse called Answer Me, who was owned by a local vet, a grand character. He would give me a few shillings for exercising his horse every Saturday, and when he entered it into a race near Hawick I decided to put some of my money on it. It came in first and I picked up my winnings. There was, however, hell to pay with my father, who saw all his grim forebodings coming to pass. He flatly told me never to go back to the stables. I disobeyed him, of course, I am sorry to say, but didn't gamble any more. It was the horses and the riding that I was interested in and, like rugby, it is something that I continued to enjoy throughout my life and encouraged my children to take up. So all the things that I enjoyed as a youngster stayed with me as I grew up, and made me what I was to become.

The major event of my childhood took place in Kelso when I was about ten years old. It didn't last very long, but I think it had a profound effect on me – I honestly think it changed my life completely, although it took some time for its true impact to be felt. An aeroplane appeared in the sky over Kelso one day, manoeuvring low over the town a few times to attract attention and then flying off to land at the point-to-point course. It was an Avro 504, a very common and popular aircraft at the time, a biplane with two open cockpits, powered by a single rotary engine at the front and a big curved skid, like a bent ski, mounted between the landing wheels as a substitute for a nose wheel. Several thousand of these planes had been built during the First World War and they had served as fighters, with a machine gun mounted above the top wing. This one, presumably an ex-services aircraft and without its machine gun, was flown by a professional pilot, a 'barnstormer' I suppose you could call him, and he was offering joy rides for 10 shillings. He looked like Biggles, the flying-ace action hero of boys' stories, dressed in his breeches and high, laced-up flying boots, with a leather flying helmet and goggles and a long, white silk scarf that flew in the wind. Was he impressive!

As for the experience of flying, I was astounded by it. This was like riding in the locomotive but infinitely more thrilling. There was the noise, the smell of hot oil and high-octane petrol, and the speed seemed immense as we took off into the air, high above the countryside, with the town far below us. It was the stuff of dreams, like a glimpse of another world that made it impossible, once I was back on the ground, to view my surroundings in the same way again. But I thought it was inevitably a once-in-a-lifetime experience, not something I could ever repeat as easily as I could go riding a horse. Now that I think back on it, that pilot has an enormous amount to answer for.

2
Childhood Lost

It's hard to tell if the world seemed to be becoming more threatening and difficult because it was, or if it was just because I was growing up and paying more attention to things going on around me.

I have already talked about the effect that the General Strike had on me when I went to County Durham as a seven-year-old. By the time I was sixteen I was certainly paying more attention to the news on the radio and in the newspapers, and you couldn't help noticing that the economic situation was affecting everybody. The great crash in 1929, when stock markets around the world collapsed and millions of people were thrown out of work, was impossible to ignore; it was a daily topic of conversation between my parents and other adults. The effects of that financial disaster were still with us in the mid-1930s and we were living in very depressed economic times. There were a lot of unemployed people in the streets, hardly anybody was hiring agricultural workers, and it was not easy to find a job. There wasn't the demand for new cars, so business was difficult for my father.

I wanted to go to university in Edinburgh, but my parents couldn't afford to pay the fees and pay for my keep while I studied. I applied for a bursary, took some examinations and was interviewed, but apparently I did not make the grade, so I was not offered any financial assistance. With this very negative news I had no choice but to leave school at sixteen and start looking for work along with many others. Through some of my father's connections in the coach business I was offered a job in the office of a bus company in Kelso. It was a job I hated. My life started to become depressing. I still played rugby for the town, which I enjoyed, and continued to ride horses at the local stables and accompany the hounds hunting, much against my father's wishes, but these activities did not compensate for the feeling that my life was wasting away in a boring job as a clerk.

I thought that I might be able to improve my position if I saved up enough money to put myself through university. As an extra source of income I joined up with some of my old classmates to form a small dance band. I played the violin and the banjo, and we toured around, performing at weddings and giving concerts at dances in local church and community halls. One of the band members, the only one who could drive, would use his father's milk-delivery van to get us around to wherever we had to appear. I continued to live at home and paid my mother half my wages each week, which was 18 shillings, or 90 pence in today's money. I had to buy my own clothes and fares out of the money I had left. At the end of the week there was precious little to put by for my university fund.

While I was languishing in the bus company, there seemed to be a great deal happening in the world outside. There was no television, of course, but the cinema was extremely popular and provided great entertainment. Not only was there a supporting picture before the main feature, but there were also the newsreels, Pathé or Movietone, which dealt with the main news of the day. Germany appeared to be extremely dynamic and exciting, not suffering as we were from high unemployment and poverty. They were building roads and constructing Zeppelins that crossed the Atlantic. It didn't seem to be the same country that had been so badly defeated in the First World War, when many of the population were on the verge of starvation.

In the winter of 1936 a couple of hundred unemployed shipyard workers set off from Jarrow on Tyneside to march on Parliament, over 300 miles away in London. They wanted to highlight the poverty and desperate circumstances of the industrial cities and coal-mining areas of the north. In some parts of England and Scotland, such as Clydeside, there was 70 per cent unemployment. But in the summer of the same year we had seen newsreels in the cinema of the Berlin Olympics, which appeared to show that Germany under Hitler was booming, with plenty of jobs, holiday camps for the workers and recreational activities for youngsters, all organized by the state.

Other news from overseas was more disquieting. Italy had invaded Abyssinia, causing the Emperor Haile Selassie to flee to safety in Britain. Under their dictator, Mussolini, the Italians were seeking to expand their empire in Africa and were enlarging their navy. Civil war had broken out in Spain, and Italy and Germany had sent some of their forces to fight on behalf of General Franco, who was trying to remove the socialist government in Madrid. Of course, none of these events stopped me getting up in the morning, having breakfast and going to work; I was at least fortunate in having a job to go to.

The biggest event, however, and the most talked about, was the abdication of Edward VIII, forced to choose between the crown and the woman he loved, Wallis Simpson. It was the subject of considerable gossip the length and breadth of the country, with expressions of great disapproval of affairs with married women and of divorce in general. There was no doubt a great deal of hypocrisy over the whole issue. I was not a prude about sex, and never have been; in fact, I was beginning to be extremely interested in women, young as I was. It was at about the time of the abdication that I had the first encounter with a woman that made me realize they knew what they wanted and were quite capable of getting it. During one of my rugby matches I injured my foot and the wound became infected. I went into the local hospital to have a small operation on my big toe and had to stay in for several days. I was extremely well looked after by the night nurse, who was a lovely woman. I won't go into details, but even now I can remember the rustle of her starched aprons and the warm feel of her breath as she leant over me. If we had ever been dis-covered she would have been instantly dismissed, and probably prevented from ever working as a nurse again. Why she took the risk I don't know, but when it comes to romance and sex, reason flies out of the window. It certainly made Edward abdicate the crown and become the Duke of Windsor instead.

There were other incidents that relieved the soul-destroying boredom of the office in the bus depot, and one in particular stands out, though at the time it did not seem particularly out of the ordinary. Southern Scotland was used to falls of snow in the winter months, but in 1937 the weather was par-ticularly severe. I was in the bus office one day – I think it was shortly after New Year – when we received a phone call late in the afternoon. The scheduled bus service from Newcastle to Edinburgh, which went via the town of Jedburgh, had not arrived there. Clearly something had happened, but there had been no news of an accident. The situation was worrying: it was snowing quite heavily, it was very cold and it would not be long before it got dark. The depot manager asked one of the bus drivers, a chap in his fifties called Turnbull, and me if we would set out along the route to see if we could discover what had happened. Turnbull was a wonderful chap the way he prepared us; he must have known what to expect. He secured boots for both of us, an extra pair of breeches, jerseys, greatcoats and piles of rugs. We loaded them into a small bus, along with torches, ropes and shovels, and we set off, driving as quickly as we dared into the teeth of a blizzard along the Kelso to Jedburgh road. It was by now eight o'clock in the evening and pitch dark. Eventually we could go no further; the snow was piling up in the road and we decided that we would press ahead on foot. We covered our heads with the rugs, leaving small gaps in the folds so that we could see ahead. The gale-force wind was whipping the snow almost horizontal, creating a complete white-out. Great snowdrifts were building up. Our torches barely penetrated the darkness more than a few feet, but we set off. Turnbull and I were roped together, and he led, trying to make a path in the middle of the road where the snow was mostly waist deep. We knew that if we wandered off the road we might stumble into a ditch or fall into a field and be over our heads in a huge snowdrift. Our situation was getting dangerous, and we moved forward slowly and cautiously. I remember thinking how isolated we were and how very careful we must be. Strangely, neither of us considered abandoning our search, although it would have made much more sense to head back to our own vehicle and return to safety in Kelso. There is a strange conflict in people, and very often a sense of duty or responsibility will provide as powerful an impetus as a sense of self-preservation. Accompanying this is an equally strong motivation not to give up or admit defeat. Whatever was going on in our heads, we never discussed the possibility of turning back.

We couldn't hear ourselves against the wind and had to put our heads close together to speak to each other, fighting down the noise of the gale. My companion, who had driven that road many times, used the telephone wires as a guide; it was a blessing that they had not been brought down by the heavy snow. Without them we might easily have wandered off the road and headed into the surrounding countryside, not to be found for days. We struggled on, and as we neared the summit of a steep hill we noticed that the snow suddenly felt different underfoot. We had been walking through very dense snow, when suddenly old Mr Turnbull realized that we were walking on a firm surface that seemed to be higher than the surrounding verge.

We paced out the length of this mound – and then it hit us that we had found the bus. We dug down with our hands to where we thought the door would be. It took some time, but we eventually broke through the snow and banged on the window. Inside there were about six passengers, the driver and the conductor. They were not in very good shape. The bus had skidded to the side of the road and after coming to a halt had quickly been covered by a snowdrift. They were badly shaken and of course extremely cold. Nobody on the bus had warm enough clothes to venture out into the blizzard to seek help. They had kept the engine going for warmth, but that had run out of petrol and they had started to cut open the seats and used the stuffing to build little fires on the bus floor. It was surprising that they had not succumbed to the smoke and fumes.

It took a lot of coaxing to persuade them to come out into the blizzard, but they could not stay there over night. They were so cold that I doubt they would have survived for another twelve hours. Eventually we persuaded them that they would be safer coming with us, and they clambered out to be roped together and led back down the hill that we had made in the snow to our waiting bus, where we wrapped them in blankets. One lady insisted on putting up her umbrella as she left the stranded bus. I tried to dissuade her, saying it would be of absolutely no use, but she wouldn't listen. Naturally, as soon as she got outside it was whipped away by the wind, never to be seen again.

So we made our slow journey back to Kelso Hospital, where they were given food and hot drinks and checked by a doctor.

Turnbull and I received a letter of commendation from the bus company, and a reward of £5 each! Looking back, it seems remarkable that just the two of us ventured out on this rescue mission to find a lost bus and its passengers. Nowadays there would have been a mountain rescue team, an emergency helicopter in the air and the mobilization of police and ambulance services, but we did the job ourselves without much thought for the dangers involved.

For the most part, working in the bus office day after day made me more determined to find an alternative, and when I was eighteen years old I saw an advertisement in a newspaper asking for applications to the Naval Air Service Reserve. This was a new organization, being set up because, after a long fight, the navy was finally going to take control of its own aircraft and the men who repaired and flew them. The Naval Air Service had existed in the First World War, but in 1919 all its aircraft had been handed over to the Royal Air Force. The latest change back to Admiralty control was due to take place in 1939. If I had understood this a bit better at the time, I might have been spared some depressing months.

The advert that I saw was the first stage in setting up a reserve force. Successful recruits would be taught how to fly and would be required to spend several weeks per year on duty in the Reserves, for which they would be paid. The idea, of course, was that in the event of a war there would be a group of trained men who could be called up rapidly to enlarge the regular service. When I saw the advert I suddenly thought that, at last, here was a way that I could learn to fly – something I had secretly set my heart on ever since I climbed out of the cockpit of the Avro 504 that had flown me over the rooftops of Kelso. In those days the prospect of flying was so remote for ordinary people that I had buried the desire deeply, but seeing this advert brought me fresh hope. I would be absolutely crazy not to apply: I might be able to learn to fly after all, and I could say goodbye to my boring life in the bus office.

I wrote off and, within a couple of weeks, received a note asking me to appear for interview in front of a board in Govan, Glasgow. It was a long journey, involving a bus to Edinburgh, then another bus to Glasgow, then a long tram journey from Glasgow to Govan. About eight other applicants were being interviewed at the same time as me and they all seemed very confident. The members of the interviewing panel were all dressed in civilian clothes, but they had ruddy faces, I assumed from a lot of time spent out in the open air. The gentleman at the head of the table had mutton-chop whiskers, and two of them had full beards. To my eyes they seemed very nautical. When they introduced themselves, I realized that they were fairly senior men.

They invited me to sit down and I was asked some simple questions about my local town and the job I was doing, and was asked to read a logbook. The interview then took an odd turn, as the chairman of the board, who seemed by far the oldest man there, realized that I lived next to the Tweed and Teviot rivers. The rest of the interview became a discussion about trout and salmon fishing, the effectiveness of various fishing flies and the best techniques for tying them. I was very interested in fishing and I had caught my first salmon when I was eight or nine, although entirely by accident. It came on to the end of my line when I had been hoping to get trout, and it was too strong for me to land. Eventually my trout rod broke and I wound the line round a bush near the river and raced home to fetch my father, who helped me gaff it. I told them this story, and the chairman brought out his fly box and we talked about the best flies to use in different parts of the river. He knew far more than me, but I was content to listen and make the odd comment. Then the interview was over. It was very strange, and I did not know what to think as I journeyed back home to Kelso.

Back I went to the office again, with nothing but winter rugby to look forward to. I heard nothing from the navy and was once more beginning to sink into despair, when one day I read yet another advert – as you can imagine, I was scouring the newspapers in desperation. This time it was for recruits to the Southern Rhodesian Mounted Police. I knew little about Southern Rhodesia, or Zimbabwe as it is now called, but clearly this offered enormous possibilities: travel to a far-off land, a marvellous climate and, most important, the opportunity to work with horses, which, after rugby, was one of my greatest passions. So I applied and was invited to an interview at Rhodesia House in the Strand in London.

I had been to London once before, in a school party that had visited the Houses of Parliament, but this time I was more able to appreciate how different it was from Kelso! I found it daunting as I got off the train at Kings Cross and asked a porter for some directions, my small case with a few clothes in it clutched in my hand. I was staying at the YMCA, near London University in Bloomsbury, and the porter directed me to the nearest bus, but there seemed to be hundreds of them outside the station, and more taxis than I had ever seen before. I decided to walk and found that my destination was not that far from the station, but I had never seen streets so busy and crowded. I should have been excited by the huge bustling city, the hub of the Empire, but to be honest it was dirty, and for a young lad with not a great deal of money it was not very inviting.

The staff at the YMCA were a great help and I managed to find my way to the interview. It seemed to go well – they appeared impressed with my knowledge of horses – and on leaving I was confident that my life was about to change for the better.

Back in Kelso, I did what I had been longing to do for the past two years: I resigned from my job at the bus company. This caused some problems with my parents, principally my father. The economic situation had not improved greatly and there were still a lot of unemployed people looking for work. He thought I was being reckless in throwing away a secure job without any firm prospects, and neither of them wanted to see me join the navy, or go thousands of miles away to central Africa. I suppose deep down they felt that my ambitions were too great for my talents and that I would end up disappointed. They knew how hard life could be, and they valued the settled life they had established in Kelso. But I could not be persuaded: I gave up my job. That year I travelled as a reserve with the Scottish rugby team to Ireland, but, unfortunately, we lost.

This was the winter of 1938/39 and, now without a job, I decided that I would move down to London. Not that I liked the place, but I thought it would be only a matter of time before I was offered a passage to Rhodesia. Also, staying with my parents in Kelso, unemployed and just kicking my heels while I waited for a letter, was not very attractive. My father had been good to me, but relations between us had soured somewhat. He told me that I would be back within six months, but I thought, 'Will I hell.' So back I went to the YMCA and managed to find a low-paid job in the parcels department of Harrods.

Weeks passed and I heard nothing further from the Rhodesian High Commission or the Southern Rhodesian Mounted Police. I was very depressed, and beginning to wonder how long I could stick it out before going back home with my tail between my legs, when out of the blue I received a letter from the Royal Navy. It was a request to go to Queen Anne's Mansions for a medical exam. The address turned out to be a row of Georgian houses just off Harley Street in the West End. The letter was not what I wanted to receive. I had abandoned any thoughts of taking up flying, having convinced myself that I would be accepted into the Southern Rhodesian Mounted Police. This was the aim on which I was now focusing my ambitions, and I waited impatiently for the letter of acceptance with details of how I would be expected to travel to Rhodesia. However much I wanted to learn to fly, all that the navy could offer was a part-time job in the Reserves, while the Mounted Police was full time, a career with long-term prospects, clearly much more of a vocation. It was, after all, nearly six months since I had attended that rather strange interview with those sailors in civilian clothes in Glasgow and it seemed odd that I had heard nothing more. But there was no reason why I should refuse to take a medical, so I duly presented myself before the men in white coats, coughed, had my eyes and hearing tested and kneecaps hit with a hammer, and then went back to my dismal job at Harrods.

Within a week or so of this appointment I received a second letter telling me to report on board HMS *Frobisher* at Portsmouth naval base to begin my training. This caused a bit of soul-searching. I still had heard nothing from Rhodesia House and, despite my reservations about the navy, it did offer an alternative to the storeroom at Harrods, so I went.

On the train going down to Portsmouth my thoughts were mixed. I was still coming to terms with the sudden interest shown in me by the navy, and I was apprehensive about what I was letting myself in for. I had absolutely no idea what naval training entailed and was beginning to wonder whether this really was a wise move. I managed to find my way to the naval office in the harbour, from where, with my small suitcase, I was eventually given a lift on a motor launch out to the ship at her moorings. My feelings of trepidation were compounded as I approached *Frobisher*. She was a big cruiser that had been detached from the Atlantic fleet a few years previously and designated for cadet training. The boat I was on tossed about in the harbour and, as we got closer to the ship, I could see that there were rust streaks on her hull, and she looked grey and forbidding above me. This was the very first time that I had seen a warship, or been out on a small boat. The experience was unsettling.

I learned later that *Frobisher* was scheduled at that time to be taken out of her training role with a view to her being mothballed. If I had known that, perhaps I would have been less surprised and confused when, after I had climbed up the gangway on to the ship, the duty officer immediately issued me with a travel warrant back home. I returned to the mainland once again on a small boat, only to find I was too late for a train back to London. The harbour office sent me to a naval dormitory in a large building that housed the Sailors' Rest – known as 'Aggie Weston', after the woman who founded them – and there I bedded down for the night.

I felt upset, rejected and close to despair in that strange bed, in a building full of sailors who ignored me. I had been uneasy as I approached that forbidding ship, and now the journey from London had proved to be a complete waste of time. Very little had gone right with my life since I left school at sixteen; I felt that I had no idea what to do with myself; and, worse, it seemed that nobody else had any use for me either. The truth was, of course, that the Naval Air Service was in a complete state of flux. The handover from Royal Air Force to Admiralty control was still going on, and how and where the training of naval pilots was going to take place had not yet been properly decided. It was one thing to advertise for people, it was another to set up a proper organization. The impact of this on me was to make me very downhearted.

Next morning I arrived back in London. I had foolishly given up my job in Harrods believing that I would be doing my naval training for the next three months, so I was now unemployed. I was determined not to go home, as my father would have said, 'I told you so.' I just could not face the defeat and humiliation. So I was forced to sign on the dole and look for a job. It was a very depressing experience and I was at an extremely low ebb. I was eking out my savings, living in the YMCA, walking the streets, visiting some of the sights like St Paul's Cathedral and the Houses of Parliament, but I was like a piece of wood floating in the Thames, a piece of flotsam drifting here and there. I had come a long way since my carefree days with my little terrier Wiggy running along beside me, and none of it was for the good.

While I was in a state of limbo in London, the newspapers and news programmes on the wireless were describing events with an ominous tone. The Spanish Civil War had ended in victory for General Franco, and there had been a very tense period in 1938 when Hitler demanded that the Sudetenland, Czechoslovak territory in which a large number of German-speaking people lived, should be ceded to Germany. There was a feeling that another war might start over this and a general military mobilization got under way as the crisis built up. Air-raid shelters and trenches started to be dug – I remember noticing the piles of fresh earth as shelters were built in Hyde Park. Gas masks were given out to the civilian population, and hundreds of lorries carrying winches and towing trailers full of gas canisters were parked around the city. These were mobile installations to launch barrage balloons – small, hydrogen-filled balloons that rose into the air tethered by steel cables, the idea being that they would prevent enemy bombers from flying low over cities and factories. They floated high over the city, like hundreds of huge, strange fish, the sunshine glinting off their silver surfaces. People expected war to start quite quickly.

Then in September 1938 the British Prime Minister Neville Chamberlain flew to Munich to discuss the situation with Hitler, returning with a deal that looked as though it might be a peaceful solution. It gave Hitler everything he wanted, including the Sudetenland, and Winston Churchill was bitterly opposed to it. However shameful Chamberlain's appeasement of Hitler might have been, most ordinary people were relieved that another war had been averted. The dreadful slaughter of the First World War was still very much on people's minds; it had been over for only twenty years and millions of people had been affected by it. There probably wasn't a family in the country that had not lost someone in the trenches, and it was still seen as a great and unnecessary tragedy. Most towns and villages had erected a monument to those who had died in what we called the Great War; I remember the big ceremony in Kelso when I was younger for the unveiling of the town's memorial to the local men who had never come back from France. Nowadays there is a ceremony at the Cenotaph in London, and in towns and villages around the country, on the Sunday nearest to Armistice Day, but in the 1930s there were local ceremonies of remembrance on 11 November itself, whatever day of the week it fell, and the two-minute silence at eleven o'clock was very strictly adhered to. Buses and cars stopped and people stood still in the streets. At the time you were aware that this silence was being observed all over the country. It was a very emotional moment. So the threat of another war filled people with dread.

The relief of the Munich Agreement didn't last long. In March 1939 Hitler took over the rest of Czechoslovakia. By then we had had time to become accustomed to the threat of war, and I think people thought now it was bound to happen. The question was, when?

Meanwhile, I was tramping the streets of London, signing on and looking, unsuccessfully, for a job, when I received yet another letter from the Admiralty, this time telling me that I would be sent for training, probably at Drem in Scotland, which was an RAF flying training school at the time. When I read it, I made up my mind that I would now go home to Scotland, face my father and wait for further instructions about training. My return in August didn't go too badly – my letter from the Admiralty was proof that at least my life had some direction.

It was in Kelso on 1 September that I heard on the news that the Germans had invaded Poland, and I knew that war was inevitable. My father and mother and I were gathered round the wireless set on the 3rd, which was a Sunday, to hear the Prime Minister announce that once again we were at war with Germany. It was a profound moment, where every person listening knows that their life will be utterly trans-formed, for ever, and there will be great changes in the world and that the future has suddenly become completely unknown. I knew that I would be part of the war, and that the question of what to do with my life was probably no longer in my hands. My parents must have felt a great deal of unease, but they kept it to themselves. My father in particular, with his experience of Gallipoli, must have had his own thoughts, but he had never discussed them before and didn't do so now.

It was clear that I would probably be starting my training in the navy much sooner than expected, and indeed almost the next day I received another letter from the Admiralty. In contradiction to the last one, it contained orders and a travel warrant for me to take the train south to Gosport, west of Portsmouth harbour, and to appear at St Vincent barracks, which was the Royal Navy boys' training establishment. Once more I said goodbye to my parents and old schoolfriends to catch the train to Edinburgh and then south. I felt that I had been kicked from pillar to post in the past months, but was sure that now all that was behind me.

3

Up, Up and Away

Unlike on my previous visit to Portsmouth, my destination was not a warship. HMS St Vincent was what was known in the navy as a 'stone frigate', a shore-based establishment of bricks and mortar. In fact, St Vincent was a collection of four-storey red-brick buildings facing a large asphalt parade ground. It was not very inviting. After finding my way there via the Gosport Ferry, I stood outside the entrance for quite a while, wondering what I had let myself in for. Things were a bit different from my last visit to the training ship HMS *Frobisher*. We were at war, and I was in the navy for the duration. I knew that once I entered the base through the arches there would be no going back. It seems strange, but after all the trials and tribulations of being accepted into the navy, I now could not bring myself to take the final step, so I delayed and delayed. Then another chap approached and stood next to me. He too was carrying a small suitcase. 'Are you going in?' he said in a Welsh accent, looking at me. I confirmed that I was. His name was Glan Evans and he came from Swansea. He too was filled with doubts and we both stood, silently, for another moment. At last, almost in unison, a Scot and a Welshman crossed the portal into St Vincent. From that moment we shared a great fellow feeling, and he remained the best friend a man could ever have. He was also a terrific scrum half.

Our fears were groundless. St Vincent was a boy sailors' training establishment, but when war was declared the young lads, who were about fourteen or fifteen years of age, were evacuated to the Isle of Man, out of range, it was hoped, of German bombers. Such was the fear of bombing that in the two months leading up to the outbreak of war, a programme of evacuating young children from the big cities had been put in motion, and eventually around two and a half million were taken from their families and sent to stay with strangers in the countryside. I imagine it did save some lives, although it was a very unpopular policy. But we had all heard about Guernica and what the German bombers had done to that town, and we expected that the same type of destruction would be visited on all our major cities by the German air force, the Luftwaffe.

So St Vincent was now set aside for training officers of the Fleet Air Arm. I think we were the first batch. The whole process of training was in a state of chaos, caused not only by the start of hostilities but by the fact that up until May 1939 the pilots and aircrew of naval aircraft had been trained by the Royal Air Force. Now it was suddenly the navy's job.

We were housed in G block, about forty of us, and they were a great bunch of lads. A wonderful officer by the name of Lt Commander Arthur Tillard introduced us to naval training. He was the first officer we saw with the naval wings on his sleeve. We were extremely lucky to have someone like that in charge. He was killed in a Walrus aircraft flying out of Arbroath later on in the war, and it was a very sad loss. Glan and I soon met up with a few other cadets who were slightly less English than most of our fellow recruits – they were South African: Buster May, Eric Margetts and Robert Lawson. For some reason it was us that Lt Commander Tillard would round up if there was anything needing doing – he seemed to realize that we worked well together and would get things done. After a few weeks we called ourselves the 'Black Hand Gang', a silly name from a popular comic, but it stuck and other people started to refer to us by it and continued to do so throughout the war.

As members of the Fleet Air Arm we would be officers in the Royal Navy, as well as pilots and flying crew. We would be expected when necessary to carry out the duties of officers on board a ship, so we had to learn to be sailors first. We were taught naval traditions and the rules of seamanship by time-served petty officers, old salts who had spent a lifetime in the navy and knew everything there was to know about life on board ship, and the very particular types of etiquette and behaviour that allowed officers and men in closely confined quarters to get along and organize themselves efficiently. These petty officers were the perfect teachers, confident, able to deal with anything that life threw at them, and by and large tolerant of our initial mistakes. We were taught the basic principles of every aspect of war at sea, from navigation, small-boat handling, gunnery, signals and fleet manoeuvres.

Instructors would visit from the other naval establishments dotted around Portsmouth and Gosport. Our gunnery instructor, Chief Petty Officer Wilmot, was based in the gunnery school at Whale Island. He was an amazing fellow. Signals, not only the traditional flags used by the navy but also Morse code for wireless telegraphy and signal lamps, were taught by Chief Petty Officer Oliver. They stand out in my memory as being excellent teachers and extremely amusing, who both enjoyed their tot of rum. It was hard work, but we learned quickly. There were plenty of sports as well, with a shooting team, rugby and swimming. We enjoyed ourselves, but it was serious all the same. The war had started and, while the expected bombing of civilians hadn't occurred, there were already casualties at sea.

One of the navy's aircraft carriers, HMS *Courageous*, was hit on 17 September by two torpedoes fired from a German U-boat. She had been patrolling in the channel approaches, south-west of Ireland, using her aircraft to search for submarines. The U-boat spotted her first. *Courageous* sank quickly, taking over five hundred sailors to their deaths, along with two squadrons of aircraft. We didn't dwell on these things, but it certainly served to remind us that we too might one day be on an aircraft carrier in the sights of an enemy submarine. In addition to *Courageous*'s sinking, a U-boat penetrated the fleet's main anchorage at Scapa Flow in October and a battleship, *Royal Oak*, was torpedoed and sunk, again with a great loss of life – over eight hundred men. This incident was particularly galling as Scapa Flow was meant to be a very secure base for the Home Fleet, but of course they had grown complacent during peacetime. The anti-submarine defences were strengthened, but it was a case of bolting the stable door. There were also daily losses of cargo ships to U-boat attack, and British ships were falling victim to German raiders, warships called pocket battleships that were very fast and could travel great distances without refuelling. Three of these were active in the South Atlantic and the Indian Ocean, preying on ships travelling outside the convoy system that had quickly been set up. So we young lads of eighteen and nineteen were studying away to join a service that was already seeing serious action, and not necessarily coming out on top.

We were trying to complete a condensed course in just three months and the original group of forty or so chaps in St Vincent was whittled down by around a third as a result of tests and examinations. After two and a half months the navy assumed that we had learned all we needed to know, or at least all we were capable of absorbing, and we were sent off on the next and most important part of our training – our initial flying instruction.

Half of those remaining on the course went to Elmdon in the Midlands while the other half went to Belfast. The odd part of this selection was that the men who, like me, were keen rugby players were all sent to Belfast. After about two weeks my friend Glan 'Taff' Evans and I organized a moderately good fifteen and played many of the local teams, with me hooking and my new Welsh pal as scrum-half. We had some wonderful matches, but one in particular sticks out in my mind. Taff was penalized three times in a row for the way he put the ball in. Frustrated, he picked it up and took it to the referee, saying, 'What bloody rules are you playing – Cardiff or Swansea?' He wasn't penalized again during the game.

We had a great time and the locals were extremely hospitable. We were billeted in private houses near to Sydenham airfield, which is now Belfast City airport. Living off the base and able to come and go after our day's training was a great improvement on St Vincent, and I made the most of it.

I met a girl, a petite blonde, and we arranged one night to meet outside the Plaza ballroom in the middle of Belfast. I had unfortunately not told her that the navy had decided we should wear civilian clothes when on leave in Belfast. My mother had sent my best kilt and sporran, so I wore these for my date. I arrived at the Plaza and saw my girlfriend on the other side of the road, so I waved and shouted. When she saw me she ran off as hard as she could in the other direction. It must have been my good luck after that to meet up with another young girl.

We had been invited to a Christmas dance sponsored by the Gallagher's tobacco factory at the Plaza, and after a few dances I was singled out by a very peroxide blonde who was a brilliant dancer. She asked me if I could 'jitterbug', a popular dance at the time, but something that I had never done. After half an hour in a nearby room she had showed me all the moves. So, accompanied by enormous amusement from my friends, we entered a dance competition. We managed to make it to the last four and then came second, so we ended with the prize of a well-stocked Christmas hamper. Then I met a lady called Ruby and we started going out together. She was great company and very attractive.

But learning to fly was the reason I had joined the navy and I would have been happy to be here, Ruby or no Ruby, despite the fact that the airfield itself was not particularly attractive. It was part of the shipbuilding company Harland and Wolff, whose massive mobile crane was visible from all over Belfast. Most of the base had been built on land reclaimed from Belfast Lough and it had a surface of hard-packed cinders. In winter a cold, bitter wind blew off the water, cutting through anything that I was wearing. I was being taught to fly in an aircraft called the Miles Magister, which was a single-engined monoplane with two open cockpits, one for the pupil, the other for the instructor. To start the engines we had to turn them over, swinging the propellers by hand to circulate the lubrication oil and forcing the petrol mixture into the cylinders, and this could be very difficult on a cold morning with everything covered in thick white frost.

There was quite a lot of classroom instruction, as well as practice take-offs and landings with the instructor. The Magister was a modern aeroplane, having been designed in 1937 as a purpose-built trainer for the RAF, so it was a very good plane to learn on, fun to fly and with none of the vices common to more high-performance planes that could take the inexperienced pilot by surprise. I learned a lot of my basic acrobatic skills in it.

I made good progress and thoroughly enjoyed flying. There was something absolutely unique about the sense of freedom that I experienced, the thrill of soaring high above the ground. On the practice flights one could see right over Belfast to the hills beyond. Looking down, I could see the shipyard, now full of warships under construction, one of them a big aircraft carrier that I was later to serve on, although at the time I had no idea what it was. Flying is exhilarating, and I have never lost that sense of joy I felt as the plane became airborne, kept aloft by nothing more than the rush of air over the wings. Other feelings could quickly take over, however, when I was flying off a carrier on an operation. But that was to come later; for now I couldn't wish for anything better.

The time for my solo flight came quickly. My instructor, Flight Sergeant Jack, thought I was ready and I remember a sense of mixed pride and nervousness as he climbed out of his cockpit and sent me off on my own for the first time. I took off to do two circuits of the aerodrome before making a final approach and landing. As I flew around I was so happy to have at last achieved my ambition that I could not contain my joy and was singing the hymn 'Onward, Christian Soldiers' at the top of my voice. I still can't believe it, but I did – I had such a great sense of achievement. I felt that I had accomplished more in the few months since I started my training than in the whole of my early life.

I also felt that deciding to join the navy had been the right thing to do. The navy was getting some excellent publicity as a result of some daring exploits. One of the German pocket battleships, *Admiral Graf Spee*, had been tracked down and there had been a major battle. *Graf Spee* had sailed for several months around Africa, in the Atlantic and the Indian Oceans, and had sunk nine British merchant ships, one of the most well known being *Doric Star*, run by the Blue Star Line. The German warship was finally spotted in the South Atlantic by three British cruisers, *Ajax*, *Achilles* and *Exeter*, and they opened fire. The British ships were hit, but kept up the chase and *Graf Spee* sought sanctuary in the harbour at Montevideo in Uruguay. She too had been hit and suffered damage. After three days she was scuttled in the harbour and the crew interned. The British ships were badly damaged and there were severe casualties on board, but *Graf Spee* was better armoured and had much more powerful guns than our cruisers, so it was seen as a major victory, with the British taking on a superior enemy and winning the day.

The aftermath was even more exciting. The captain of *Graf Spee* had behaved very decently, usually allowing the crews of the merchantmen that he intercepted to man the lifeboats before he fired on their ships. Some of them, however, had been taken prisoner and put on to *Graf Spee*'s supply ship, *Altmark*. Some weeks after *Graf Spee* was scuttled, *Altmark* was spotted in Norwegian territorial waters, heading south to a German port in the Baltic. The crew of HMS *Cossack*, a destroyer, tried to board *Altmark* but were stopped by a Norwegian gunboat, which was attempting to enforce Norwegian neutrality. The captain of *Cossack* knew there were prisoners on board, despite what *Altmark* and the Norwegian gunboat captain said, and he ordered his gun crews to open fire if the Norwegians threatened his ship. During this stand-off the captain of *Altmark* tried to ram *Cossack*, but instead his ship ran aground. *Cossack* sent over a boarding party to find that there were three hundred British sailors held prisoner in the hold. They were freed and brought back to Britain. The papers were full of the story, naturally, but the icing on the cake as far as we were concerned was the report that, as they broke into the hold where the prisoners had been kept for weeks, the boarding party shouted out, 'It's OK, lads, the navy's here!'

All of us felt a great deal of pride. There we were, newly qualified pilots, walking around in our uniforms, smiling at the girls and basking in the reflected glory of *Cossack* and the ships that sank *Graf Spee*. We felt we were the bee's knees. We soon came down to earth with a very big jolt.

Having finished our initial flying training and collected our wings, we were sent off for further training, this time to the RAF station at Netheravon, in Wiltshire, near Salisbury Plain. It was February 1940, and it was a particularly hard winter. Where we had previously been billeted in civilian houses, we were now housed in wooden barracks with bunks for twenty people. They were heated by two old pot-bellied stoves, one at each end of the barracks. I was not at all impressed by this, but thought to myself that it was only for a short while. If I had known how bad it was going to get, perhaps I would have got myself sent somewhere else.

Our training was now going to be on two aircraft, the Hawker Hart and the North American Harvard. The Hart had been designed by Sir Sydney Cam, who also designed the Hurricane fighter that was in front-line service with the RAF. The Hart dated back to 1927, with a fixed undercarriage, biplane wings and a two-seater open cockpit. When it first entered into service it was described as a light bomber, although it was one of the fastest aeroplanes around at the time, faster than most fighters. When I started flying it was obsolete, but it was still a good plane on which to learn long-distance navigation skills and bombing techniques. The Harvard was produced in the United States and was much more modern, being an all-metal, low-wing monoplane with a retractable undercarriage and a Perspex-covered cockpit. It was a sturdy, reliable aircraft with an air-cooled radial engine that could take a lot of punishment. Some of these planes are still flying and they even race them in America. We used the Harvards for instruction in formation flying and for some basic aerobatic and fighter tactics.

We shared the camp with the RAF, and there were some

Women Royal Auxiliary Air Force members there too. One night in the mess there was this absolute stunner, a tall, elegant blonde with Sergeants' stripes, who, I was told, rebuffed any advances. I approached her and to my amazement we hit it off. I had noticed her around the camp before and had been told that she was called Jane. I discovered that her real name was Margaret; Jane was just a nickname because of her long legs, like Jane the comic-strip pin-up in the *Daily Mirror*. Towards the end of my stay at Netheravon we used to play tennis together and there was always a good crowd to watch her play in her shorts.

My good luck in finding an attractive female companion wherever I got myself posted was beginning to become the envy of some of my fellow trainees, but we soon realized just how unlucky we all were as the weather, which was already severe, got much worse. There were high winds, a heavy snowfall and the roads to the airfield became blocked. The bad weather didn't slacken and the roads in and out of the camp remained impassable, so food and coal couldn't be brought in and soon the only place to go where we could get a hot drink was the NAAFI. It was so cold in our wooden barracks that we slept in our sheepskin flying suits. The stoves were inadequate anyway, but after the camp had been cut off for seven days there was no more fuel for them. We resorted to breaking the black-out frames in the windows and burning the sticks of broken wood. We had to melt water that had frozen in the fire buckets and try to wash ourselves with it, one leg at a time in each bucket. After the wooden frames were used up there was nothing.

Then a more serious situation developed. People started to fall ill with all sorts of ailments. The sickbay became full and patients had to be housed in the church. I was then told that there was a call out for funeral parties, because people were falling ill with influenza, pneumonia and German measles and the camp was starting to experience fatalities.

It was a dreadful situation and shows just how unable the country was to cope with the needs of wartime. We were lucky in a way that the war in Britain had so far been relatively peaceful, because the armed forces and the government had still not made a full transition to a war footing. We seemed to get no direction from the camp's officers, and nothing was being done to evacuate the sick or improve the food and heating situation. One of my companions in the Fleet Air Arm, Rupert Brabner, was actually an MP, who had been elected in July 1939. He managed to leave the camp for London and of course went straight to the Admiralty. The next thing that we were aware of was the arrival of an emergency hospital train at Netheravon station. The whole base was evacuated and we were given two weeks' leave. When we returned, the place was much improved and so was our position in a predominantly RAF camp. The final confirmation of the respect we had gained came with a concert we put on in the days before we left Netheravon. It was the usual stuff of comedy sketches and old favourites on the piano, the high point that I can remember being the appearance of my Welsh friend Glan dressed in a short skirt and with pan lids for a brassiere; the turnout was amazing.

Rupert went on to serve in various squadrons, and was on board HMS *Eagle* when she was sunk in 1942, but survived. After this he became a very young under-secretary in the Air Ministry. He was on a delegation to the United States in March 1945 when his Liberator aircraft disappeared over the Atlantic, and he died at the age of thirty-three.

Just before we left Netheravon for good we were sent with our planes to South Wales, where we did a final bombing and gunnery course from an RAF base called Stormy Down near Porthcawl. This was designed to finish our initial combat-flying training, and it also marked a watershed in my education about the female sex. While we were at Porthcawl we lived in a good hotel overlooking the seafront. We were amazed by the number of young girls who were booking in as well. They were there to work on the bombing range, operating the cameras that filmed us as we dive-bombed the targets floating in the bay. On a visit to a local beach I met a rather good-looking girl in a bathing suit, who told me she was staying at the same hotel. Our friendship blossomed and a room key changed hands. This young lady gave me my first experience of someone who was interested only in sex, without any emotional feelings. This is usually thought to be a particularly male attribute, but I am not so sure. Anyway, after four nights of exhausting sex with her I staggered into my pilot friend Dickie Chambers' room and gave him the keys to her room. I was physically drained, I felt used, and I had become tired of it. As I say, it was an education. Poor Dickie was killed not long after in the Shetlands, but I gather both he and the girl became quite attached and were very happy with the arrangement during the rest of the time we were in the hotel.

The final part of the navy's effort to turn me into an officer and a gentleman was a course in the Royal Naval College at Greenwich. Eighteen of us went there, from the original draft of forty or so that had started in St Vincent some months before, so I must have made the grade in a few things. The college is a magnificent building, with a majestic sweep of colonnades facing the Thames, and even more remarkable is the fact that it was originally built as a seamen's hospital. The painted hall is stunning and would not be out of place in a palace. Some of the buildings were quite badly damaged in the Blitz, but this was after we arrived. We were being trained to do a man's job, to become leaders in charge of ratings who might well have many more years' seniority than us. At heart, however, we were young men of between eighteen and twenty, irrepressible, full of fun and, however grave the situation, always on the lookout for the next drink or attractive female.

It was our boast that we would never allow a deserving case to go unattended.

As a precaution against damage from air raids, some parts of Greenwich had been boarded up. The statue of King William on its plinth in the main quadrangle had been completely surrounded by a brick wall and roofed over. One night before leaving we decided that we would leave our mark on the college. There were some small naval cannon lined up along one side of the colonnades, and we got some ropes and pulleys and purloined a couple of ladders. A group of us dismantled one of the cannon, then hefted the barrel and gun carriage on to the top of the brick tower that surrounded the statue, which was about 30 feet high. We then reassembled the cannon and removed all traces of the lifting tackle. Next morning there was a constant stream of people wandering through the quad to look at this cannon perched high in the air.

Of course we were quickly identified as the guilty men. Commander D'Oyly, the captain, called us into his office. We expected the chop, but he was quite calm. He questioned us closely about how we had managed to dismantle the cannon, lift it above the statue and then assemble it again in the dark. 'Well,' he said, 'I am very pleased that you have learned something from your seamanship lessons!' He was right. None of us would have had the foggiest idea how to do it before we had joined the navy. He then said, 'You will take it down before you leave.' We knew that this was not a request and we quickly chorused our desire to restore the cannon to its proper place. Nothing more was said about the incident, but I still have the photograph that one of us took before the cannon was removed.

I had one unpleasant incident at Greenwich, which made me extremely angry. Lord Gort, a senior army general, and a female companion were invited to a dinner, and there was a lottery to find out who was going to have the honour of joining them at the top table. I drew the short straw and sat next to her throughout the proceedings. After two abrupt questions, about my rank and my family, she utterly ignored me. My nervous attempts to start a conversation were cut dead, so I sat there feeling humiliated, sinking lower and lower in my chair as the evening progressed. I have never forgotten her rudeness, and I was pleased to be present when she later received some of her own medicine.

So we became sub-lieutenants in the Royal Navy Volunteer Reserve, the lowest form of officer life, but officers none the less. We were given a few days' leave. In one final daring coup one of my South African colleagues, Buster May, sweet-talked the Wren who was issuing the travel warrants and secured us warrants to travel home via Belfast. So it was a few days with Ruby, whom I hadn't seen for several months, then home to Kelso.

4

The Shooting Starts

In the final weeks of my training at Greenwich Naval College the world started to change very rapidly. The Germans mounted a huge assault on Western Europe, and we found ourselves looking down the barrel of a gun, sometimes quite literally.

It started at the beginning of April 1940 when Hitler launched an invasion of Norway and Denmark, both of which were neutral countries. German warships sailed with a large number of soldiers on board to capture the capital of Norway, Oslo, and several other towns along the coast. The seizure of Oslo didn't go according to plan, the harbour defences sank the leading German destroyer, and the Norwegian government and royal family escaped northwards.

The Royal Navy had put to sea when the German fleet was spotted, and there was a battle with some of the invading ships at Narvik, which lay at the head of a large fjord, Ofot Fjord, in northern Norway. Two German destroyers were sunk and three others damaged, as were two British destroyers. The German warships had succeeded in landing their troops, but were bottled up in the fjord, and unfortunately for them Britain had selected Narvik as the point where they would land British and French troops to fight the occupation. A few days later the battleship *Warspite*, with a fleet of destroyers, entered Ofot Fjord. The German destroyers were taken by surprise, and all eight of them and a submarine were sunk or scuttled in the ensuing battle. It was a great victory for our lads. The Fleet Air Arm had also come out of it well, because it was a Swordfish aircraft catapulted off *Warspite* that bombed the German U-boat. It was the first U-boat to be sunk by an aircraft in the war, and Narvik was the first naval battle.

A few days later the Fleet Air Arm pulled off another historic victory when a group of Skua dive-bombers that had taken off from Hatston in the Orkneys attacked a German cruiser. *Königsberg* had been part of the fleet that landed troops in Bergen, and she had been damaged by shells fired from the Norwegian shore batteries. She was moored against the harbour wall, awaiting repairs. The Skuas scored several direct hits, setting the cruiser on fire and rupturing the hull below the waterline. This was the first time that a warship had been sunk by air attack.

But from then on the boot was on the other foot. The Germans reinforced their troops by air, sending several squadrons of bombers and fighters to Norway. Within a few days the Royal Navy was being attacked by these German aircraft. German bombers, twin-engined Junkers Ju88 and Heinkel 111, sank a modern Tribal-class destroyer, HMS *Ghurkha*, and hit a battleship, HMS *Rodney*, although not much damage was caused. The vulnerability of the fleet to the German aircraft meant that they could not sail close to the shore to bombard German positions or to attack their shore communications. The aircraft carriers HMS *Ark Royal* and *Furious* had sailed with the fleet to provide air cover, but the problem was that the aircraft they carried were no match for the modern German planes with which they were coming into conflict.

*

I had still not completely finished my training, so I had been posted to another Fleet Air Arm base at Eastleigh, near Southampton, where I was being given instruction in naval fighter aircraft. Here I was flying the same aeroplanes that the navy was relying on to fight off the Luftwaffe over Norway, and it was quite clear to me that they would not be up to the job. We had Blackburn Skuas, Rocs and Gloster Gladiators. The Skua was a single-engined aircraft, an all-metal mono-plane with a covered two-seater cockpit. There were four machine guns in the wings, and the observer at the rear had a rearward-mounted machine gun to fight off attacking aircraft. As well as this, it could carry a 500lb bomb. It was a good dive-bomber, but as a fighter it was outclassed by the German Messerschmitt 109, which had a much better performance. Even the twin-engined Messerschmitt, the 110, which was also classified as a fighter bomber, could outrun it, although it probably wasn't as manoeuvrable as the Skua in the turn.

The Roc was a completely useless aeroplane. It looked like a Skua with a gun turret mounted at the rear of the cockpit. It had no forward-firing guns at all. Finally there was the Gladiator, which was a biplane with a fixed undercarriage and an enclosed cockpit. The Gladiator, however, despite its obsolete appearance, was my favourite aircraft. It was wonderful to fly and very good for aerobatics. But un-fortunately, like the Skua, it was not up to the performance of modern fighters.

One morning at Eastleigh I was told to take a Gladiator up and I decided to see how high I could get. The Gladiators had been fitted with an oxygen supply for high altitude, so I went out over the Solent and started to ascend, switching the oxygen on at about 12,000 feet. It was a beautiful day, and as I went through some clouds I came out into early-morning sunshine. I continued to climb, reached 29,000 feet and

would have gone higher if I could, but the controls were starting to feel vague and I lost any positive feel. I thought it wise
to start my descent and took her down in a gentle banking
turn, heading back to Eastleigh. I hit some cloud at 6,000 feet
and continued my shallow dive through it, coming out underneath at 3,000. I could see the coast, but while I was checking
my position in relation to Eastleigh I suddenly became aware
that I was in the company of some other aircraft.

As tracer bullets started to whip over my upper wing, it
quickly dawned on me that these aircraft were not friendly.
Then a fast monoplane fighter shot past me and I saw the Iron
Cross markings of a Luftwaffe fighter. I decided to follow at
full throttle, when more bullets started to go past. I looked in
my mirror and saw another aircraft approaching fast, its gun
ports twinkling as the pilot tried another burst. I made a very
tight climbing turn to the left and the attacking plane shot
underneath me. I could see that it was a Messerschmitt 109,
and as I pulled round tightly I saw the German pilot's face as
he looked up at me out of his cockpit. It was my first face-to-
face contact with the enemy.

I realized that I was no match for these fast fighters, with
their no doubt much more experienced pilots, so I kept climbing into the cloud. I stayed there for about ten or fifteen
minutes before venturing out, and by this time the German
fighters had decided to head back. During my flight to
altitude Eastleigh had come under attack and had launched its
barrage balloons. Under these conditions we were instructed
to fly to Worthy Down, near Winchester, which was our
reserve station.

I was lucky, because the Messerschmitt 109s were at the
limit of their endurance and did not have the fuel reserves to
fly around and wait for me to appear once more. Also, there
was a good chance that a group of Hurricanes or Spitfires
might be sent up to take them on. If I had been flying over

enemy territory, however, I would not have had that advantage. This was the problem for the crews of the Skuas and Gladiators in Norway. The aircraft carriers HMS *Furious* and *Glorious* had ferried some RAF Gladiators and Hurricanes to fly from an airstrip at Bardufoss to provide air cover for the allied troops. Both carriers remained on station, sending out anti-submarine patrols and bombing missions. It was a strain on the crews, because in northern waters there was daylight for almost twenty-four hours, so the carriers were the target of lots of dive-bombing attacks from the Luftwaffe. There were a lot of casualties in the Fleet Air Arm during this period, because not only were their machines inferior, but if they were shot down over land they were usually taken prisoner. The German army did not have it all its own way, however: Norway is particularly difficult terrain to fight in. But the war there was overtaken by other events.

Hitler invaded Belgium and Holland on 10 May, and then crossed into French territory. The British Government decided to pull our troops out of Norway. There was a squadron of Hurricanes still operating there and, because every modern fighter was now precious, a decision was made to recover them on to an aircraft carrier and get them back to Britain. I was told that they could have gone on to *Ark Royal*, but her deck-lifts were too narrow, so they opted instead to try to fly on to *Glorious*. Remarkably, they succeeded. Unfortunately, *Glorious* was seen on her journey back to Scapa Flow by two German warships, *Scharnhorst* and *Gneisenau*, battlecruisers with large-calibre, radar-controlled guns. The two destroyers escorting the carrier, *Ardent* and *Acasta*, tried to attack the German vessels, but they were hit and sunk, although *Ardent* managed to fire a torpedo at *Gneisenau*, forcing her to break off the action. But *Scharnhorst* fired shell after shell into *Glorious* and she went down with most of her crew, and with her aircraft, including the Hurricanes. Around twelve hundred men were killed.

Scharnhorst had also been slightly damaged by the attack from *Acasta* and anchored in Trondheim fjord for some repairs. The air group on *Ark Royal* was ordered to mount an attack on the ship while she was at anchor. In my view this was a risky operation, and I gather that many on the *Ark* thought the same. However, if there was a possibility of crippling the warship, which was a powerful threat where she was, then I believe that there was no option but to try it. Two squadrons of Skua aircraft took off for a daylight attack. The RAF should have bombed the local German airstrips to prevent Luftwaffe fighters taking off, but the plans went totally wrong. The Skuas were met by Messerschmitt 109s, which tore into them. Our planes made some direct hits, but the 500lb bombs carried by the Skuas couldn't penetrate the deck armour of *Scharnhorst*. People on the *Ark* at the time still remember the day when they waited for the planes to come back and only seven out of the fifteen returned. Sixteen pilots and observers had gone missing. To lose the equivalent of a whole squadron like that is a severe blow to an air group, very damaging to morale, and it was probably a good thing that the *Ark* returned to Scapa Flow.

So there we were, in the space of a few days, with the loss of another aircraft carrier and her aircrew, as well as eight Skuas and some very experienced pilots. The results of this operation probably helped to influence a decision I made a few months afterwards, but for now the disaster in France completely overshadowed what was happening to the Fleet Air Arm. The German army had stormed through the French lines and the French were retreating. Holland and Belgium had surrendered. The British army had been surrounded and there was an all-out attempt to rescue them from the beaches at Dunkirk. For almost a week we listened to the six o'clock news on the radio, and read the *Daily Mirror* and *Daily Express* for news of what was happening to our troops. As an individual you went about your daily duties, but I thought that we were approaching an extremely serious and difficult time. These were very worrying events. Winston Churchill had become Prime Minister after the invasion of France, and there was a feeling that the lot who had got us into this mess were no longer in charge, so there was less of a sense of despair than there could have been at what was really a humiliating defeat.

I remember listening to the wireless as Churchill made his speech about fighting on the beaches, never surrendering. I think it helped that there was no attempt to pretend that things were better than they were. It was a clever way of making people feel too proud to contemplate surrender.

Our base at Eastleigh was part of the Supermarine factory, which produced Spitfires. It was a juicy target, in easy flying range for the Luftwaffe now situated in northern France, hence my contact with the two Messerschmitt fighters. Subsequently, there were frequent raids on the factory and the airstrip and incursions by German fighters became very common.

'Air raid imminent' warnings were received on a red telephone in the air duty office at the base. Almost immediately the barrage balloons would be released and they would shoot up into the air at an enormous speed, causing the tethering wires to smoke with friction as they unwound rapidly on the rotating cable drum. Of course, once the balloons were lazily bobbing about in place the airfield was out of use; no planes could take off and none was allowed to try to land. I was often diverted to our alternative airfield, Worthy Down, because an air-raid warning had Eastleigh on alert. Sometimes these precautions did not work. During one of my stop-offs at

Worthy Down I was with three other pilots in the air-watch office, waiting for a call from Eastleigh telling us it was safe to make our way back there. It was a lovely summer's day and we were idly chatting, probably about our plans for the week-end and the local girls we were interested in, when we heard this aircraft. We recognized the engine noise almost simultaneously – we had heard it too many times during raids – and we all shouted, 'Jerry!' There had been no air-raid warning, but we all rushed for the door, my three companions turning left while I turned to the right, heading for a slit trench near the aerodrome fence. I had run not more than a few yards when a bomb dropped behind me and exploded with an immense bang. I remember flying up in the air, then plummeting back on to the ground face down, with stones and gravel falling on top of me until I was almost covered. I could hardly breathe, the blast had winded me so much, and I was stone deaf, but I managed to crawl a few yards and fall into the slit trench. It was obviously one of those lone raiders that used to sneak over the Channel in broad daylight. It came back on two other passes, machine-gunning anything that appeared in the pilot's sights.

When it finally flew off the all-clear sounded and I staggered out of the slit trench and down to the officers' mess. The building was just a heap of red bricks; rubble and dust covered the ground and bits of wooden beam and window frame were scattered around. There was a horrible smell of explosives. I never saw my three companions again; they had all been killed by the single bomb. Their bodies were never found.

I went to the sickbay and was checked out by the medical orderly, but apart from a ringing in the ears there was nothing physically wrong with me. I flew back to Eastleigh with my uniform ripped and dirty. This incident had quite an effect on me – I suppose I was suffering from some sort of shock. I was very disturbed by the sudden deaths of my three companions and my lucky near-miss. It brought me up with a round turn, as they say in the navy. If sometimes during my training it had been easy to forget that others were engaged in a life-or-death struggle, this bomb was a harsh reminder. I found it hard to get to sleep at night for some time after, and was quite alarmed by sudden noises. I have sometimes read that young men have no fear of death, but if this incident happened too quickly to feel fear at the time, then I certainly felt it afterwards as I searched the wreckage for any signs of life.

Next day I had to borrow some clothes and set off to Geives, the naval tailor in Portsmouth, for a new uniform, which I had to pay for out of my own funds. Luckily I was properly dressed, because the next day we were called out to a parade and, quite unannounced, we were inspected by His Majesty the King. I wonder what the reaction would have been if I had stood there in my dust-covered, blast-torn uniform?

It was not long after this that I had my next meeting with the enemy. I had been instructed to take a Lieutenant Crane to Kemble to pick up some spare parts. We were going to fly up in a Skua, so we took off and flew north. I was in the pilot's seat and he was in the rear in the observer's position. It was a lovely summer's afternoon and we flew at about 5,000 feet. As we were passing over Marlborough College there were shouts in my headphones and, looking in my mirror, I saw Crane pointing frantically behind and there was this twin-engined Heinkel coming for me. As we were on a simple housekeeping flight, our aircraft had not been armed and we had no ammunition. I gave the engine full boost and headed down, but still he came on and I thought if I turned left or right he would open up on me from his forward turret. It was then that I noticed Swindon and the big railway marshalling yards, so I dived down at a very steep angle and pulled out about 50 feet above the rails. I could no longer see him, and neither could I see Crane. We flew as low as I dared and landed at Kemble, about 10 miles further on. I taxied over to some RAF Hurricanes whose pilots were on standby and told them where I had encountered the Heinkel. Within five minutes three of them were in the air. Lieutenant Crane had been thrown to the floor of the cockpit in my dive, and he struggled out as we stopped. We obtained the spare parts from the stores and then he said, 'I am pulling rank, so you can go in the back.' That was the thanks I got for shaking the raider off my tail.

Shortly after, although the lightning hit-and-run raids continued, what became known as the Battle of Britain started in earnest, with heavy bomber raids on London and other cities all over Britain, including Portsmouth and Southampton. The main targets were the docks, but of course the bombs fell everywhere, and many of the poor civilians would move out to the surrounding countryside every night to avoid the heavy raids.

The squadron that I was in then, 759, was referred to as 'The broken-down actor and windy jockey squadron'. We had Ralph Richardson, Laurence Olivier, the film star Robert Douglas and the jockey Frankie Furlong of Grand National fame as members. If it hadn't been for the constant raids it would have been great fun. Ralph Richardson was an instructor and once told me, 'If you see a plane flying over the airfield going like this,' and he mimicked a plane rising and falling with his hands, 'then it's me. I suffer from kangaroo petrol.'

Ralph in particular was great company, and of course they could all drink like fish in the wardroom at night. We had some very enjoyable parties, but sadly the airfield was becoming just too dangerous and the navy decided to move us all out to various places. The experienced pilots were sent to boost the ranks of the RAF, where they were thrown into action in the Battle of Britain.

This was a strange period, at times both frightening and bizarre. The weather was extremely good – it was a glorious summer. Here we were in the midst of a deadly war, with blue skies and the sun shining. I had a forty-eight-hour pass from Eastleigh – in fact I had two for successive weekends. For the first one I was invited by one of my fellow pilots, a chap called 'Lucky' Sutton, to visit his family at Kingston upon Thames. About four of us went and we were made extremely welcome by his parents and had a good night out at the local club.

The next weekend's leave saw the same group travel to a fellow pilot's home in a village in mid-Kent. We ended up on the Friday night in the local inn, being stood drinks by every-one. The next day after lunch we went with our host to the village cricket match. I always remember on this July day sitting on a grass bank outside the pavilion, watching a rather boring match. I have never been an enthusiast of the game, but there was a great deal of local interest. Then I noticed the sky: there were aircraft at about 10–15,000 feet having a terrific dogfight. The noise of machine guns was faintly audible and there were great swathes of vapour trails stretched across the sky. A fight to the death was taking place above our heads, and my heart went up to the boys in their cockpits, knowing how they would be desperately turning, their mouths dry, anxiously checking their mirrors, their speed, their legs aching through pressure on the rudder pedals, their planes shaking as the guns fired. I was the only one looking up; nobody else was showing any interest in what was going on above them – they were concerned only with the cricket. It was difficult to comprehend.

Shortly after this the squadron was disbanded. However,

before our transfer one strange incident occurred which had a profound bearing on my life, although if I had known at the time just how it would affect me I would have been even more disturbed by it than I was.

I was on afternoon duty in the air-watch office with a senior officer. It was another nice summer's day, and I think it was probably the weekend because everything was quiet. There were just the two of us, smoking and chatting. On the table were the telephones linking us to the adjutant's office and the switchboard, and of course the red 'alert' handset. In a rack on the wall were three sets of loaded Verey pistols, two with red flares and one with a green. Suddenly the red phone rang for an air-raid alert. So we sprang up and switched on our air-raid siren, which was on a lattice tower. As the horrible wail of the siren started up, my partner on duty noticed a Hudson aircraft taxiing out from the Saunders Roe hangar on the other side of the aerodrome. It kept coming out and lined up at the end of the runway, turning into the wind. We both knew how efficient our barrage-balloon operators were by now; they would spring into action as soon as they heard our siren. I rushed into the watch room and grabbed both the red Verey pistols, rushed out and handed one of them to my companion. He immediately fired it into the middle of the airfield where it burst lazily, leaving a trail of red smoke. It didn't seem to deter the pilot of the Hudson, and realizing he was opening up to take off, I fired the second red Verey pistol. Sure enough, the balloons were soaring up. To our alarm, the pilot of the Hudson ignored both our danger signals.

'The idiot, what is he doing?' I shouted, but there was nothing else we could do. The aircraft started rolling, reached speed and took off. He must have been at about 200–300 feet altitude when he reached the airfield perimeter where several barrage balloons were stationed. I was tensed, waiting for the inevitable, horribly powerless to prevent what I knew was going to happen. I didn't see the pilot make any attempt to manoeuvre. One wing struck a cable, bits flew off and the aircraft dived into the ground, where it exploded. We stood there for I don't know how long, as smoke from the burning wreckage climbed into the sky. I felt sick. We learned later that the plane had crashed on to a house in Nutbeam Road, destroying it and killing both the Mayor and Mayoress of Eastleigh who lived there.

The closure of the squadron meant that I had to make a choice about what I wanted to do next. I knew that I did not want to continue training on Skuas. What I knew personally about them, and what I heard about them in action, made me think that they did not have much of a future in the Fleet Air Arm, and their replacements, the Fairey Fulmar, did not look any more promising.

One of the functions of the Fleet Air Arm that had been stressed at different times during our training was to attack enemy ships, sinking them or damaging them sufficiently that they could not escape our fleet. There was a slogan that summed it up: Find, Fix and Strike. We would locate the enemy by searching vast areas of the ocean from the air, work out his position and then mount a strike from the air using bombs or torpedoes. This seemed a way forward that would enable me to fight back against the enemy. The war was happening all around me now, and I felt restless and out of it. The cricket match at which I had been a spectator while the war was being fought out thousands of feet above my head had upset me. It was fine for the civilians, who were doing what they could, but I was meant to be a pilot, not a spectator.

So I made a formal request to be transferred to a training course for TSR aircraft, which stood for Torpedo Spotter and Reconnaissance. I went north to another naval shore-based establishment, HMS Sanderling at Abbotsinch, which has now become Glasgow airport. Here I was taught how to dive-bomb, drop depth-charges and launch torpedoes into the Firth of Clyde off the Isle of Arran.

I often decide on a course of action and then wonder whether I have made a mistake, and I certainly felt that at HMS Sanderling. The problem was not the course; it was the aircraft I was flying. I was piloting the slowest pre-war biplane still in front-line service. I refer of course to the Fairey Swordfish. This aircraft seemed like a hangover from the 1920s, although it had actually come into service in 1936. It was a biplane, and it had all the struts and wires reminiscent of the First World War planes like the Avro 504 that had first excited my interest in flying. But the Battle of Britain was being fought by fast monoplanes – Hurricanes and Spitfires. They were all metal, whereas the greater part of the Swordfish, the wings and the rear fuselage, were canvas covered. It was powered by a single radial engine that gave it a top speed of barely 110 miles an hour. The Spitfire could manage over 300 quite easily. The Swordfish was a big air-craft, with a crew of three. The pilot sat in a forward open cockpit, which was high above the centre line and gave a good field of view. Behind was another cockpit, set slightly lower in the fuselage, in which there was first the observer/navigator; then behind him the telegraphist air gunner, or TAG, who worked the radio and could fire a rear-pointed drum-fed Lewis gun. Apart from this, there was a forward-firing machine gun mounted in the fuselage behind the engine. The huge wing area gave the Swordfish the ability to carry a bomb load of almost 2,000lb, which was impressive for a single-engined plane. It was manoeuvrable at slow speed and could pull out of a dive without any trouble.

I felt that I was riding a carthorse instead of a steeplechaser at first, but the more I flew it, the more I began to appreciate its qualities. It was nicknamed the 'Stringbag'. Several reasons are given for this, the most obvious being that at first glance it looks as though it is held together by string. This is deceptive. The main struts were made out of stainless steel, the rigging was very strong steel cable, and the frames were made of steel and duralumin, an aluminium alloy produced for aircraft production. No, I believe the Stringbag got its name because, like the old lady's shopping bag, it expanded to accommodate whatever was demanded of it. It carried bombs, depth-charges, torpedoes, smoke flares, and they even mounted sixteen rockets under the wings in the later stages of the war. There are stories of some squadrons moving rapidly from airstrip to airstrip in the desert in North Africa, securing motorbikes underneath the fuselage of their Swordfish and then carrying them to a new location. It was a tough plane and could take an awful lot of damage, as many aircrew were to discover and be grateful for. Its low speed was also an asset, it seemed, as our instructors told stories of Swordfish in the Norwegian campaign being attacked by Messerschmitt 109s. The British pilots employed the tactic of making 180-degree turns at sea level towards the attacking plane. The Swordfish had a much smaller turning circle than any fast fighter, and moreover it had such an advantageous lift ratio that you could reduce its speed to just 70 knots in the turn and it would continue on a perfect line. Most planes need more power to complete a turn, but not the Swordfish. The hapless Messerschmitt pilot would not know why his target had suddenly disappeared from view as he sped past.

During my time at Abbotsinch I was able to meet up with some of the friends I had made since entering St Vincent so many months before. My friend Buster May from Durban was one. During our stay we produced a concert party that gave two performances at the local Empire theatre in Paisley. It was a fantastic success, so much so that we were allowed to travel for free on the local corporation trams and we were treated in every bar we went to – and we went into many, I can tell you!

The wartime forces were a great melting pot; people from the strangest occupations and places, all over the Empire, were thrust into uniform and told to get on with it. It produced the most amazing juxtapositions. One of the junior ratings who looked after our billet, and who was obviously a wartime recruit, asked for a grand piano to play in the concert. On the night he appeared in immaculate white tie and tails and performed a solo act which was just unbelievable. After a couple of classics he asked the audience for requests and they would not let him leave the stage. He was so popular that his original slot of fifteen minutes stretched to forty-five, after which the MC had to go out and tell the audience to let him finish. It was a remarkable performance, and did a great deal to boost the popularity of the navy.

When my South African friend was due to leave, we decided we would have a weekend on the town, so on Saturday night we went off to Glasgow for a meal at a popular restaurant called Rogano's. We decided after the meal to look for some local female talent and were told that the best place was the Locarno dance hall. This was a very respectable establishment, where the doormen inspected you to make sure that you were smartly dressed before letting you in, and where no alcohol was served. Eventually we teamed up with two nice-looking, well-dressed girls for some enjoyable but fairly chaste dancing. Towards the end of the evening they told us that they were going home together, so we were forced to say goodbye. The girl that I had been dancing with asked if we would like to come along to a tea party at her parents' house the next day. We accepted. The following day, to my annoyance, Buster, feeling perhaps slightly more predatory, decided that as he was leaving on

Monday a tame afternoon in a suburban house was not for him. I, however, felt under some obligation to go. Knocking at the front door, I found about twelve people of both sexes gathered in the parlour, chatting over sandwiches and cups of tea. I was asked by my hostess to join a Ludo game where a young lady needed cheering up. She had, I was told, recently lost her boyfriend, who had been a pilot in the RAF.

As soon as we were introduced I realized that she was someone special. Her name was Marjorie Cochrane and she lived in a small town south-west of Glasgow. There was something about her that I had not met in any other woman. Eventually, when we were on our own, I was able to get her to talk about her boyfriend and she said that he had been killed in a plane down south in Eastleigh about three months ago. I didn't know of any accident at Eastleigh other than the one I had tried to stop. We talked further, and it became clear that her boyfriend was the pilot at the controls of the Hudson. I explained that I had tried to prevent him from taking off. All she knew was that his passengers had been some very important people from the Air Ministry in London. It was a remarkable coincidence. I was so struck by her that before the evening was out I told her that I was determined to marry her. I think she thought I was mad, but I am pleased to say that we were married in June 1944 and remained so for almost sixty years. It was the best decision that I ever made in my whole life.

I learned a lot at Abbotsinch. Dive-bombing in the Swordfish was very different from doing it in a Skua. This manoeuvre was enough to show what a reliable aircraft the Swordfish was. At the beginning you do a banking turn and head the nose of the plane down in a dive. The plane starts to accelerate, and the wind starts shrieking as it rushes through the struts and wires. At this stage it's quite possible for the air-speed indicator to show 200 knots: you are falling fast, the needle of the altimeter going from 8,000 feet to 7,000 feet like the second hand of a clock, but you are still able to keep perfect control of the aircraft. Plummeting down, it is possible to wait until the frightening height of just 200 feet is reached before pulling back on the stick and levelling out. During our training I avoided diving to such a low height, but I did it later and can vouch that it can be done.

There were complicated patrol patterns to learn, depending on whether we were meant to be locating a surface vessel, hunting a submarine that had been detected by a merchant ship or mounting an anti-submarine patrol along the line of advance of a convoy or fleet of warships. Finally, of course, there was the torpedo practice, where we launched a dummy torpedo at our target ship. She was an elderly destroyer but still capable of the rapid manoeuvres that any self-respecting warship would carry out to avoid a torpedo in the water. Of course, she was not carrying guns that were directing their fire at the crew of the attacking aircraft. But the key was learning to judge the speed of the ship by the size of the bow wave, and then to calculate the required deflection for a torpedo that would be launched from a distance of 1,000 or so yards and would travel at a speed of 29 knots to its (one hoped unsuspecting) target. It sounded simple, but the truth was that so far in the war torpedo attacks on moving warships had never been successful, despite several attempts.

One such attack had taken place while I was still at Eastleigh with 759 Squadron. The French government's surrender in June 1940 meant that the French fleet in the Mediterranean might be absorbed by the German navy, boosting its strength overnight and threatening our fleet, which was based in Alexandria in Egypt. The main base for the French warships was Toulon on the French mainland, but they also had ships with our fleet in Alexandria, as well as a big base in Oran in Algeria. It was these ships that the Admiralty felt they should do something about.

The operation against the French ships in Oran was to prove important, because it was the start of a battle that I was eventually to join and it formed a big part of my war service. The incident was given great publicity – it was all over the newspapers – but what I later discovered had taken place caused several people I served with, including the commanding officer of a squadron I joined, 818, to make some crucial decisions about the attack on *Bismarck*. Apart from that, it's important to realize that while I was deciding about what aircraft I would fly in the Fleet Air Arm and embarking on various training courses, others were putting into practice what I was being taught and were finding that there was a big difference between peacetime exercises and what was possible when the shells were exploding, with your aircraft as a target.

In July 1940 HMS *Ark Royal*, our most famous aircraft carrier, was sent down to the Mediterranean base in Gibraltar to be part of a small unit called Force H. This was a very powerful force when it was first created. As well as the *Ark* there was HMS *Hood*, probably the most famous warship in the Royal Navy, a battlecruiser, though most of us thought of her as a battleship. The only real difference was that she was slightly less armoured than a battleship and so was a bit faster, but she had extremely large guns and was, we thought, quite formidable. There were also the real battleships HMS *Valiant* and *Resolution*, each with big, 15in-calibre guns, accompanied by several cruisers and nineteen destroyers. This may appear to be a big fleet, but it wasn't that large compared to either the Italian or French navies.

Force H had been assembled with the immediate aim of making sure that the French fleet in Oran didn't become a threat to us by remaining in the Med and coming under German control. We were going to 'escort them off the premises', so to speak.

The force was commanded by Rear Admiral James 'Slim' Somerville, who was based on *Hood*. I was later to serve under him on more than one carrier and the general opinion of him was that he was an absolutely first-class commanding officer, who was not only respected but liked. His orders from the Government were to tell the French to steam their ships to a British port and throw in their lot with us against Germany, or alternatively to sail to a French port in the West Indies, or, finally, to scuttle them. If they chose not to do any of these things, then we would sink them.

The French naval base was really in two separate locations. The harbour at the city of Oran was home to submarines and small patrol boats, while further west along the coast was Mers-el-Kébir, where the larger cruisers and battleships were moored. The two that we wanted out of the way in particular were, I gathered, *Strasbourg* and *Dunkerque*, which were recently built and fast.

The captain of the *Ark*, Cedric 'Hooky' Holland, another officer I liked, and who had a great sense of humour, had at one time been an attaché in the embassy in Paris and was selected to go to discuss terms with the French admiral on one of his battleships in Mers-el-Kébir harbour. The French were given a deadline by which either they must agree to comply or we would open fire. From the British point of view, there was very little to discuss. It was important that, if we were to move against the French fleet, the action should be decisive and must not allow the French warships to put to sea and escape, or fight back. The planning was quite meticulous, carefully timed from the expiry of the ultimatum. Our battleships would launch a massive barrage against the French ships in the harbour, and Swordfish from the *Ark* would launch torpedoes and bombs against them as well.

Early on the morning of 3 July the first two Swordfish took off to start their patrol to the west of Force H. When the light improved they would begin standard anti-submarine searches. Almost immediately after this another six Swordfish took to the air to search the sea up to 150 miles to the north-east and as far north as the Spanish coast. (I became quite friendly with a telegraphist air gunner who took part in these patrols, George Dawson of 810 Squadron, one of those on the *Ark*.) A fighter patrol of three Skuas was then put into the air, and a reconnaissance Swordfish took off to carry out a patrol over Mers-el-Kébir and Oran harbours, keeping watch over the activities of the French fleet. It was also ordered to give any assistance, especially in the way of transmitting signals, to HMS *Foxhound*, the destroyer that had taken Captain Holland to meet with the French admirals. *Foxhound* was patrolling slowly outside the breakwater at Mers-el-Kébir, while Captain Holland had gone into the harbour on a small boat.

By now the negotiations were dragging on and the squadrons started to make preparations for an attack on the harbours. The plan called for six Swordfish to mine the entrance of Mers-el-Kébir to stop any of the French ships escaping. Dropping mines was something that I went on to practise at Abbotsinch. They were shaped much like a torpedo, without the motor and the propeller at the back, and were mounted in the same position on the aircraft's fuselage. Once the mines were released they would hit the water, sink to the bottom and then become armed. They would be set off by a fuse triggered by the magnetic field of a ship passing over them. They contained 1,000lb of explosive, so were very potent, although their value was not just in the damage that they could cause to one ship: particularly in a situation like Oran, the knowledge that mines had been laid would also deter ships from passing through the harbour entrance. So dropping just one mine in the right place could bottle up a whole fleet until the mine was cleared. That, at any rate, was what we hoped and were told in our training!

While the mine-laying aircraft were ranged at the end of the flight deck, the reconnaissance Swordfish, which had been constantly circling over the French ships, reported back that there was now a lot of activity amongst the moored vessels. Tugs had appeared and were laying tow ropes to some of the battleships, and it looked to the observers as though they were raising steam. Their estimate was that the ships would be ready for sea in half an hour.

At a few minutes after 1300, at orders from Somerville, the six Swordfish took off on the mission to drop the mines on the harbour of Mers-el-Kébir. They circled while a flight of six Skuas joined them to give them some defence against attack from French fighters. There was no opposition from any aircraft or from the ground; they seemed to have taken the French completely by surprise. An hour later, fresh orders came through from Admiral Somerville in *Hood* to mine the harbour at Oran as well. Two Swordfish were loaded up to do this, in the hopes of bottling up the submarines and destroyers moored there.

As the minutes ticked away, no one on the *Ark* was clear about what was happening. As a matter of fact, there was growing confusion at quite a senior level about the state of the negotiations. Captain Holland was talking to the French Admiral Gensoul, trying to find a face-saving formula that would allow the French to surrender their ships and avoid bloodshed. Admiral Somerville was under pressure from the Admiralty to settle the issue quickly and stop the French from wriggling off the hook. The time for launching the attack passed, and 'landing on' – as we called landing back on the carrier – was suspended.

Then, without any warning, the British battleships opened fire. Somerville had told Holland to break off negotiations and head out to the open sea. George Dawson in 810 Squadron, who had been on a reconnaissance patrol, searching the coast of Spain, told me that all during his patrol he had been listening to broadcasts from the French Radio Lyons. Their news bulletins had been repeating the British demands, so it was clear to him that they had been quickly passed to the French authorities and were by now common knowledge. He was not at all sympathetic to the French admirals and couldn't understand how they had allowed themselves to get into the position they were in.

He was now one of those Swordfish crews anxiously waiting to land on when he was startled by the huge crash of *Hood*'s heavy guns going off, blasting out clouds of black smoke tinged with white flashes. He could see the impact of the shells in the harbour at Mers-el-Kébir, and after a few minutes of this barrage there was a massive explosion from the harbour, and the smoke and debris from what was clearly a substantial target poured high into the air, reaching an altitude of, he thought, 1,000 feet or more.

The giant blast was caused by a battleship, *Bretagne*, blowing up. A shell must have hit a magazine to cause such devastating damage. Then almost immediately a destroyer also disintegrated as it too blew up. The harbour was by now covered in smoke from the explosions of the French ships and our shells, with the result that the observers in the spotting Swordfish found it hard to see anything. One of them thought he could see ships preparing for sea, despite the fact that the harbour entrance had not been cleared of the mines laid earlier in the day. Some other ships had also been seriously damaged. *Dunkerque*, which had received some hits, was being driven on to the beach to save her from sinking, and so too was *Provence*, another battleship of the same class as *Bretagne*.

Two flights of three Swordfish had now taken off, with racks under their wings carrying four 250lb bombs and eight 20lb anti-personnel bombs, to dive-bomb the remaining

French warships in the harbour. With this striking force already in the air, one of the Swordfish spotter planes confirmed what they had suspected ten minutes earlier: *Strasbourg* had raised steam and was powering through the carnage in the harbour, determined to make its escape. A signal was sent to Somerville in *Hood*, while the crew of the Swordfish watched the harbour boom open and the raked bows of one of the fastest ships in the French fleet passed over five 1,000lb mines totally unscathed and headed for the open sea. She was escorted by eleven destroyers that had also managed to escape any damage from British shells or from the mines. The Swordfish signalled to the *Ark* that *Strasbourg* was coming into gun range, and the *Ark* immediately changed course and went at full speed away from her. But escape was uppermost on the French officers' minds and they headed east as fast as they could go.

One of the most important targets at Mers-el-Kébir was now escaping, so an urgent signal was sent to the Swordfish on their bombing mission to change course and make their attack, not on the ships in the harbour but on the fleeing warship, which was rapidly putting distance between herself and Force H.

This, of course, is one of the tasks that I was training for at Abbotsinch, although ideally the Swordfish would be armed with torpedoes. In circumstances like this, however, you do what you can with what you have. The Swordfish changed course and made an approach to the French battleship. Completely unobserved, they turned into their dive, releasing their bombs at 4,000 feet. Then the anti-aircraft guns on the French destroyers opened up, projecting a dense barrage of fire, which the planes managed to avoid. One or two possible hits were observed by the crew of the Swordfish, but the warships steamed on apparently unscathed. The 250lb semi-armour-piercing bombs had little effect on the armour plating of a battleship – something that had been discovered in the attack on *Scharnhorst* in Norway.

Somerville had been told that *Strasbourg* and *Dunkerque* were our most important targets. *Dunkerque* seemed to be beached in Oran, but *Strasbourg* was steaming away, most likely heading to Toulon to meet up with the rest of the French fleet. We needed to stop her, and a torpedo attack was rapidly organized. Six Swordfish from 818 were ranged on the flight deck, torpedoes slung in their cradles under the fuselage. The warheads had been fitted with Duplex pistols, fuses that would be triggered to explode on impact or if they were affected by the magnetic field of a ship. Ideally, they should explode beneath the waterline or under the keel of a ship, and the running depth of the torpedo can be adjusted to take account of this. Here they were set to run at a depth of 20 feet.

The planes took off at 1950, when the light was beginning to fade. They had a good fix on *Strasbourg*, however, and they flew along the coast about 15 miles off shore. It was now twenty minutes after sunset. Their ruse seemed to be success-ful. The torpedoes were launched from a position between two escorting destroyers, with deflections for an estimated speed of the target between 28 and 30 knots. The attack went almost unnoticed, until the gunners on the destroyers woke up as the last two Swordfish dropped; they burst into action, but it was too late. The Swordfish had carried out a classic, well-planned attack, but sadly there was no sign of any hit to *Strasbourg* – even if there had been, the darkness and funnel smoke obscured the evidence. The main focus of the *Ark*'s efforts, and of Force H itself, had managed to escape and even now was steaming to safety.

Even though *Dunkerque* had been hit and was now beached in shallow water inside the harbour at Mers-el-Kébir, it was difficult to ascertain just how badly damaged she was, or how easy it was going to be to refloat her. Britain wanted to make sure that she was out of action for a long while, so two days later a new plan was put into operation: the *Ark* would carry out another torpedo attack. Around 100 miles from the Algerian coast a dozen Swordfish, six from 810 Squadron and six from 820 Squadron, were armed with torpedoes and ranged on the flight deck. *Dunkerque*'s position made it difficult for an attack. She was close to the shore in shallow water, protected by a mole. To make a beam attack would require an approach either over the breakwater or over the town. The twelve aircraft would attack from two directions and so formed up into two sections. One group of nine would make its approach low over the sea out of the rising sun, dropping their 'kippers', as the torpedoes were known, just inside the breakwater, while the other three would approach over the town and attempt to hit the port side of the warship.

The nine aircraft coming in from the sea waited until they could see the rays of the rising sun hitting *Dunkerque*, then they started their dive, separating into two groups, one of six aircraft and one of three. They took the French by surprise, and their approach was purposeful and steady, without any of the anti-aircraft guns firing at them. Five out of the first six torpedoes, which had been set to run at a very shallow 12 feet, hit the target, although one failed to explode. It was seen to ricochet off the side of the warship, then continue running along the side of the ship on the surface until it hit a jetty, where finally the warhead, armed with a Duplex pistol, did explode, blowing fragments of wooden decking and massive heavy piling high into the air. The sixth torpedo missed the target and ran up on to the beach, where it too blew up.

The lead pilot, Captain Newson RN, took the group on another, lower approach, from 2,000 feet, but as they made a turn to launch their attack the anti-aircraft guns started firing and the pilots were forced to take violent avoiding action until they were over the breakwater. Captain Newson forgot to press his master switch, so his torpedo failed to drop, but the following two aircraft released theirs successfully. They then turned and made a low-level, erratic getaway, being fired on as they did so. As they flew behind a headland, the observer of the rear plane saw the smoke and red fireball of a large explosion rise into view. He thought it came from where *Dunkerque* lay beached, and could only have been caused by a magazine exploding.

The final attack, led by Lieutenant David 'Feather' Godfrey-Faussett of 810 Squadron, an extremely good pilot and a man for whom I had a lot of respect, made its approach over land, hitting the coast at Cap Falcon, keeping to the landward side of the high promontory of Point Mers-el-Kébir and then swinging over the town at very low level. Even with this stealthy approach they were fired on by anti-aircraft guns from another battleship in the harbour and from the shore batteries to the east. Godfrey-Faussett dropped first, but although his observer thought the torpedo hit the target, there was no explosion. The second Swordfish dropped at a longer range. The torpedo ran straight and true, but hit not *Dunkerque* but a tug, which disintegrated in a ball of flame. The third torpedo hit *Dunkerque*, but again it failed to explode.

These three Swordfish were the last aircraft to attack, and there had been enough time for the French to be on a high level of preparedness. Not only were the shore-based batteries ready for the approach of the last three Swordfish, but the French air force had managed to get some fighters airborne and these were now flying over the harbour being engaged by the Skuas. The pilots of the Swordfish were unaware of this fight going on overhead, but as Sub-Lieutenant Pearson, Godfrey-Faussett's wingman, was flying at about 100 feet above the waves, he noticed strange splashes on the surface on his port side, slightly ahead of him. It dawned on him with a shock that he was being fired on from behind by a fighter. The burst of adrenalin that had hit his nerves as he jinked through the anti-aircraft fire over *Dunkerque* had slightly dissipated, but now he realized he was in mortal danger yet again. Almost immediately his observer told him that a fighter had just turned away – then he added in a slightly tenser voice that another fighter was coming at them out of the sun on the starboard side. It was a French Dewoitine D.520. These were modern fighters, fitted with a 20mm cannon and four machine guns. They had the same speed as a Messerschmitt and were equally if not more manoeuvrable, allegedly having a turning circle smaller than the German fighters.

Pearson knew he was in trouble. By now every Swordfish pilot realized that there was only one way to get out of this situation, and that was to use the aircraft's superior slow-speed manoeuvrability. He was already flying at a height of 100 feet above the sea, a situation that most fast fighter pilots find uncomfortable. As soon as his observer told him where the fighter was, Pearson made a tight turn into him and a burst of bullets churned up the surface of the sea to port. The fighter came round again and made another attack. Pearson repeated his manoeuvre, with the same results. The fighter broke away, then made a stern attack. Pearson knew that his Swordfish was being hit, and he made a tight 180-degree turn to fly underneath the French fighter, who gave up the chase, perhaps nervous at how low he was getting – a tight turn at slow speed might be fatal at barely 100 feet above the sea. Then Pearson saw another Dewoitine: for the first time he realized there were two of them. He was nowhere near out of the woods. Yet again, gunfire poured into the ocean as Pearson, sweat pouring cold down his back, his mouth dry, yanked his plane into the tightest possible turn and kept it there, his engine thundering away until the Dewoitine appeared through the disc of his whirling propeller. Then he pressed the button on his stick. The single fixed machine gun in the nose of the Swordfish added another metallic hammering to the cacophony around him as bursts of flame stabbed out of the recessed barrel. Fifty rounds were fired, filling the cockpit with the acrid smell of cordite. It was unlikely that a single one of his bullets did any damage, but the second French pilot didn't want to give Pearson another chance and he too was gone, clawing for the sky with all of his aircraft's 330-miles-an-hour speed – faster than the Swordfish and carrying enough cannon and machine guns to rip it to shreds, but outwitted and outmanoeuvred.

Elated, amazed at what he had just done, the young sub-lieutenant flew on to rendezvous with the *Ark*. Once the plane was down in the hangar, the riggers started totting up the damage. A cannon shell had smashed through the fuselage cowling on the port side of the cockpit and burst on the starboard aileron. One bullet had smashed the radio transmitter and another had twisted the ring of the TAG's rear-firing Lewis gun. It had been a very narrow escape for the observer, Lieutenant Prendergast. Some frames in the fuselage had been damaged, and several ribs in the lower wing had been hit, as had the centre-section rear main spar. The torpedo-release mechanism had also been hit and destroyed.

Dunkerque, meanwhile, had been hit by five torpedoes and was most definitely out of action. It had been another highly successful day, but the vagaries of the torpedo warheads were obvious, and they were unsettling. *Dunkerque* had been a stationary target, and out of nine torpedoes that had been observed to hit her, three had definitely failed to detonate. Whether this was the reason for *Strasbourg* appearing to shrug off what seemed a perfectly timed and coordinated attack two days earlier was hard to know.

It was an open secret when I joined 818 Squadron that pilots on the *Ark* were doubtful about the efficiency of the new Duplex triggers, but Admiralty instructions were clear: they were to be fitted and used unless there was no alternative. The torpedoes carried by the Swordfish were the Mark IX and were referred to as 18in torpedoes, which was the diameter of the warhead and body. These were smaller than those launched by our submarines, the Mark VIII, which had a 21in diameter, at 40 knots were faster and had a far greater range of 7,000 yards. More important, the warheads were very different. The airborne 18in carried a warhead of 250lb of explosive, compared to 750lb in the bigger Mark VIII. Some modern warships had thick enough armour, or specially constructed bulges in their hulls designed to limit the effect of a hit by a torpedo, and our small warhead would not necessarily cause enough damage to sink one of these ships. At best, as I was to be told during my training at Abbotsinch, all we could hope to do was damage a ship sufficiently to slow it down, or get enough hits in at the same time to cripple it. An unreliable warhead was merely adding to our problems.

5

Hard Lessons

I shouldn't give the impression that flying a Swordfish against enemy fighters or anti-aircraft guns was a piece of cake. It was remarkable that the planes that tried to hit *Strasbourg* or attacked *Dunkerque* were able to make it back to the safety of the *Ark*'s flight deck in one piece. It took a very cool head and some fantastic flying skill to avoid two modern fighters in the way that Sub-Lieutenant Pearson had done over Mers-el-Kébir. The outcome wasn't always guaranteed: if you got into a fight you could easily end up dead. George Dawson of 810 Squadron told me about the horrible mess that he got into when the *Ark* was sent down to Dakar, in French West Africa. This happened in the middle of September 1940, when I was just starting my training at Abbotsinch.

General de Gaulle, who led the Free French in Britain, believed, for whatever reason, that the troops in the French colony might come over to his side if he presented himself and made a personal appeal to their loyalty to France. The plan was that he would go down there in a small force of British warships and *Ark Royal*, with around 6,000 Royal Marines and Free French troops, to make a public proclamation and negotiate with the French governor. As with Oran, the

negotiations would be backed up with the threat of taking the
port by force if they came to nought. Dakar was an important
port on the west coast of Africa, and if German submarines
started operating out of it they would cause a lot of damage
to our convoys sailing round the Cape of Good Hope to India
or the Red Sea. Another reason why it was worth taking
Dakar, so it was rumoured, was because a lot of gold from the
central banks of Poland and Belgium had been shipped there
for safekeeping when Germany first invaded France. There
were stories that up to £60 million in gold bullion was stashed
away there.

So *Ark Royal* sailed down to West Africa with two battleships, HMS *Barham* and *Resolution*, with an escort of five
cruisers and ten destroyers. They arrived in Freetown, in
Sierra Leone, on 16 September, and then a few days later
sailed for Dakar. Whatever the attitude of the Vichy forces to
General de Gaulle might have been, it was unlikely that they
would welcome a visit from the Royal Navy after our actions
in Oran. Their fleet in Dakar had been reinforced by a
modern battleship, *Richelieu*, which had sailed from Brest
dockyard to avoid being captured by the Germans, and two
other cruisers that slipped past Gibraltar from Mers-el-Kébir.

The first attempt at persuading the French forces in Dakar
to leave Vichy and join De Gaulle didn't go well. *Ark Royal*
had embarked two French aircraft at Gibraltar and when they
took off and landed at Dakar airfield, their pilots and
passengers, all Free French officers, were straightaway
arrested and jailed. Then two ships' boats that attempted
to enter the harbour with De Gaulle's representatives were
fired upon and several of their passengers wounded. This
marked the start of a general French offensive. They knew of
course what had happened at Mers-el-Kébir, and it is
hardly surprising that they decided to get their retaliation in
first.

Their shore batteries opened fire on the British warships, and *Richelieu*, with her huge 15in-calibre guns, also started blasting away. The battle lasted intermittently over two days, with *Barham* suffering a hit by one of *Richelieu*'s shells, and *Resolution* being torpedoed by a French submarine. The French lost two submarines and a destroyer.

In the middle of this battle, General de Gaulle decided that he would attempt a landing along the coast and deliver an ultimatum to the Vichy forces. It was a hopeless effort in the circumstances. The landings were hampered by fog and two French cruisers managed to leave the harbour, raising the possibility that the Free French troops would be cut off and their reinforcements from the troop ships sunk by the cruisers that were now steaming along the coast. The Vichy forces also managed to send troops to the landing area at Rufisque, and they started to fire on the Free French soldiers. De Gaulle realized that the situation was lost and he would gain nothing from large numbers of French casualties, so the landings were abandoned and the Free French troops already on the shore were taken off.

Ark Royal had flown off some Swordfish to provide aerial spotting for *Barham* and *Resolution* during their attempt to shell the shore batteries and Dakar harbour, with the immobile *Richelieu* at anchor, but they met some organized resistance. French fighters were already on alert and maintaining combat air patrols over the coast. When the landings were abandoned, the two French cruisers turned and tried to return to port. Seeing an opportunity to weaken the Vichy forces, and under orders from the Admiralty, eight Swordfish from 810 and 820 Squadrons were ranged up to carry out a torpedo attack on the cruisers. They met some very fierce anti-aircraft fire, and five of the Swordfish failed to make it back. The observers that managed to return to the *Ark* reported that they believed they had managed to get two hits,

but in the mayhem of the crossfire and their violent getaway
they could not be sure.

All this was happening while I was engaged in my training
at Abbotsinch, carefully guiding my Swordfish over the
waters of the Clyde, waiting for the cameras mounted on
the wing of my aircraft and on the target ship to tell me if I
had carried out a successful drop or not. Perhaps if I had had
an idea of what was happening in the harbour at Dakar at
that very time I might have been more apprehensive about my
decision to transfer to Swordfish. I would certainly have been
less complacent about my good results from the training
course.

Back on *Ark Royal* in West Africa, the final operation was
to be a dive-bombing attack on the French shore batteries,
and George Dawson was the TAG on one of the Swordfish.
Armed with 250lb bombs, they had originally been briefed to
dive-bomb the 9.2in gun batteries located on the island of
Gorée, lying to the east of Dakar, which effectively covered
the entrance to the port. George was strapped in ready for
take-off when a last-minute change of orders was handed to
their observer: the Swordfish were now directed to bomb
Richelieu. George, in the last plane of the flight of six, had not
been told of the change of target and was alarmed when he
realized that they were flying past the island and heading into
the harbour. A French fighter followed them in and started
firing. The Swordfish was hit, bullets thudding into the cockpit and the metal-covered forward part of the fuselage.
George was uncertain whether it was from the fighter or
whether it was anti-aircraft fire from the French ships at
anchor, but it seems unlikely that the French guns on the
ground would risk hitting their own plane. He was slightly
wounded by some shell fragments in the arm, but kept his eye
on the fighter, waiting for the opportunity to get in a burst of
fire from his Lewis machine gun. He had warned his pilot

immediately, but the Swordfish had not taken any evasive action. George then noticed that they were leaving a trail of smoke. He turned round to check where it was coming from and saw a horrific sight. His observer, Sub-Lieutenant Cross, was still seated, his eyes glazed and blood pouring from his mouth. Looking further forward and up to the cockpit, he could see the pilot, Sub-Lieutenant Wheeler, with his head flopping on his shoulder as if he were asleep, his yellow Mae West lifejacket covered in crimson blood. The Swordfish was flying crazily, doing violent zooms and dives, and the pilot's head rolled with the plane's gyrations. Then his arm came out of the cockpit and George saw that it was almost severed below the elbow, hanging on by just a piece of skin.

When the plane turned upside down, both George and Cross were thrown out, but Cross was either dead or too badly injured to open his parachute. George managed to grasp his ripcord and his chute opened; he floated down into the water of the harbour while 15in shells from *Barham* exploded all round the port. He managed to swim ashore, where he was arrested and taken prisoner. In the police cells where he was initially locked up he met the crews of the two other Swordfish in his sub-flight who had also been shot down. The lead Swordfish, flown by Lieutenant Jackson, had managed to drop its bombs, but then a bullet had ignited their liferaft's flares and set the main wing on fire. The third Swordfish had also been hit, then pounced on by a French fighter, and the pilot, the young Sub-Lieutenant England whose plane had been hit in the attack on *Dunkerque* at Mers-el-Kébir, had been killed. So too had the TAG, Sub-Lieutenant Moore. The observer, who was wounded, had, like George Dawson, managed to swim to shore where he was also captured.

Five Swordfish from the *Ark* were lost that day. The operation was clearly a disaster, and the *Ark*, with the rest of the British ships, returned to the UK, where the *Ark* docked in Liverpool for a refit. The lesson was clear: Swordfish could be very vulnerable, despite their great manoeuvrability and robustness, and attacks on shore-based installations could prove extremely risky. Whether I would ever be involved in any, I would just have to wait and see.

Having completed my training in torpedo-dropping and dive-bombing at Abbotsinch, I was sent to Naval Air Station Arbroath, where we practised carrier landings on the tarmac runways. Here again the slow speed of the Swordfish is an advantage, although landing on land is completely different from landing on a carrier. A Swordfish stalls (stops being able to fly) at a speed of 50 knots, but at sea the carrier after all is moving forward at perhaps 30 knots, so the relative speed of the aircraft as it flies over the stern is just 20 knots. There is also the effect of any wind, which will aid in reducing the landing speed of the aircraft to perhaps 15 knots. That, at any rate, is the theory.

But for all my praise of the Swordfish, it was while flying one out of Arbroath that I had my first crash, and I was lucky that it was not fatal. I was flying with my friend Sub-Lieutenant Ed Dunkley on a navigation exercise and we were looking forward to making some observations of wild deer as we travelled west along the South Grampians. Flying at a relatively low altitude over the rugged hills just due north of Kirriemuir, the engine began to run erratically. I started to adjust the mixture, but the engine hiccupped, sputtered and cut out. I went through the procedures in the cockpit to restart it – check all the switches are on, pump the fuel primer to get more fuel into the carburettor – but nothing I tried would revive it. Naturally it's noisy in the open cockpit of a Swordfish, with a big nine-cylindered, 700 h.p. radial engine hammering away in front of you, but now all I could hear was the sound of the air rushing through the struts and over the wings. We were in trouble.

I obtained the best angle of glide to keep our speed up for as long as I could. I shouted to my passenger that I would try to get down, but this was rather a forlorn hope among the steep mountains over which we were now gliding. I remembered having seen a large house to the south and hoped that it might be set in some open ground, or a paddock. I turned and we glided over to it, but I could see there was no grass or any sort of open country. We had lost height and were rapidly running out of anywhere to go.

Then I noticed on my right a narrow firebreak between the trees. This was our only chance. I turned, losing even more height, and headed straight for the gap. As we got closer the trees came up to meet us and the firebreak, which was fenced with a gated entrance, seemed impossibly tight. It's hard to say what I felt. One part of the brain is full of fear about the possibility of pain and injury, while the other part takes over and tries to stay in control, in the vain belief that somehow the inevitable might be avoided. That, I suppose, is what the training is all about. A Swordfish might look fragile, but it weighs over 2 tons without any payload, so we hit very hard. The wings smashed against the trunks of the trees with a loud crash and I was knocked unconscious. The next I remember was a female voice shouting at me and shaking my shoulders.

When I managed to regain focus I could hardly believe what I saw. There was a lovely young lady standing over me in the cockpit with her skirts raised, enquiring if I was hurt. It left nothing to the imagination. I undid my harness and she pulled me over the side on to the grass, which was quite close as we had lost our undercarriage. Then I remembered my friend Dunkley. The girl and I got him out and saw that he was bleeding from a head wound and very frail. With assistance from some other men who had arrived, we took him to the house and bandaged him up. I then asked to phone Arbroath, but our crash had pulled down the telephone lines, so someone was dispatched to go a considerable distance by bicycle to the nearest phone at Kirriemuir. Meanwhile, the butler of the beautiful apparition I had seen on regaining consciousness appeared with an extra-large decanter of whisky.

Dunkley was laid out on the settee, with his head bandaged, but I, fully recovered, had a very good evening in the company of the young girl, with a good meal and plenty of dance music from a wind-up gramophone. I particularly remember listening to 'In the Mood' by Glenn Miller. Very appropriate!

All's well that ends well, but it was a chastening experience. Mercifully, the engine of the Swordfish was normally extremely reliable, and engine failures like the one I had experienced were definitely out of the ordinary, but it certainly brought home to me that I was going to be spending a lot of my service life flying over large areas of ocean in a single-engined aircraft. There was an investigation into the crash, of course, and I was told later that the engine had failed due to sabotage. I received a letter from the squadron's commanding officer, who told me that they had discovered sugar in the fuel tank and that similar accidents had happened to two other Swordfish, neither of which had been fatal. Who did this, or for what reason, I never discovered but, as someone pointed out, there was a host of motives. The saboteur could have been an IRA sympathizer, an admirer of Hitler, or perhaps a Communist, because at the time Hitler's non-aggression pact with Stalin was still in force. Anyway, I was glad that the incident happened right at the end of my time at Arbroath, because it is obviously very disturbing to know that people are deliberately trying to make you crash.

During my stay in Arbroath I bought a second-hand car, a Morris Isis, and I used it regularly for Saturday-night trips to the dances at the Seaforth Hotel in Arbroath. Because there was no late-night public transport, the car was always full of Wrens; often it was so overloaded that the mudguards would be scraping on the tyres.

As my period of training was finally over – it was now December 1940 – I knew that I would be posted somewhere, and that I was most likely to be sent to serve on one of the air-craft carriers. In the RNVR we had, I think, originally been intended as useful bodies who would relieve full-time aircrew and properly trained Naval Reserve officers so that they would be able to serve in the front line. Casualties had been high in the Fleet Air Arm, however. The navy had been fight-ing since the very first day of the war, the Fleet Air Arm had seen a lot of action in Norway, and Swordfish squadrons had been extremely active in the Channel on mine-laying missions. In the few months leading up to Dunkirk, more than fifty Swordfish crewmembers had been killed or gone missing on operations, and then of course the fatalities caused by the sinking of *Courageous* and *Glorious* were considerable. Swordfish were even used over the beaches of Dunkirk; eight of them were shot down in a period of five days at the height of the evacuation. It was obvious that some of us would be filling their shoes.

We were given a week's leave before our postings came through and I wanted to go home, to see my parents and take my car to be looked after by them while I was away. There were one or two problems I had to solve before I gave the car to my father. It was dark blue and someone had written in white paint on the back 'Honky Tonk the virgin's hearse'. This would go down badly with my parents and the other upstanding folk in Kelso. I found it extremely difficult to paint it out before driving the little Morris down to the Borders.

My journey was not without incident. Three of my friends

from the Naval Air Station came along with me. One of them, whom I remember very well, was a South African, Guy 'Brok' Brokensha, who had flown Skuas on *Ark Royal*. He had taken part in the attack on Mers-el-Kébir, and flown as part of a protective escort for the Swordfish who had torpedoed *Strasbourg*. He had become engaged in several dogfights with French fighters, during one of which he was turning to open fire when all his forword-firing machine guns jammed, as too did that of the observer in the rear cockpit. He manoeuvred his way out of it, though, and later helped shoot down a couple of attackers and was put forward for an award. In the same way that I had formed up with the 'Black Hand Gang' at St Vincent, I naturally seemed to get on well with anybody, like Brok, who was from the colonies. Brok was senior enough to be an instructor at Arbroath, but this didn't get in the way of our friendship.

The three wanted me to give them a lift down to Edinburgh, dropping them off in Princes Street on my way home. Brok was courting an attractive girl from Wick, whom he later married. I was happy to oblige, but I asked them if they would fill the tank with petrol. Before we left I also took the precaution of filling the spare jerrycan that was carried on the running board. In a breach of regulations, I used aviation fuel from the base. This was dyed pink, in the same way that agricultural diesel is today, to prevent unauthorized use and to make it harder to divert to the black market, which was quite rampant because of rationing.

We had a nice drive to Edinburgh and I went with them to a hotel off Princes Street. When I left them to continue my journey to Kelso, however, I discovered that my rascally friends had welched on their deal and put hardly any petrol in the main tank. I got as far as the post office at Waterloo Place when the engine spluttered and died. Cursing my friends, I gave thanks that I wasn't in a Swordfish, when I noticed that a policeman on traffic duty had seen me come to a stop and was walking methodically in my direction. He was very sympathetic, keen to help a young flyer in uniform get on his way to see his parents before going abroad. 'Don't worry, sir,' he said. 'I'll soon sort this out.' Then without warning he grabbed the spare can and started to fill up the tank. I sat there quaking, my fingers tightly crossed, hoping that he wouldn't notice that the petrol he was pouring into the tank was strictly for military use and should never have left the base. If he did notice, he said nothing, and with a wave and shouted thanks I motored off for my few days' leave in Kelso.

I had one bad time there. While flying out of Arbroath I would occasionally make a detour to Kelso and fly over the main square. On one of these trips I had seen my father and decided to 'beat up' the Horse Market, heading directly at him in the square. I can remember him looking at me in horror, his hands high in the air! When I got home he certainly told me all about it and how he managed to stop the police reporting me!

When I returned to Arbroath after the leave I received notice of my first posting to a front-line squadron. I was amazed at my luck, for I was being sent to what we all thought of as the crack carrier in the fleet, *Ark Royal*. She was very well known and, as I have already made clear, always seemed to be in the thick of any action. I was clearly going to have to meet some very high standards. The *Ark*, however, was in the Mediterranean and first I was going to have to travel to Greenock and embark on HMS *Argus* for the trip down to Gibraltar. As soon as I received the orders I phoned home and asked my parents to see that my trunk was sent immediately to the railway station at Paisley where I would collect it.

*

If *Ark Royal* was one of the most modern carriers in the world, then *Argus* was one of the oldest. Her keel had been laid down in Beardmore's shipyard in Glasgow in 1914 and she was originally intended to be a passenger liner for an Italian steamship company. Instead, the navy commandeered her and modified her into an aircraft carrier and she entered service in 1918. She was an odd-looking ship, with a big, flat flight deck laid over her hull. I heard her referred to unkindly as a floating shoebox. There was neither the funnel nor the bridge structure you would expect to see in most carriers. The funnel gases were directed so that they came out under the flight deck at the stern, and there was a small retractable bridge that rose and fell on the edge of the flight deck according to whether flying was taking place or not. She was lying in the Clyde in midstream when I first saw her, and I was taken out to join her from the pier by one of her boats.

I had travelled through Paisley on the train from Arbroath, but my trunk had not arrived. Each day I went back to the station for it, but never managed to locate it. After an agitated phone call to my mother, I was assured that the trunk had been forwarded promptly. On the third day I was told that we were due to sail on the morning tide to join up with a convoy. I panicked. My trunk had still not arrived. The station office had been trying to find it for two days now, with no success. That afternoon I rushed to the station again, to be told that my trunk had finally been located in Glasgow Central and had just arrived on the local train. Relieved, I spent a small fortune on a taxi to help me carry it as far as Greenock pier. Dashing to the signals office at the end of the pier, I asked the petty officer on duty to signal *Argus* for a boat to collect me and my trunk. I was horrified to get a signal by return saying that all boats had been hoisted and stowed and the ship was due to get under way. I was in a serious sweat now: this was my first posting on board a vessel and I could imagine the repercussions if I failed to make it on board. It was a serious disciplinary offence, but there was also the shame, and damage to my reputation, as well as my own pride. Then I noticed a fellow in a motorboat and asked for help. After some wrangling about the price of petrol, a fiver was waved – a good week's wages in those days – the trunk was loaded on board and we set off in pursuit of the carrier.

As we got closer I could see a commander on the quarterdeck and I shouted to him to help me. In retrospect, what he must have thought, seeing a young RNVR sub-lieutenant in a speedboat, bouncing about in the wake of his ship and yelling at a senior officer for a hand as though he were a railway porter, beggars belief. He merely replied, with a voice that carried remarkably well, 'Come along the starboard side.'

There was an opening in the side of the hull, just above the waterline, that I assume had been originally intended for passengers' luggage when the ship was designed as a liner. I urged the boatman to go flat out and, as we passed the quarterdeck and drew level, a seaman opened the baggage port. The huge ship above me was gathering speed and my boat started to bounce about in the wake and the increasing chop of the estuary. The boatman and I heaved the trunk on board, then I stepped on to the gunwale of the speedboat and, sensing the boat rising up on a crest of a wave, threw myself into the hatchway, where a couple of seamen caught me and dragged me safely aboard.

One of them straightened my uniform and adjusted my cap as though I were a small boy, while the other saluted and said, 'Captain's compliments, sir, and he will see you in the wardroom.' I was on an aircraft carrier at last, but it was quite clear I had not made a very good impression.

6

Active Service

The journey to Gibraltar on board *Argus* was anything but pleasant. The weather was poor all the way, with strong winds, seas and the occasional rain squall. Also, there was a shortage of accommodation for junior officers. At one time *Argus* had been considered inadequate for front-line service, and would probably have been scrapped had not the war started. Even then, initially she had been set aside for aircrew training, but the loss of *Courageous* and *Glorious* meant that she had been pressed into service. For several months she had been used in the Atlantic for anti-submarine patrols, and as a carrier to ferry aircraft to the Mediterranean. This is what she was doing while I was on board her. On this particular voyage she was carrying eighteen Swordfish, which were going to be assembled in Gibraltar to be flown on to Malta. Normally, I was told, Hurricane fighters were carried on the flight deck, and when *Argus* was in the Mediterranean they would fly off to provide air defences for Malta, the island located just east of Sicily in the middle of the Mediterranean. Malta was being pounded heavily by air raids from the Italian and German air forces, and there was quite a high casualty rate amongst the Royal Air Force.

We had the Hurricane pilots and maintenance staff on board, so I, a very junior reserve sub-lieutenant, was given a hammock, which I had to sling in the afterdeck. I gathered from some of the Fleet Air Arm chaps on board that *Argus* was very much a navy ship – in other words, the complement of Swordfish and their crews was seen as a bit of a nuisance. Fortunately, I was not going to stay on board.

It may seem odd, but I had been in the Fleet Air Arm for a year now and this was the first time that I had been on an aircraft carrier, or been to sea. All my flying had been from land-based airstrips and I had lived in barracks or civilian billets. This was my first introduction to sailing and a carrier, and it was not a very good first impression. I never got used to sleeping in a hammock, and for the first few days I found it hard to get around the ship. I was not used to negotiating ladders and companionways while the ship was being knocked about by rough seas. The food was not very good, and cockroaches were everywhere. I found my sea legs, of course, but the food did not improve.

Landing on the mole at Gibraltar was another shock, as I tried to adjust my balance to dry land having just acclimatized to the constant pitching of a ship at sea. This was a minor distraction, however, as I looked at the ship that I was now about to join. *Ark Royal* looked magnificent. She was huge, towering above me, and compared to *Argus* looked extremely modern and elegant. Her sheer sides rose up to the flight deck, and there was a swooping grace to her bows and an enormous flared flight deck at her stern. She had recently returned from her brief refit in Liverpool after the Dakar operation, and her paint still looked relatively fresh. I felt a sudden burst of happiness that I was going to serve aboard her. *Ark Royal* was really a very famous ship by now: there had been magazine articles and newsreels about her since her launch in 1937, and if you thought of aircraft carriers you thought of *Ark Royal*.

She had already come through so much that it was hard to imagine anything happening to her.

I boarded her and was met by a young rating who took me to my squadron's office, which was beneath the flight deck on the port side. I thought if I had had a job finding my way about *Argus*, then the *Ark* was going to be twice as bad. She seemed to be more than double the size, with two hangar decks, and was much longer. There were three Swordfish squadrons, one Skua squadron and one Fulmar squadron on board when I joined her, so there were over fifty aircraft. My new home was going to be 818 Squadron and I met the commanding officer, Lt Commander Trevenon 'Tim' Coode, who seemed a decent chap. He was friendly and said that I had a good report from my training squadron at Abbotsinch. Then he said, 'It doesn't say how many deck landings you have done.'

'None, sir!'

He looked completely perplexed and started to say something, then thought better of it. I could see the squadron writer, a chap called Percy North, and the rating who had brought me to the office looking at each other as if to say, 'My God, another one.' I was aware of the absurdity of the situation. If there is one unique aspect of naval aviation, it is that pilots take off from and land on the flight decks of aircraft carriers at sea. Here I was, on the most famous aircraft carrier in the world, in the middle of a war in the Mediterranean, and I had never taken off from a flight deck, let alone landed on one.

Lt Commander Coode put my papers down on his desk and said, 'We'll have to do something about that, but go along to your cabin. We'll join up in the wardroom later and you can meet the rest of the squadron.'

I was taken to my quarters. However much of a disappointment I had been to my CO, he hadn't made a meal of it, for which I was grateful, and my cabin was far superior to the hammock I had had in *Argus*. Here I had a bunk, with properly laundered sheets, and the cabin had its own wash basin with hot water.

Later I went to the wardroom and met my fellow pilots. They seemed to be mostly regular navy officers, with a sprinkling of Reservists like me. There were one or two veterans, people like Lieutenant Alan Owensmith, a good pilot, who had been shot down over Norway and had taken part in the mining of Oran; and Lieutenant 'Feather' Godfrey-Faussett, who had attacked *Strasbourg* and made a brilliant attack on the beached *Dunkerque* at Oran. I was to discover that his name was automatically on the flying list for any operation. There were also some real characters. An observer in 820 Squadron, Lieutenant Val Norfolk, was naturally known as 'Duke', and would knock back pints of a cocktail called a Horse's Neck, made of cognac and ginger ale. Another was known as 'Maxie' Mayes, a real dandy who refused to wear a Mae West lifejacket because it spoiled the line of his uniform, which he had, of course, had specially made. These characters were always ready to start a sing-song in the bar. Others were quiet, almost shy, like 'Tan' Tivey, who was one of the quieter RN types, and the CO of 820 Squadron, James Stewart-Moore, who was an observer, not a pilot.

Interestingly, in the Fleet Air Arm it was rank, not function, that decided who was in charge of an aircraft or a squadron. Apparently most of the new recruits to the Swordfish squadrons on the *Ark* had joined while she was having her refit at Liverpool and, although all of them had completed several deck landings, they were fairly inexperienced. There was a hierarchy of sorts; for example, certain areas near the bar were reserved for more senior officers, whereas sub-lieutenants like me were expected to occupy an area down the other end. There was an inevitable distinction between the regular navy officers and the Reservists and hostilities-only types. They wondered what to make of us, but even so the wardroom was a relaxed and friendly place and I was made to feel welcome. It seemed that the *Ark* was a genuinely happy ship.

My CO was as good as his word. Next day the *Ark* slipped out of Gibraltar to escort *Argus* to where her fighters would take off for Malta, and Lt Commander Coode told me that the commander air had given him permission to take me up on a familiarization flight. He sat in the cockpit while I perched in the observer's seat. With the *Ark* heading into the wind, our take-off was rapid and we flew in a circuit round the carrier, then made our approach. I paid close attention, looking over Lt Commander Coode's shoulder. There was a bit of turbulence from the funnel gases and the wash of the big bridge structure on the starboard side, but nothing severe. It was a question of adopting a three-point tail-down attitude and approaching at about 60 knots, then, as you passed over the round down at the end of the flight deck, you would close the throttle and the plane should drop, allowing the tail hook to catch one of the arrestor wires, and you would thump on to the deck. The trick, of course, was not to misjudge the speed of the ship and either overshoot or undershoot the point where you had to cut the power. We landed, then Lt Commander Coode undid his harness and turned round: 'Get into the cockpit. This is my plane, so don't bend it.' Then he left me to get on with it.

I knew that he was paying close attention, and that there were a lot of spectators on the 'goofers' gallery' that ran level with the flight commander's station on the island – the structure at the side of the flight deck with the bridge and funnel. Their cameras were at the ready, waiting for me to make a total hash of it. There was a 'batman', as the deck landing officer was known, by the side of the flight deck on the port side who was an experienced pilot and whose job it was to indicate to approaching planes whether they were too high or too low, or wandering off the centre line. I followed his signals, got it right and made a very competent landing.

Walking off the deck to the squadron office I met the batman, the very tall Lt Commander Pat Stringer, and I said, 'That was a very good landing we made today, sir!'

He looked down his nose at me, a tyro Reservist, and snorted. That put me in my place.

The reason I had been drafted out to 818 was that there had been a few accidents in the past month. I was introduced to the rest of my crew: the observer, 'Dusty' Miller, and the telegraphist and air gunner, or TAG, Leading Airman Albert Hayman. Miller looked presentable enough, but Hayman seemed to be a tough-looking brute. He had a broken nose and a cauliflower ear, and I thought, 'What have they given me?' I could think of nothing to say except, 'So are you good at your job?', which was a pretty cheeky thing to say, considering I was a raw sub-lieutenant without a single operational flight to my name.

Quick as a flash, Hayman retorted, 'Are you any good at yours?' They could hardly have failed to hear that I had just made my first deck landing. He went on, 'I've been shot down twice over Norway, and I don't intend to let it happen again.'

He was a dead shot, and both of them were stalwarts. I clicked with Miller; we were never close friends in the wardroom, but we had a rapport in the cockpit that worked. Hayman was a junior rating, so we never met socially, but I trusted him. I saw how good he was one day in Gibraltar. There was an old racecourse in the north, close to the border with Spain, which we had turned into a runway; the modern runway is still there. Known as North Front, this was where some maintenance work would be carried out and we would fly off sometimes from here for anti-submarine patrols in the Straits if the *Ark* was in the harbour. The army also used the runway as a firing range. We had just picked up a Swordfish and Hayman wanted to align the sights of his Lewis machine gun. I asked the sergeant in charge if we could use one of his targets, taxied down to the end and had just turned the aircraft to give Hayman a clear field of fire when, without any warning, a burst of fire ripped apart the target. 'OK, boss, we can go now,' he said and so I opened the throttle. We had never even come to rest. He was a first-class operator.

As well as the *Ark*, the battleship HMS *Renown* was based in Gibraltar. This was now the flagship of Force H, still commanded by Rear Admiral James Somerville, the *Hood* having returned to the home fleet. His nephew was an observer in the Fulmar squadron on board the *Ark*. There was usually a cruiser, HMS *Sheffield*, and two or three destroyers accompanying us. We worked most closely with *Sheffield*. The *Ark* did not have radar installed, relying on *Sheffield*'s radar for locating enemy aircraft. Commander Henry Traill, the commander air in the *Ark*, a fresh-faced officer whom I later found friendly and approachable, and the radar opera-tors in *Sheffield* had worked like this for several months, first of all off Norway and now carrying out the same procedure in the Med. The radar operators would plot the range and bearing of suspected enemy aircraft on a board identical to one maintained by the commander air in the *Ark*. It also marked the positions of the *Ark* and *Sheffield*, and the positions of any aircraft from the *Ark* that were in the air. Information about enemy aircraft would be radioed to the commander air's office and he would inform *Sheffield* when aircraft were launched or recovered, so a continuous plot of the situation in the air was maintained on both ships. All the information between them was exchanged via radio using

Morse code, so it required a high level of collaboration. I think *Ark Royal* had been the first carrier to work out this way of directing aircraft by radio – remarkable when you think that she didn't even have her own radar!

We left port a few days later to fly off the Swordfish that had been brought down by *Argus*. These had observers with them and so, like all Fleet Air Arm crews, would not find it that difficult to navigate for several hundred miles to their destination.

When RAF Hurricanes were involved, however, the pilots had a difficult task ahead of them. Their anticipated long flight over the sea was not something that fighter pilots particularly relished. It isn't easy to navigate on a long journey using dead reckoning whilst also flying a plane; it needs special training, and there is always the anxiety of relying on a single engine, with absolutely no chance of making an emergency landing. Once they had taken off from *Argus*, that was it – they couldn't land back on. The plan usually was that we would sail just far enough into the Med to launch the Hurricanes, hoping to avoid being spotted by Italian reconnaissance planes. As soon as the Italians knew that aircraft were being ferried to Malta, the Italian air force would lie in wait for them and catch them as they approached the island. The Hurricanes were easy meat at that stage in their journey. They were unarmed to save weight, and they would anyway be at the very limit of their fuel, with no extra resources to engage in a dogfight. The launch point was finely calculated, depending partly on how strong the winds were and in which direction they were blowing, because this would influence how far they could fly on their fuel load.

Two days after we had left Gibraltar we were in position. I was not scheduled for any flying duties, so I had got up to observe the take-off. One thing that I was beginning to appreciate was how busy the flight deck of a carrier was. At daybreak three Swordfish were ranged at the end of the flight deck for take-off, to carry out the first of the anti-submarine patrols ahead of the small fleet of ships. A permanent patrol was maintained throughout the day, so every two hours Swordfish were landing and taking off. In addition, other Swordfish would be launched to patrol an area and inspect any ships in the vicinity, and to look out for enemy vessels. As the *Ark* got closer to Sicily, where a large number of enemy aircraft were based, Skuas and Fulmars were launched to maintain a combat air patrol, ready to intercept any enemy bombers picked up on *Sheffield*'s radar. When we were at heightened readiness, there might be sixty or more landings and take-offs during the day.

On this particular morning the Swordfish took off on their first patrol, and then the two Skuas were in the air, circling while the Swordfish bound for Malta set off east into the early dawn. Long before they had vanished from sight, the ships had turned and we were heading back to Gibraltar. Later that day we received a warning that a fleet of enemy aircraft was approaching, so two sections of Fulmar fighters were launched to intercept them. They broke up the formation and I saw the Italian planes drop their bombs some way away, sending up great spouts of smoke and seawater, the explosions reverberating in the distance. My first taste of action in the Med.

When we returned to harbour I was told by my CO that I was scheduled to carry out my first anti-submarine patrol, keeping a close lookout in the Straits not only for enemy submarines but for any strange cargo ships that might be entering the Spanish port of Algeciras on the other side of the bay. I was going to use one of the two catapults built into the front of the flight deck, as I had never carried out a catapult launch before and needed the experience. These could rapidly accelerate the plane to its flying speed. I sat in the cockpit, the engine running at full boost, and when I was sure that the oil pressure, the revs and everything were fine, I gave a signal and an engineering artificer in the walkway at the side of the flight deck released a lever. I shot forward, there was a slight dip and then I was slowly climbing, leaving the ship behind me. Another first!

Like all the other aircrew, I was also expected to carry out ship's duties, like inspections, and quite often be officer of the watch in harbour. Many of my colleagues in the Fleet Air Arm found this irksome, but I did not mind; it helped us to become part of the ship.

It was not long before I was listed to make an appearance on the bridge, which caused me some anxious moments, as I had forgotten most of what I had learned about seamanship in my first months at St Vincent. When I arrived I was aghast to see so many senior officers standing around. I resolved to make myself as inconspicuous as possible, but the captain, 'Hooky' Holland, noticing a new face, asked me my name. I replied, then he said, 'Well, Lieutenant Moffat, would you report to me how many cables we are from *Renown*?' I must have looked like a rabbit caught in the headlights at this question. Thankfully, a nearby lieutenant commander noticed my panic and said, 'I think this is what you are looking for, Moffat,' and helped me unship a portable viewfinder with which I could read off the range of our flagship, *Renown*. After a bit of fumbling I was able to make my report to the captain. He thanked me with a slight grin on his face.

My other duty when I was not flying was to go to action stations to man one of the ship's clusters of 0.5in machine guns. Strangely, this duty influenced my flying, as I will explain later.

It took me a few days to realize that Force H and its commanding officer Admiral Somerville had been under a cloud for the past few weeks. Nobody on the *Ark* was pleased about this. Somerville was extremely popular, and respected – two things which don't always go hand in hand. He had been labouring with two courts of inquiry because of recent operations. The first was a delivery of twelve Hurricanes, plus two Skuas to guide them, to Malta on 17 November 1940. Only four Hurricanes and one of the Skuas managed to reach the island. There was no sign of the other aircraft, and the nine pilots plus the observer from the Skua were all missing. There was little hope that they would be found. It seemed that there was no hard evidence why so many of these planes had gone missing; it was assumed that they had hit a strong headwind and run out of fuel.

The second, more serious inquiry was into a convoy and involved some of *Ark Royal*'s squadrons. The operation, this time at the end of November, was to escort some merchant ships and over a thousand members of the RAF to Alexandria in Egypt. The RAF men were embarked on two cruisers, HMS *Manchester* and *Southampton*, which, because of the large number of passengers they carried, were not in a position to turn and fight if there were any attacks from the Italian navy. These convoys were not like the large, slow collections of merchant ships that steamed across the Atlantic. The Mediterranean was in many respects a far more hostile area, with most of it in range of shore-based aircraft in Sicily and Sardinia. There were Italian submarines on the lookout for targets and, whilst these tended to gather in the narrow waters to the south of Sicily, where any ships bound for Malta had to pass, they were quite capable of lying in wait anywhere in the western Mediterranean. There was also a threat from the surface warships of the Italian navy, which possessed several fast cruisers and battleships. The dangers were great, so cargo and supplies for the British forces in Egypt were sent via the long route round the Cape of Good Hope. The convoys that we escorted through the

Mediterranean were small, generally composed of fast modern merchant vessels carrying very urgent strategic cargoes.

In the *Ark* we did not necessarily see the ships we were escorting, because Force H would take up a screening position between them and the north-east, from where the main threat was expected to come. The Italian and German air wings based in Sicily and Sardinia would have reconnaissance planes searching for us within a day of our leaving Gibraltar; if we were spotted, then the next day there would be a concerted effort to bomb us. It was, I gathered, usually much more determined than the half-hearted attempt I had recently witnessed. The general principle adopted by the Italians was that, once Force H was sufficiently damaged, or distracted by attacks from the air, then their surface warships would move in on the transports. Naturally, the main target of their air-craft was always *Ark Royal*.

When I flew off on a patrol, the main task was searching ahead of our line of advance for signs of enemy submarines, but I might also be ordered to fly farther to gain sight of the Italian fleet if we suspected it was at sea, or to maintain a visual contact with the merchant ships. In all these operations it was the Swordfish and their crews that were the workhorse of Force H. I had volunteered to fly Swordfish because of what I saw as their exciting torpedo-carrying role, but I quickly learned on the *Ark* just how much flying the Swordfish had to do, and how much of it involved patrols and reconnaissance.

On this operation in November, which was codenamed Operation Collar, Force H was going to escort three cargo ships as well as the two cruisers carrying the RAF personnel. The merchant navy ships did not stop at Gibraltar; they went past and we had to make a rendezvous with them. On the morning of 26 November a Swordfish was sent off to locate them, while another flight was ranged up to be sent on anti-submarine patrol. This pattern was kept up all during that day.

Next morning there must have been some intelligence report that there were enemy ships at sea. I know now that a great number of enemy signals, both Italian and German, were being received and deciphered, but at the time this was obviously secret. We were never given any information about intelligence matters, but I do know that the *Ark* could pick up Italian radio traffic, and if there was a lot of activity on frequencies associated with the Italian navy, then it was easy to draw the conclusion that something was up!

That morning nine Swordfish were sent out on a wide-ranging patrol, searching the seas as far as 100 miles to the east and north. These reconnaissance patrols could be a test of endurance. You had to cover the area methodically, making sure the navigator was keeping track of the position; he would be constantly monitoring the wind speed and its direction so that he could take account of drift and keep in mind the route to be taken back to the carrier. The area on the horizon had to be scanned, because it was important not to be close to any ship we spotted, otherwise the target would be alerted and would take evasive action. Once a ship was spotted, a report was sent back to the *Ark*, and the Swordfish would then settle down to a cat-and-mouse game of staying in contact while trying itself to remain unnoticed, until relieved by another aircraft.

Later that morning, one of the patrolling Swordfish from 820 Squadron signalled back to the *Ark* that it had spotted a group of warships. Ten minutes later these were confirmed as two battleships and an escort of destroyers. The Italian fleet was at sea, and it was heading towards Force H.

There was immediate activity in the *Ark*. At the first report of a sighting there were six Fulmar fighters in the air, on a combat air patrol, and two relief shadowers were on their way to take over trailing the Italian warships from the three Swordfish that were still in contact. The remainder of the reconnaissance aircraft had to be landed on, as did a third section of fighters that needed refuelling. As soon as these aircraft landed, a strike force of Swordfish had to be ranged and launched. The Fulmars landing on would be taken down on the forward deck-lift, where they could be re-armed and refuelled in the hangar decks, while the Swordfish would be brought up on the rear deck-lift. They had been armed with torpedoes the night before in readiness, all nine of them, and they were ready to go. Two more Swordfish were now armed and made ready.

Meanwhile, the crews were being briefed and told about their expected targets. The latest information was that, as well as the two battleships with their escort of destroyers, there was another group, some miles way, of three heavy cruisers also protected by destroyers, bringing the total possibly to as many as seventeen warships. This was a sizeable fleet, bigger by far than Force H. The observers quickly mugged up on the identification silhouettes, the pilots checked the latest weather updates, and the TAGs made sure that Force H and *Ark Royal* had the up-to-date identification codes for friendly ships. The orders from the commander air to the operation leader, who was Lt Commander Mervyn 'Johnnie' Johnstone of 810 Squadron, were to attack the battleships if at all possible, and because of this the torpedoes had been set to run at a depth of 34 feet. This was the second torpedo strike from the *Ark* in just five months.

When the crews came out on to the flight deck the folding wings were already locked in place and the riggers and mechanics made final checks while waiting to start up the engines. All the propellers were turning before the attack leader would start his take-off. The noise was overpowering, and the aircraft behind the leaders trembled in their propeller wash. None of the riggers and other ratings manhandling the aircraft was on their feet at this point; they were kneeling by the chocks, keeping their heads down, trying to prevent themselves from being blown over.

Then one by one they were off. The signal to prepare for an attack was received on the *Ark* at 1030; in an hour the planes in the air had been recovered and eleven swordfish had been launched and were on their way to attack the Italian fleet.

In the meantime, *Renown* and the rest of Force H were steaming at full speed towards the enemy, preparing to open fire once they were in range. The guns of both sides started firing while the Swordfish were still twenty minutes away, and they could see the first British shells landing, the second salvo in amongst the cruisers. Then the Italian cruisers stopped firing and started laying down a thick smokescreen. The two Italian battleships had not yet begun to fire, but instead were still steaming towards Force H, and the attacking Swordfish approached them at about 6,000 feet. They were identified as *Vittorio Veneto* and *Giulio Cesare*. Lt Commander Mervyn Johnstone went into the dive and launched his torpedo at the rear battleship from about 1,500 feet, then pulled away. The remainder of the Swordfish aimed at the forward battleship. There was heavy gunfire from the battleships and the escorting destroyers, but none of the Swordfish was hit. Some of the pilots saw a column of brown smoke rise up from the far side of the leading battleship, but it wasn't until they all returned to the *Ark* that they could be debriefed and a possible hit on one of the targets was reported to the captain of *Ark Royal* and Admiral Somerville on *Renown*.

The Swordfish landed on at 1315, by which time the Italian ships had abandoned the fight and were heading at maximum speed for Cagliari on the Sardinian coast. They were still being shadowed by a Swordfish with an observer, my friend

Sub-Lieutenant Henry 'Maxie' Mayes, and he reported at around 1330 that he had been fired on by an Italian cruiser, a San Giorgio class, which was stationary in the water, and it appeared that there was a fire in the after part of the ship. He thought that she had been hit by a large shell in the after turret. Mayes circled her for about half an hour before heading back to the *Ark*.

While the first torpedo attack had been taking place, there was another round of intense activity to prepare aircraft for a second attack. At 1410 nine Swordfish took off in pursuit of the Italian battleships. On the bridge they decided that they would prepare a force of Skua aircraft to carry out a dive-bombing attack on the stricken cruiser that Mayes had seen on fire. This decision was a risky one. Some of the Fulmars in the air had already made contact with Italian bombers approaching the fleet at around 10,000 feet, and detaching the Skuas to carry out a dive-bombing exercise would leave Force H with just one squadron of Fulmars for air defence. Moreover, most of the crews had carried out at least one if not two patrols already.

Twenty minutes after the second wave of Swordfish took off, ten Italian bombers staged an attack on *Renown* and Force H. They dropped a long stick of bombs from a height of 13,000 feet, the closest of which exploded over a mile away, but, sadly, one Fulmar was shot down. The Italian battleships were continuing their dash to the Sardinian coast, and if there had been any damage caused by the first attack it was not apparent when the second wave of Swordfish approached them, led by 820 Squadron's CO, Lt Commander Stewart-Moore. They approached from the west, and by this time they were coming out of the sun. Stewart-Moore saw that the battleships were in the lead, escorted by ten destroyers, followed by the three cruisers and four more destroyers. He had been told by Commander Traill, the commander air, that he should go for the battleships if possible, but ultimately to use his own judgement. At the back of both the commander air's and Stewart-Moore's minds was the relative inexperience of most of his pilots compared to those in the first wave. He looked at the position of the ships and realized that, if he wanted to continue his approach to the battleships in the van of the Italian ships, he would be seen by their escorting cruisers, who would have plenty of time to raise the alarm. He would also be vulnerable to their anti-aircraft fire as his Swordfish flew past them at a relative speed of just 50 knots. However, the final fact that influenced him was that they were now only about 30 nautical miles from Sardinia and he could see Italian aircraft circling over Cagliari. If he delayed until he could reach the battleships, then he would be placing his Swordfish in danger of attack from Italian fighters. He elected to attack the cruisers, and signalled the other nine aircraft of his intentions.

They went down in a shallow dive from 10,000 feet, then about 2 miles out dived to the surface, where they made their approach. The forward cruiser was shielded by the destroyers, so Stewart-Moore picked the last cruiser in line and dropped his torpedo. By now the cruisers were alerted and were firing at him. They changed course, turning into the attack, and the following Swordfish turned also to keep them beam on. The cruisers executed a broad circle and, as they did so, all the torpedoes were dropped. The destroyers were also firing and the Swordfish zigzagged away to avoid the anti-aircraft shells. As they made their getaway, several of the observers thought they could see a mound of water rise up along the side of the cruiser, as if it had been caused by an underwater explosion, and brown smoke poured out of one of the funnels, but they saw nothing else to indicate that a torpedo had scored a hit.

Seven Skuas had taken off from the *Ark* at 1500 hours to administer the *coup de grâce* to the damaged stationary cruiser that Sub-Lieutenant Mayes had sighted earlier. When they got to the reported position, however, they found nothing, so continued to search. About 6 miles away they saw another group of three cruisers, of the Condotierri class, armed with 6in guns. They were steaming in line astern at about 16 knots and were, it seems, entirely separate from those attacked by the Swordfish led by Stewart-Moore. The Skuas climbed to 9,000 feet, then dived on the warships, which were taken completely by surprise. The bombs were dropped on the last cruiser of the trio at around 900 feet, but out of seven 500lb bombs aimed at this ship, no hits were seen. As they flew away, pursued by bursting shells from the cruisers, they saw a wide oil slick, but nothing to indicate that the damaged cruiser they had originally been looking for had sunk.

This was the last attempt to damage the Italian warships that day, but it was not by any means the last of the action. Shortly after the Skuas had taken off, three waves of Italian bombers, flying at around 14,000 feet, headed for *Ark Royal*. Each wave of five aircraft dropped ten bombs, and they fell extremely close; at one point enormous gouts of water were cascading on to the flight deck from both sides of the ship. The noise of the explosions and the fire from the sixteen 4.5in anti-aircraft guns was deafening. The *Ark* steamed furiously through the bombardment, heeling over in sharp turns, avoiding stick after stick of bombs plummeting down. The ship's photographer had some photos of the *Ark* taken from *Renown*, and she was completely obscured by the explosions. When I saw them later, I wondered how long it would be before I was in an attack like this.

After the last attack by the Skuas, and this retaliatory attack on the *Ark* by the Italian bombers, Admiral Somerville did not pursue the Italian fleet as it retreated. Their warships were faster by several knots than *Renown* and the British cruisers. He was also concerned that to try to close on them would inevitably take Force H and the *Ark* very close to the airbases in Sardinia. *Ark Royal* was his biggest asset in Force H, and if she were lost then Gibraltar might as well close down. He considered it his main duty to continue to protect the three cargo ships and the troop-carrying cruisers, escorting them to where they could be handed over to the Mediterranean Fleet, which had steamed out of Alexandria to meet them.

It was Somerville's decision to abandon the pursuit of the Italian fleet that led to calls in London for his court martial, and the convening of a court of inquiry into his conduct. Everybody in Force H was 100 per cent behind him, of course. As part of this inquiry, evidence was also taken from the COs and pilots of the squadrons that attacked the fleet. There had been three attacks by aircraft from *Ark Royal*, but two separate torpedo attacks by twenty Swordfish and a dive-bomber attack by seven Skuas had failed to slow any of the Italian ships down.

It was an unsatisfactory result, and the general feeling was that there were two problems. Many of the pilots in the Swordfish squadrons were inexperienced. There was also a lack of training in torpedo attacks. The Swordfish squadrons were stretched, with patrol, reconnaissance and anti-submarine duties to be performed throughout the day, and there was little time to devote to training. I gathered this was going to change, and we were scheduled to do more of it. But there was a general feeling as well that there was a problem with torpedo attacks on high-speed targets. The results were not as decisive as had been expected during peacetime exercises. Many in the wardroom felt that there might be something wrong with the torpedoes, but nobody was in a position to do anything about it.

I felt that the inquiry was a bit of a cheek. The target, of course, was Rear Admiral Somerville, but it was felt to be a veiled criticism of *Ark Royal*, particularly as many questions were asked about orders given for the attack and the tactics adopted. I didn't take part, but questions were asked of some of the pilots that suggested that the admirals on the board of inquiry didn't know very much about flying, or about torpedo attacks. Everyone carried on as normal, of course, but there was a sense that something was being left unsaid. Fortunately, the court of inquiry exonerated Somerville of any wrongdoing.

7
Gotcha

The mood on the *Ark* was affected not only by the court of inquiry sitting in Gibraltar, but by the news of a stunning attack on the Italian fleet at its harbour in Taranto. I was still in Arbroath at the time, waiting for a posting to a front-line squadron. I was very excited, as was everyone in the Fleet Air Arm, because at the time it looked like a real knock-out blow. In our view it showed how vital naval aviation was, and how much of a threat a properly trained squadron of torpedo bombers could be. At last, we thought, the navy will wake up and begin to take notice of us. When I got on to the *Ark*, however, there was a slightly different attitude. Everyone was very pleased, of course, with the success of the attack, but there was also a feeling that the spotlight of publicity had shifted away a bit from the glamour boys of *Ark Royal*, especially as the efforts against the Italian warships in November had not resulted in any losses on their part. But this operation and the earlier attack on *Strasbourg* had been spur-of-the-moment things, rapidly assembled groups of aircraft flown off to intervene in the middle of a surface action. The raid on Taranto, on the other hand, had been planned for years.

The Mediterranean was a very important area for Britain.

Our interest in it had never diminished since Nelson beat Napoleon in 1798 in the Battle of the Nile. Egypt and the Suez Canal gave access to the Middle East and India, so control of the route from Gibraltar through the Med was vital. The Mediterranean Fleet before the war had been second in size only to our Home Fleet. To be in command of it was an important step to very high rank in the navy.

When Mussolini came to power in Italy he wanted to expand the Italian empire in North Africa and the Horn, and started to build up the Italian navy. The Italians began modernizing their First World War battleships and building new ones. Their submarine fleet, in particular, became very large. In short, Italian influence in the Mediterranean was expanding and there was a good chance that they would soon challenge Britain for control of the sea.

Admiral Sir Dudley Pound was in charge of the Mediterranean Fleet in 1935 and, before he moved on to become First Sea Lord in the Admiralty under Churchill, he started drawing up plans to attack the Italian fleet if it ever came to war. There were several important ports around the Italian coast, but Mussolini had promoted the construction of a major new one in the town of Taranto, a natural harbour in the large Bay of Taranto inside the heel of Italy. It was naturally defendable and with the construction of large breakwaters to create an outer harbour it was hard to attack in any way other than from the air.

In 1938, at the time of the Munich crisis, Pound's plan was looked at again by Captain Arthur Lyster, who was then in command of HMS *Glorious*, at the time attached to the Mediterranean Fleet. As a result of his concern about an alliance between Germany and Italy, Lyster started to put some of the groundwork of the plan into place. The two squadrons of Swordfish on board *Glorious* started carrying out exercises in night flying, and nighttime torpedo attacks.

They started to look at improvements in launch and recovery techniques, and after two months Lyster and his commander air came to the conclusion that, with the right preparation, a surprise attack on Taranto was possible. *Glorious*, however, was later replaced by HMS *Eagle* in the Mediterranean Fleet and was sent with the *Ark* to operate off Norway, where of course she was sunk by *Scharnhorst* in June 1940.

The Royal Navy in the eastern Mediterranean needed to be strengthened and, in August, HMS *Illustrious* was sent down from the UK, travelling through the Med to help boost the air cover available for Admiral Andrew Cunningham's fleet in Alexandria. *Illustrious* was a modern carrier, designed and built after *Ark Royal* expressly to serve in the Mediterranean. The proximity of Italian airbases caused the Admiralty to call for a carrier that would be better protected against air attack, so *Illustrious*, and all the carriers that followed her, were designed with armoured flight decks, armoured anti-aircraft gun turrets and a thick belt of armour around the hull. Because of this increased weight above the waterline, she had to be built with a single hangar deck to reduce her freeboard. The consequence, however, was that she could not carry as many planes as the *Ark* and had a total complement of just thirty-six aircraft. On board *Illustrious* was the man who had worked on the fine planning of the Taranto operation, Captain Lyster, who had now been promoted to Rear Admiral and was going to take command of both *Illustrious* and *Eagle* under Cunningham. With both carriers, Lyster thought that he had enough Swordfish aircraft to carry out an attack on the Italian fleet in its harbour.

A lot of preparations had to be made before the plan could be set in motion. Lyster did what he did when he was in *Glorious* in 1938: set in motion a programme for the aircrew, deck-handlers and riggers to be trained in night operations. There are a lot of extra dangers when the aircraft are brought up out of the hangar and ranged at the end of the flight deck at night. Any mistake, stumble or misjudgement could damage a plane or kill or injure someone.

It took several weeks before Lyster was confident that the planes could be assembled and take off safely, and that they could navigate and recognize their target in the dark. Once the crews were in an efficient state, good reconnaissance was the next essential. The attack would be successful only if there were sufficient Italian warships at anchor in the harbour. The RAF flew regular reconnaissance missions over Taranto from Malta, using American Glenn Martin bombers, and the photographs that they were bringing back showed that the harbour was full, with plenty of valuable targets. The strike was planned for 21 October, Trafalgar Day, when there would be a full moon.

Then, with a few days to go, a fierce fire broke out in *Illustrious*'s hangar deck, destroying several of the Swordfish that were needed for the attack. The attack was postponed until another full moon.

It was fortunate that it was, because the continued reconnaissance flights now showed that there had been some drastic improvements in the air defences around Taranto. The Italians were increasing their number of anti-aircraft gun emplacements and they had put sixty barrage balloons around the outer harbour, with a line of them moored from barges in the middle of the harbour. In addition, they had lowered some torpedo nets around the battleships moored there to create a defensive enclave on the eastern side of the port. This meant that there was a very limited line of approach for the Swordfish to get a clear shot at their targets.

The operation was now scheduled for 11 November, when again a few days before there was another problem, this time in *Eagle*'s fuel-storage system, which supplied petrol for the Swordfish. It had sprung several leaks and was in need of urgent maintenance. Several Swordfish from *Eagle* had carried out forced landings because their fuel was contaminated by seawater, and it was clear that *Eagle* could no longer take part in the operation. In order to prevent any more delays, five of her Swordfish and eight of her most experienced crews were embarked on to *Illustrious*. A total of twenty-one aircraft were going to take part in the attack, and those from 813 and 824 Squadrons on *Eagle* were included in the second wave of nine Swordfish.

At 2200 on the 11th *Illustrious* was in position to begin the take-off of the first wave. Some last-minute information from a late reconnaissance flight had revealed that a sixth battleship had just anchored. The aircraft had been fitted with auxiliary tanks to give them extra range. These were installed in the cockpit where the observer normally sat, so the observer moved into the TAG's seat. These tanks were ramshackle things; I remember they quite often leaked, and it was not a comfortable feeling to think that 60 gallons of high-octane fuel were right behind you.

The Swordfish took off, but the last one of the last flight was damaged in a collision on the flight deck and needed repairs to its fabric covering. The crew were anxious to get away and pressured the riggers to hurry up. The plane was repaired and they took off on their own thirty minutes later. There was enormous expectation about this raid: it was a major attack against the Italian navy and everybody involved was completely keyed up. After the weeks and weeks of training, nobody wanted to be left behind.

The large battleships and cruisers in the Italian fleet were moored in the outer harbour, and the first wave of the attack was going to split up so that the planes could approach the ships from two different directions. Hopefully, it would divide the anti-aircraft defences by giving them two different targets to aim for. The leader of the second wave, Lt Commander

Hale, decided that he would keep all nine of his aircraft in one formation, make an approach from the north-west and then turn south. Approaching at this angle meant that they would increase their chances of hitting one of the ships at its mooring, because their silhouettes overlapped each other: it would be like hitting fish in a barrel. It did, however, mean flying over a concentration of anti-aircraft guns and then through a line of barrage balloons.

As they flew over the sea at 7,000 feet, they entered thick cloud and were suddenly flying blind, relying on their instruments to maintain a straight and level course. When they passed into clear sky again, four of the Swordfish were no longer to be seen. There was nothing to do but hope they would find Taranto, so the diminished group pressed on. As they got closer they could see that the anti-aircraft defences were already alert and firing shells and tracer into the night sky. The sky ahead over Taranto looked like a giant fireworks display. One of the missing aircraft had been flying faster than its companions and had reached the target first.

The leader of the first wave, Lt Commander Williamson, flew parallel to the outer breakwater, then turned and dived to release his torpedo. As he turned to get away, he was hit by machine-gun fire and lost control, the Swordfish plunging into the water. Luckily, he and his observer were not injured; they were rescued and became prisoners-of-war. His torpedo, however, hit the water, functioned perfectly and motored towards its target. It struck the battleship *Cavour* just forward of the bridge and the ship started to settle in the water.

The next aircraft of the first wave were now desperately jinking to avoid the exploding shells and tracer, the whole area was surrounded by winking flashes of gunfire pointed in their direction, and they were in no position to be fussy about their targets. Two torpedoes missed *Cavour*, exploding harmlessly. Lieutenant Kemp flew in low along a line of cruisers that began firing on him. He held his plane steady and launched his torpedo at a huge ship looming in front of him. It ran true and tore a hole that was later found to be 49 feet long in *Littorio*. Another pilot, Lieutenant Swayne, chose a different course, coming at *Littorio* from the other side. He too had a hit and *Littorio*'s hull was ripped open again. Some of the Swordfish were armed with bombs and they took what targets they could identify. Captain Ollie Patch dropped his bombs in a steep dive on a cluster of destroyers in the inner harbour and got away as quick as he could. Another Swordfish couldn't identify any ships, so dropped his bombs on the seaplane base, where there was a huge explosion and the hangars and fuel tanks started blazing furiously into the night sky.

The second wave had to fly into this mayhem. They were detected some way out and the defenders' fire was redoubled. One of the aircraft released flares, shining bright white magnesium light over the whole harbour. The pilots could smell the reek of burning petrol and gunsmoke. Hale, the leader, also aimed for *Littorio* and succeeded in ripping a third hole in her. The second plane in to the attack, flown by Lieutenant Bayly, was hit and crashed near *Gorizia*. His body was recovered the next day, but his observer, Lieutenant Slaughter, was never found. Another torpedo found *Duilio* and blasted open her hull below the waterline. The crew, already desperately working up the ship in preparation to escape the inferno, realized that there was no alternative but to beach her to stop her sinking altogether.

Lieutenant John Wellham had taken off in the last wave. As he flew close to the harbour he started his dive, but nearly collided with a barrage balloon at 4,000 feet. He did a tight downward turn, then tried to straighten up. As he did so he felt the control stick almost ripped out of his hand and found that he could not lift the port wing. Something, a cable from the balloon or a piece of shrapnel, had damaged his aircraft, but it was impossible to say what. He struggled for control of the Swordfish but, when he managed to regain some response to the stick, he realized that he had been losing height and was diving straight into the city of Taranto. He levelled out into a right turn, but found that the plane would fly only with one wing down and at a slight yawing angle. It was not ideal for an accurate torpedo drop, but he pressed on and, with every gun in Taranto apparently firing at him, he dropped his torpedo at what he hoped was *Vittorio Veneto*, then zig-zagged wildly and headed for the clear night sky as fast as he could. He was hit again, but got away and turned towards the position where they would rendezvous with *Illustrious*. He managed to get down on to the flight deck, but once in the hangar his rigger found that his port aileron rod was split in two and there was a jagged hole in the lower port wing. A large piece of metal had broken several wing ribs and cut the controls. He had been lucky.

After both waves had landed it was clear that two Swordfish were missing, although nobody in *Illustrious* knew that two of the men were alive and taken prisoner. The casualties were remarkably low considering the strength of the defences and the fact that they had inadvertently been alerted. The Swordfish as well had spent more time than they had wanted over the target.

Next morning the Italians came out to see what the damage was, and RAF reconnaissance planes flew over, their big cameras clicking. *Littorio* had been seriously damaged and rested on the bottom. *Duilio*'s magazines were flooded and she had been beached. *Cavour* was also flooded, with her decks awash. *Trento* was leaking oil, which was covering the waters of the harbour, hampering any salvage efforts. The destroyers *Libeccio* and *Pessagno* were damaged and could not put to sea. The seaplane base was a mass of twisted girders, still smoking in the dawn light, and smashed sea-planes lay crumpled on the concrete ramp and apron.

It was a magnificent success, and news of the raid spread around the world. Many think that the success of the attack on Taranto influenced the Japanese Admiral Yamamoto, convincing him that the surprise attack on the US navy at Pearl Harbor would also succeed. We knew nothing of this, of course. At home, where we all thought that we had proved ourselves in spades, Taranto was a magnificent advert for the Fleet Air Arm. It showed what could be achieved if sufficient planning and preparation were devoted to an operation, and moreover if there was plenty of reconnaissance prior to the day. Without this, the lives of many of the crews might have been squandered. As it was, some of them did not have much longer to live.

8

Buckling Up, Buckling Down

I had arrived on *Ark Royal* after an intense period of activity in which she, and the other carriers in the eastern Mediterranean, had for the first time been fighting the warships of large enemy fleets. In this short space of time a lot of lessons had been learned, and a lot of changes were being made to the way we did things. Simple changes to the way aircraft were taken down to the hangar decks, the way maintenance crews and armourers were organized, could improve turnaround times and keep more aircraft in the air for longer. The Mediterranean was still a dangerous place.

After the Italian navy had been hit at Taranto, they moved the rest of their fleet to ports along the western Italian coast – Naples, of course, and La Spezia further north. This may have removed them from the area of operations of the Mediterranean Fleet, but put them much closer, merely a day's sailing away, to the route taken by convoys from Gibraltar to Malta for which we in Force H were responsible. In January 1941 we had to escort a convoy of nine transports to Malta, and also fly off six Swordfish that had been brought down to Gibraltar by *Argus* to be permanently stationed on the island. The operation was known as Excess. The route was fairly predictable and we had to keep a sharp lookout. Once again I was flying long patrols searching for ships, or hoping to spot the telltale wake of a submarine's periscope.

Even in the midst of a war, on active service, life was very much one of routine and sometimes agonizing boredom. Much of my time flying was not the heart-stopping drama of a dive-bombing attack, or the stomach-churning tension of a torpedo run, but long uneventful patrols over mile after mile of flat, featureless ocean. At times, if the sun was just striking the tops of the mountains of Spain and beginning to burn off the haze lying over the surface of the Mediterranean, then I would feel that upsurge of exhilaration that I have always associated with flying – in particular joy at my ability to pilot the plane that is taking me up so that I can see for hundreds of miles around me. The open cockpit of the Swordfish was marvellous for the full experience, which really did sometimes seem like a miracle.

But when the clouds were low and dark, and the sea was a cold, white-flecked steel grey, and the rain beat against my face, the patrols became an endurance test.

Anti-submarine patrols would often start just before day-break, when the *Ark* slipped out of Gibraltar. Very often these would need a launch from one of the catapults mounted in the front of the flight deck. They had quite a kick – I remember that first time I had a catapult launch, the deck officer warned me to brace myself in the seat otherwise my head would be thrown back. The observer and TAG in the back had a more uncomfortable ride. The TAG had to lean down and fold his arms in front of his face over the breach of his stowed Lewis gun.

Before a patrol we would get dressed in very warm clothes, with three layers of gloves, starting with silk ones, then woollen ones, then our sheepskin flying gloves; similarly with layers of socks under our flying boots. We wore specially made sheepskin suits over our flying overalls. I felt like the Michelin man at the end of it. Then we, my observer and TAG and I, would walk out to the aircraft. The flight deck could be very slippery, especially early in the morning, so you needed to watch your step. Not only would it be wet from dew, but after a few days at sea it would get salty and then a layer of rubber from aircraft tyres would be deposited, so it could be very dangerous. The armourers and riggers would be waiting to start strapping us in. My rigger was a character. He would sit astride the fuselage behind me, shouting at me to 'get yourself in here', yanking away at my shoulder straps and singing at the top of his voice, 'Oh Ma, I like your apple pie', some song I had never heard before, but he was one of those regular navy ratings who would look you in the eye with the utmost confidence and I trusted him, as every pilot had to trust the mechanics and riggers who worked on their plane. I never had any qualms about them: they were thoroughly reliable.

Several planes would be ranged up according to the flying orders for the day, but if you were the first anti-submarine patrol, then your Swordfish would be at the front. This shortened the take-off distance slightly, and you knew that there would be a slight dip as you went off the front of the flight deck, but you would then start to gain height.

I always found starting the Swordfish a bit nerve-racking. There was no electric starter motor, and the nine-cylinder radial with its three-bladed propeller was far too big to be turned over by hand. Instead, the engine was turned over prior to ignition using an inertial starter. This was a large fly-wheel mounted in the nose, which was cranked up to speed by two of the aircraft handlers, one of whom had to stand on the leading edge of the port lower wing. They had to turn a handle that was inserted in a hole in the side of the aircraft. It took quite an effort. When the flywheel was spinning fast enough they would shout 'Now!', and I had to flick a switch in the cockpit to fire the sparkplugs and move a lever to engage the flywheel, which would then turn the engine over. If you didn't time it exactly right, the engine wouldn't fire and they would have to start winding up the flywheel all over again. If that happened there would be quite a lot of muttering, which of course I was not meant to hear. Everyone knew that I *could* hear, but I couldn't respond without making a complete arse of myself. I made damn sure that I got the timing right though.

I would go through the checks automatically. The elevator was set for 3 degrees nose-up attitude; the mixture was at rich; flaps were fully down; and the oil bypass was set on the 'in' position. Then open the throttle to 1,000 revs and wait for the oil temperature to settle. With the engine running and the oil pressure and revs looking OK, the rigger and the aircraft handlers would crouch down by the wheels waiting to remove the chocks. At a signal from the deck officer I would set full throttle and the plane would roll down the flight deck. It was best to stay level as long as possible to gain the most effect from the pressure build-up between the deck and the lower wing, although really, depending on the load and the wind speed over the deck, you could be airborne by the time you got past the bridge.

Then it would be a case of reaching the required height, depending on the cloud base, and starting a patrol pattern over the sea for the next two and a half hours. I didn't enjoy these early-morning patrols. I was still a young lad in many ways and found it hard to wake up at four o'clock in the morning. Our squadron writer, a decent chap, Percy North, who was just a few years older than me, was responsible for issuing the flying orders and would often make his way down to my cabin to wake me up. One morning he rushed in, shouting at me to get up because I was very late. 'I came in twenty minutes ago, you lazy sod. The CO'll have your guts!' I swore he hadn't woken me, and in a desperate attempt to make it in time, got dressed over my pyjamas. It didn't fool anybody: as I walked out on to the flight deck everyone could see what I was wearing and I was given extra watch-keeping duties for the next month as a punishment. But I found it so hard to get up in the mornings.

The roar of the engine and the cold sea wind in my face, however, were enough to get the blood stirring, although I did long for some action, an opportunity to drop my depth-charges. But in all the time I was flying Swordfish I never saw a periscope, or better still a U-boat running on the surface, a 'floater' as we called them.

During these patrols, the busiest man in many ways was the observer, whose job it was to navigate the aircraft, making sure that we carried out the proper patrol pattern and also that we made it back to the aircraft carrier safely. He carried a lot of equipment with him: a small mechanical cipher machine, codebooks, a Very signal pistol and Aldis lamp, maps and briefing notes, and a Bigsworth Board – a square piece of wood fitted with parallel rulers and protractors so that he could calculate the course back to the carrier and offset our heading against the wind speed. The *Ark* would have travelled more than 60 miles from the position where we took off by the time our patrol was finished. We knew what her intended course was going to be and our landing-on point was prearranged at the briefing, although of course anything could happen while we were in the air. But the task of running a complicated search pattern and making it back to a very small point on the ocean after two and a half or three hours is not as easy as it sounds.

I had to make sure that we stuck to the course given me by my observer, and he had to make sure that he recorded the changes of direction and their duration correctly. Of course, if there was a wind, and there always was, this had to be taken into account, particularly if it changed during the flight. After a while you developed a sixth sense, so that it was possible to detect any changes of wind through the controls. We carried smoke floats on racks under our wings. I would drop one of these and, once it had started smoking, I would fly right over the top of it, then turn and do a 180-degree course back over it in a timed run so that the observer could measure the rate of drift and the angle. With this he could calculate on his charts the necessary changes to our course back to the rendezvous point. It was not easy in an open cockpit, but most of the Fleet Air Arm navigators were good, and my observer, Dusty Miller, was really spot on. Once our calculations had been made it was the job of the TAG to sink the smoke float. You couldn't leave something like that bobbing about in the ocean, because it was obviously a clue that a carrier was in the vicinity and it could help build up an intelligence picture for a U-boat trying to track a convoy and its escort. So the TAG would sink it with machine-gun fire. My TAG, Hayman, would manage this with a single burst from his Vickers.

I got lost only once. We had been on a long patrol – I think it was nearly three hours – but when we got to our rendezvous point there was no sign of the carrier. I did feel anxious at that point. It was vital to keep radio silence, of course, because any transmission would have given away the carrier's position. I took us up to 3,000 feet, but still we could see nothing.

'I think we've made a mistake,' I said. Dusty didn't reply, or at least I can't remember one. It was pretty obvious. So I said to him, 'Now will you go back to your chart again, and make sure you've laid the winds off in the right direction.'

After a while he said, 'My God, you're right.' He roughly corrected it and within five minutes the carrier was in sight.

After a long patrol, the strain of maintaining a level height and course against the wind, plus the incessant noise of the engine and the slipstream whistling through the spars for two and a half hours sapped my energy. It was always a relief to see the *Ark*, a tiny ship in the distance, growing bigger as we approached. Landing on required all my attention, under the strict gaze of the deck landing officer, Lt Commander Pat Stringer. I had to check that the brakes were off, set the mixture for rich again, because you could often lean it out to conserve fuel on a long flight, and then set the carburettor intake to 'cold'. I would lower the arrestor hook and come in over the round down – the end of the flight deck at the stern – keeping my eye on the batman and trying to hit the first or second arrestor wire; hitting the last one was seen as a bit of a last-ditch effort. By the time I was waiting for the tug of the hook against the wire there was not enough speed to take off and go round again. Use the brakes at this point and it would be disaster: the plane would flip over and crash. All you could do was switch off the engine and hope the crash barrier would stop you. Then I would climb out of the cockpit while the wings were folded and the plane was moved to the deck-lift. Tired and stiff, we had made it again.

There is a story that I was told by another Swordfish pilot, Pat Jackson, who took a short-service commission when the war started. He was flying off *Victorious* and he too got lost, but his observer's error did not end as easily as mine. He flew back to the point where he should have seen the carrier, and there was nothing.

They were in the North Atlantic, with low cloud and poor visibility. It was a devilish place in which to navigate, with a lot of variable winds at different altitudes, and it was an even worse place in which to get lost. They flew around, but naturally at the end of a patrol fuel is low, and it was getting lower. The observer then spotted a boat in the sea; it was a lifeboat, submerged up to its gunwales, with the waves break-ing over it. The Swordfish was equipped with an inflatable liferaft, which was stowed in the centre section of the upper wing. When seawater penetrated a cartridge it released carbon dioxide, which then inflated the raft, breaking open the hatch that covered it. Although it saved many people, the liferaft was not something in which you would want to spend a lot of time in the North Atlantic. Pat had about ten minutes' fuel left at that point, with not a clue where his carrier was. There was this swamped boat, more solid and bigger than the liferaft, so down they went. They ditched as close to it as they could, got into the liferaft and drifted down to the submerged boat. There was a big tarpaulin covering the bottom planks and they half expected to find some bodies under it, but it was empty. There were some emergency rations and a sail. They baled the water out with their flying boots, rigged a mast and set the sail. They were closest to Greenland, but the thought of trying to land there, on a rocky coast with strong winds and ice, was not appealing, so they turned east.

Then they were hit by a storm, swamped again and had to start baling once more. The wind was against them, so they had to run before it, heading west. They were alone, in the middle of the Atlantic, wet, cold and with the barest of rations, when they saw another sail. They got closer and realized it was another lifeboat with five or six men in it. They were in the same condition as Pat and his crewmembers, except that three of the men in the other lifeboat were dead. They were Scandinavian and said they had been adrift for fourteen days. Pat gave them some ship's biscuits, but the two groups could not agree on the best course. Pat and his crew still wanted to try to head east, but those in the other boat thought it was better to go west, to Canada. They separated, each going their different ways.

Pat drifted for nine days. The TAG started to develop

frostbite in his legs, despite the fact that they took it in turns to massage each other to keep the blood flowing. But the TAG's feet and lower legs turned blue, and he started to lose any feeling in them. They then decided to head north, because they saw some birds heading in that direction. They sailed for another two days, then were hit by another storm, and it started to snow.

By now the TAG was barely conscious, and Pat and his observer were beginning to suffer hallucinations. They too were beginning to get slightly frostbitten. During the night, Pat had to dissuade the observer from trying to swim home. When dawn came, I think Pat must have been near to breaking. He had always been a religious man and he said that he prayed a lot in those last days. Then, as they crested a wave, he saw what he thought was a ship. He was sure that he was hallucinating, but he woke up the observer, who was, fortunately, lucid enough to see it as well. By a miracle, they had kept their signal flares from the Swordfish and they fired them off.

The ship saw them and turned. They managed to secure the line that was thrown to them, but they were so weak that three sailors had to climb down into the lifeboat and haul them out to safety. They had been rescued by an Icelandic fishing boat. All three survived, although I think the TAG lost his toes. Yet to this day Pat has never forgotten the poor buggers in the other lifeboat. He told the Icelandic authorities about them and they put out a search, of sorts, but they would have been adrift by then for almost a month and either had been rescued already or were dead. They were never found to his knowledge. Their fate has haunted him ever since – perhaps more than the hardships he suffered himself. I was very lucky that I found the *Ark* so quickly that day.

Yet it happened often. I had been on the *Ark* for a few weeks when I was told that a new pilot was going to share my cabin, a chap called Ferguson. He was a quiet, slightly delicate soul. As I was on early flying duties, I didn't see much of him. Within a few days his aircraft had failed to return and I found myself assembling his few possessions, photos and other personal items to parcel up and post to his parents. It was very disturbing to have to do this. It really shook me up. It was not as severe as the bomb that nearly killed me at Worthy Down, but I could not but be affected by this sudden death. He was about my age, and I thought of his mother's reaction when she heard the news, and how she would feel when she looked at the letters she had written to her son, whom she would now never see again. I hoped that his death had been quick. I thought of my parents too, waking every day not knowing if I was still alive.

Of course, living in Kelso as they did, I was fairly sure that they were safe, but there were many men on board the *Ark* who did not know what was happening to their parents, or their wives and children. They had families in London, or Liverpool or Coventry, cities that were being hit by air raids, and whenever news of the Blitz came through on the BBC a ripple of anxiety went round the mess decks.

Whether it was this, or the ambience on board the *Ark* generally, but I felt that I was beginning to grow up. There was an atmosphere of competence and confidence in which you felt that if you didn't give of your best you were letting the whole ship down. I too wanted to do my best and I started to become serious about my duties – although like most young men, I couldn't resist a challenge or a chance for some sport.

Perhaps the most powerful influence on me at the time was my squadron CO, Lt Commander Coode. I had enormous respect for him; he was an outstanding leader. He was regular navy, and although he could have been only about twenty-seven or so, he seemed like a god. I hero-worshipped him slightly, developing an almost childlike desire to emulate him.

The officers of Force H were very strong on exercises and practice. Admiral Somerville and the captain of the *Ark*, as well as the commander air, were well aware that we were not always the most experienced pilots, so at every opportunity we had training sessions. We did everything we could to speed up our landings and take-offs, so that we could land on, clear decks and fly off again in the shortest possible time – something that could be vital if we came under attack. We carried out torpedo-dropping exercises and often launched mock attacks against the destroyers and cruisers in Force H to give their gunnery directors experience in judging aircraft altitudes and speeds, something they were notoriously bad at doing.

At the end of one of these sessions I was following Lt Commander Coode in the circuit above the *Ark* as we came in to land. As he came in he did a perfect loop above the ship, then flew round to land on. I saw him and thought, 'I can do that.' I forgot to tell my two crewmembers in the back that I was going to attempt a loop, however, and down I went, then pulled the stick right back up into the climb. It was a disaster. I had failed to build up enough speed, so at the top we hung for what seemed an eternity. There were cries of alarm from behind me and everything in the rear cockpits, which of course had not been secured, fell out. Pencils, slide rules, map cases, plotting boards, ad hoc rations all descended from the air; and worse, we were close to a stall. I was told that everyone on the bridge was aghast as they looked up at this hapless pilot, with the rain of equipment falling into the sea. I managed to right the Swordfish, descended and went back into the circuit, feeling extremely embarrassed. I was given a severe talking to by the CO when I landed and made to feel about a foot tall. Naturally, I was the butt of every joke in the wardroom for days: 'Tried another loop yet, Jock?' But what made me feel more sheepish than anything was the abuse I received from Dusty and Hayman. I promised myself I would never ever do anything like that again. But I did, as we shall see.

It was rare for us to enter the Mediterranean without being attacked by the Italian air force. Sure enough, on our return in January from escorting the ships of Operation Excess to Malta, we were attacked by ten Italian bombers, Savoia Marchetti 79s, which flew straight and level and attempted to bomb the battleship *Malaya*. Two of these aircraft were shot down by the *Ark*'s Fulmar fighters and the rest withdrew. Some of the crew of the downed aircraft were rescued by one of our escorting destroyers, and I remember seeing one Italian airman standing on the fuselage of his slowly sinking bomber trying to catch a line that had been thrown to him. He was brought over to the *Ark* to be interrogated and also, I heard, for some medical treatment. I thought that when he had been rescued he hadn't looked particularly injured, so asked if he was all right. 'No,' came the reply. 'He's got the clap.'

This token bombing raid was the only sign of the Italian air force and it was not until we returned to port in Gibraltar that we heard some sad and alarming news, which explained why we on the *Ark* had got off lightly. The carrier that had mounted the attack on Taranto, *Illustrious*, had been very badly damaged on 10 January as she was providing air cover for the small convoy of fast cargo ships that we had escorted as far as the Straits of Sicily. So far, the major combatant faced by us in the Mediterranean had been the Italian fleet and their air force. The Italians had not had a great deal of success and, perhaps more importantly from their perspective, had also been getting the worst of it against the British army in North Africa. The navy had been hammering their supply shipping to the port of Tobruk in Libya and they were on the run. Some intelligence briefings had suggested that the Germans had stationed some aircraft in southern Italy, or in Sicily, but in the *Ark* we had not faced the Luftwaffe.

On 10 January, around midday, *Illustrious* had been carrying out a manoeuvre where carriers are at their most vulnerable. The combat air patrol of six Fulmars had been in the air for some two hours and the planes, low on fuel, were coming to the end of their endurance. On *Illustrious*'s flight deck were six more Fulmars, ranged and ready to take off to replace them. *Illustrious*'s radar had picked up a large formation of enemy aircraft approaching from the north at about 12,000 feet, but the Fulmars in the air did not have the fuel to engage them. The first attack, however, came from the south in the shape of two Italian Savoia Marchetti 79s, three-engined torpedo bombers, which made a low-level attack on the carrier. The captain of *Illustrious* manoeuvred the ship so that she combed the tracks of the torpedoes, which passed on either side of her. Two of the Fulmars in the patrol had descended to attack the torpedo bombers and both the Italian bombers had been shot down. The Fulmars were now at low altitude; it would take some time for them to climb again to meet the next wave of attacking aircraft. *Illustrious* changed course again, going to maximum speed and heading into the wind so that she could start launching the Fulmars ranged on the flight deck. As she did so, the first of the German dive-bombers, for this is what they were, were going into their attack manoeuvre.

This was the first time that these aircraft, the Junkers 87 – a plane we all referred to as a Stuka – had been seen in the skies above the Mediterranean fleet. They were aeroplanes that epitomized Nazi aggression and the bombing of Poland and France. They had a V-shaped crank in their wing, a high cockpit and were quite unmistakable. They had been specially designed as a dive-bomber and were extremely effective.

Captain Eric Brown, an RNVR pilot who had joined up in 1939 and was another Scot, born in Melrose, flight-tested a captured Stuka after the war. His report explains a great deal about why these aircraft were so feared by ground troops. There was a bomb-sight built into the floor of the pilot's cockpit and when the target was aligned in this, the pilot would pull back on the throttle, roll the aircraft 180 degrees and start his dive. He would descend at a steep angle of 90–60 degrees, and even with the aircraft's dive brakes extended it would reach a speed of 360 miles an hour. The aircraft designers had incorporated a system into the plane whereby extending the dive brakes triggered an automatic mechanism that would simplify the whole process of pulling out of the dive. As the Stuka reached an altitude of 1,500 feet, a light flashed red on the instrument panel, signalling the pilot to release the bomb. He would then press a button on the stick and the bomb was released, thrown clear of the propeller by a swivelling frame under the fuselage. As soon as the bomb-release button was pressed, the automatic mechanism took over. The dive brakes were retracted, the propeller pitch was changed and the controls automatically pulled the plane out of the dive and into a fast climb. When the propeller spinner rose above the horizon, the pilot could take over again. This took an enormous amount off the pilot's shoulders at a critical moment. The bomb-sight was accurate and he knew that the bomb would be dropped at the right height. He could be confident that, even if he lost consciousness because of the high G of the pull-out, he would not lose control of the air-craft. All the pilot really had to worry about was keeping the Stuka aimed bang on target. It's no wonder that these aircraft were such a devastating weapon.

Now a whole wing of Stukas and their associated fighters

were based in Sicily. Their most important target was the air-craft carrier that defended the Mediterranean Fleet.

Forty-three Stukas had taken off from their airfield in Sicily; just ten of them were now searching out the two battleships *Warspite* and *Valiant*, while the remaining thirty-three were concerned solely with hitting *Illustrious*.

Despite a massive anti-aircraft barrage, the Stukas got through. The Fulmars took off from *Illustrious* through the fountains of seawater that were thrown up by near misses. The last Fulmar to roll down the flight deck was machine-gunned by a Stuka as it pulled out of its dive. It staggered into the air, then crashed into the sea.

Illustrious's flight deck had been armoured to withstand a direct hit from a 500lb bomb, but the Stuka carried a 500kg bomb as standard, and, if they dispensed with the reargunner, the Germans could load it up with a 1,000kg bomb, the equivalent of 2,200lb of explosive. Six bombs hit *Illustrious*, and the result was catastrophic. Both the deck-lifts were hit, the rear one bringing a Fulmar up to the flight deck; that too was destroyed, killing the pilot. One bomb destroyed the steering gear and created fires in the stern. The carrier left the line and steamed in circles while the crew tried to put out the blaze and restore power to the rudder. Another bomb penetrated the flight deck and exploded below it in the hangar deck, where most of the pilots were standing by their aircraft, their normal action stations when they were not in the air. The hangar became an inferno; six of the Swordfish pilots who had taken part in the Taranto raid were killed and many others were gravely wounded.

Badly damaged and out of control though she was, the carrier did not sink and her engines continued to produce power. The fires raged, but finally the rudders were repaired and she could steer again. She headed for repairs to the nearest port, which was the shipyard at Valletta in Malta. Her

Swordfish aircraft and the Fulmars that were in the air had also flown there to land, and some of the Fulmars had refuelled and re-armed at Hal Far, the airbase in Malta, then flown back to take on the Stukas, managing to shoot down four of them. *Illustrious*, however, was not able to go back into action so quickly. In the dock at Malta, they set about recovering the burned bodies of the dead, as well as making the repairs that would enable her to escape to Alexandria, then on to a shipyard in New York for major reconstruction.

Next day both the Luftwaffe and the Italian air force targeted her again while she was in the dock at Valletta, with hits causing further damage to the ship, as well as to the dockside, and bringing death to civilians in the narrow workers' streets of Senglea. The raids continued, but so too did the work on the engines and rudder, and two weeks later *Illustrious* made a nighttime dash to Alexandria, the Suez Canal and freedom.

Like most other aircrew in the *Ark*, I thought first of those Fleet Air Arm men we knew who had been killed in such a short but brutal attack, but we all knew that this was a serious defeat, particularly after the triumph of Taranto. We wanted to do something that would show that we were still in the game and were not going to be intimidated by the arrival of the Germans in the Mediterranean. Our chance came quite soon.

9
Dambusters

Illustrious had gone for repairs to the US and *Eagle* was still out of action in Alexandria. In a dramatic reversal of fortune since its success at Taranto, the Royal Navy in the eastern Mediterranean now had no air cover at all. Before the Italians decided that it was safe to move the remainder of their fleet back to Taranto, Force H was ordered to make its presence felt and remind the Italians that there was still a threat from the west. Ever since *Ark Royal* had moved into the Med, plans had been worked up to attack Italian naval bases near Genoa, the main port on the Ligurian coast. They had never been put into action, because it was feared that the *Ark* would come dangerously close to the Italian mainland and be over-whelmed by the Italian air force. Now, because it was believed that the loss of *Illustrious* might give Italian civilian morale too big a boost, those fears were ignored and the *Ark* was going to attempt a large-scale attack on some big targets in Italy.

We were all for it. It felt that at last we were doing some-thing, taking the fight to the enemy and showing the navy that we in the Fleet Air Arm could do our bit. Unfortunately, I was personally to be disappointed.

The idea was to mount a multi-pronged attack. The Swordfish would attack the ports of La Spezia and Leghorn, while *Renown*, along with *Sheffield* and the battleship *Malaya*, would bombard Genoa. As a diversion, some Swordfish would make a highly unconventional but inspired attempt to breech a dam in Sardinia by launching torpedoes at it. It was a bit of a gamble, because Force H would have to loiter in waters that would be under constant surveillance from a long stretch of the Italian coastline. The Swordfish would also need to go in under cover of darkness, because the latest intelligence about the German aircraft that had hit *Illustrious* was that perhaps sixty had been based at Elmas aerodrome near Cagliari, just 60 miles from the Tirso dam, their target.

It was not the first time that aircraft from the *Ark* had attacked targets on land. In October and November the previous year bombing raids had been carried out on the same aerodrome that it was now believed housed the Luftwaffe. These raids were intended to do two things. It was hoped that they might confuse the Italians about the true purpose of the *Ark* and her escort putting to sea, acting as a diversion from the main mission of escorting a convoy through the Mediterranean; and they were also intended to deny the Italians the use of the aerodrome for the period when Force H was passing close to Sardinia, making the Italian air force use bases further away. This would restrict the time they could spend attempting to evade the defending Fulmars and Skuas, and so frustrate their bombing attacks on the convoy or on us, the defenders. The raid in November was typical. Nine Swordfish were armed with 250lb bombs, some with a delayed-action fuse and incendiaries. Their target was the hangars and other buildings at Elmas, while another group would attack the seaplanes that were normally moored at the jetty. Other targets were local factories and an adjacent power station, which provided power not only to the aerodrome and seaplane base, but to the local town as well. When the Swordfish left there were fires burning, and reconnaissance photos subsequently showed damage to the hangars as well as the factories.

This attack, like two others before it, had been led by Commander 'Johnnie' Johnstone, the CO of 810 Squadron, and his observer, Lieutenant 'Shaggy' Shaw, who had flown in as pathfinders to illuminate the target with flares. They were recommended for an award, as were Godfrey-Faussett and his observer. These two were amongst the best pilots in the *Ark*. Johnstone had led the unsuccessful attack on the French battlecruiser *Strasbourg*, while Godfrey-Faussett had torpedoed the beached *Dunkerque* after Mers-el-Kébir. Given the youth and fairly short life of the average Fleet Air Arm pilot, these chaps were now experienced veterans. Moreover, because the attack was scheduled to take place before first light, the pilots had to have had some experience of night flying, which again limited the choices.

The operation that was now being planned was a much greater task, with several strategic targets being struck in the same day. The initial briefings took place a few days before, and it was clear that we were going to be handicapped by a lack of intelligence. We did not have the resources to carry out aerial reconnaissance of the targets beforehand and the RAF was not able to send regular photo-reconnaissance planes over in the way that they had done for the raid on Taranto. One Spitfire flew over Genoa harbour to check what elements of the Italian fleet were moored there, but there would be no regular updates of information provided by Maryland reconnaissance flights as there had been for the Swordfish on *Illustrious*. For the most part, information about the disposition of any war-ships in the harbours was confined to what could be gleaned from radio intercepts, and anything else that the Admiralty in

London might be able to provide. They had been able to send us maps and plans of the Tirso dam, which had been built in 1924 as part of Mussolini's big construction projects. These arrived from the UK in a destroyer that was going to be part of Force H when it made the attack.

From these blueprints and maps we were able to build a papier-mâché model of the dam and the surrounding country-side, as if we were building a model-railway layout. This was a regular practice in the *Ark*, where at the beginning of the campaign, around the time of the attack on Oran, models of various harbours and airbases that were potential targets had been put together. Eight crews from 810 Squadron had been selected to mount the attack on the dam, most of them experienced in torpedo attacks, and they spent some time looking at the model, working out the best way to approach their target. It might have been a diversion, but it was an important enough target in its own right. Not only was it a politically prestigious target, being one of Mussolini's projects, but it also apparently accounted for the supply of 40 per cent of Sardinia's electricity. A few lights would go out if we managed to hit it.

I was not picked for this mission, and I was not happy about it. There was a real distinction in the wardroom between the young Reservists like me and the more experienced pilots. I was younger than most of the senior pilots, but I felt that I ought to be given a chance to show what I could do and when I realized that I was expected to sit this one out, I complained. I was far too junior to bring it up directly with my CO, but I made my feelings known to the staff in the squadron office. I was politely told that the operation was considered fairly risky, that the Tirso dam must be attacked by those with the most experience of torpedo attacks and of night flying, and that anyway the CO considered me far too inexperienced. It was hard to argue. Everyone on the *Ark* knew that I had made my first deck landing only after I had arrived in Gibraltar barely eight weeks previously. I was defeated, but my complaints didn't fall on entirely deaf ears.

Late on Friday, 31 January, the *Ark* put to sea, and we steamed at high speed eastwards to Sardinia to a point about halfway up the west coast of the island. The wind was strong, gusting from the west at speeds of up to 37 knots, which meant that the *Ark* would have to rendezvous with the Swordfish at the same point from which they took off, because they would be beating into a strong headwind on their return and their fuel state would be becoming critical.

There was low cloud and icy rain, and at one point it seemed that the weather would be against the whole operation, but at about 0400 it seemed to improve, or at least it had settled down and was not getting any worse.

The Tirso dam and its surrounding hills were on relatively low ground at about 1,200 feet and so would be below the cloud cover, which was setting a ceiling of about 1,500 feet. In these circumstances whether to proceed or not is a very close call, but the attack seemed possible, so eight Swordfish were brought up and ranged on the flight deck. They were all armed with torpedoes, which had been fitted with contact pistols in the warhead, and they were set to run at a depth of 44 feet at a speed of 44 knots. The wind and sea conditions were still rough, and it was not easy to range the Swordfish on the tossing deck, but by 0558 they had all taken off. They formed up roughly in their sections on their way in to Sardinia, which was about 60 nautical miles away. When they reached the coast it was still dark, with heavy rainfall, and as they had just another 20 miles to run to the target, the leader, Johnnie Johnstone, signalled the others to turn out to sea to wait for light. One aircraft did not see the signal, so continued inland and got lost in the cloud layer at 1,500 feet, which was about 5,000–9,000 feet thick, and he never saw land again until he returned to the *Ark*. He failed to locate the target, so didn't drop his torpedo.

The others circled for a while, then started to make their approach, crossing the coast at Cape Mannu. The largest and most obvious landmark was the wide lake that had been created when the dam was built, but the structure itself was further south, at the end of a lengthy, meandering flooded river valley.

In order to drop a torpedo at right angles to the dam, it would be necessary to fly down the course of this river valley, with its many sharp turns, until the dam came into view. Intelligence passed on to the Swordfish crews was that the dam was only lightly defended. If only it had been. The first Swordfish to make an attack flew low over the nearby town of Ghilarza, saw the lake and turned south to enter the river valley as it exited the southern point of the lake. The pilot's intention was then to fly at low level along the course of the river to the dam. As he approached, there was a bridge crossing the river at the point where it left the lake and he was faced with a fierce battery of anti-aircraft fire from guns mounted on either side of the bridge; he was forced to turn away. He once more came down to make his attack, but considered the fire so intense that he would never get through, so he jettisoned his torpedo and made for the coast.

The remaining six Swordfish crossed the coast slightly to the north, and two of them, flown by Godfrey-Faussett and Sub-Lieutenant Tony 'Bud' Beale, made an early turn south, short of Ghilarza, so avoiding coming down between the two heavy concentrations of anti-aircraft guns at the bridge. Even so, as they made for the target they were still fired on, and it became apparent that the dam was protected by gun batteries on both banks of the river. Nevertheless, they both managed to drop their torpedoes and make a good getaway, turning sharply to avoid the gunfire, which was now very heavy and closing in on their two aircraft. They stayed low and flat, trying to avoid offering a sharp silhouette to the Italian gunners, but this meant that neither could make any observations on the outcome of their torpedo drops.

A third aircraft, flown by a young sub-lieutenant, Dick Charlier, made an extremely low-level approach all the way from the coast, then followed the river at such a low height that the batteries didn't open fire. Whether this was because they could not locate him or could not depress their guns sufficiently to open fire isn't known, but he dropped his 'kipper', and it was only when he turned to make his getaway that the batteries fired on him. His observer, Sub-Lieutenant Beattie, thought the dam looked intact when they dropped and couldn't see any result from their torpedo.

The last two aircraft to go in were the leader, Johnstone, and his wingman, Pattison. They flew in a line, passing over the small village of Abbasant, and they were located and fired on by the defending guns before they had even managed to start their approach. They saw that there was a break in the cloud over the lake, so Johnstone decided to climb into the cloud for cover and then descend through the gap to make a low and fast approach over the water of the lake. Once he got into the cloud, however, he got lost and could not find the gap where he was going to descend, so at 7,000 feet, still in cloud, he decided to abandon the attack. His wingman lost him, but dived and came out of the cloud too high above the target. He turned right round, dived and came in at 150 feet, nose down, with a speed of 145 knots. The gunfire was getting intolerably close, shrapnel was ripping through the fuselage and he decided to drop his torpedo then and there. He flew right over the dam, his TAG firing his single rear gun at the anti-aircraft batteries, and managed to get away without any major damage to his aircraft.

One Swordfish failed to return, and no one else in the attacking aircraft had seen it after they took off. A few weeks later the Italians announced that the crew, Lieutenant 'Spike' O'Sullivan, Sub-Lieutenant Knight and Petty Officer Eccleshall, had all been captured and were now prisoners-of-war.

None of the attacking aircrew saw any sign of damage to the dam, or saw any significant explosion. It hadn't been breached and remained intact.

Taranto had been planned in the years before the war started, and the man whose idea it had been, Admiral Lyster, was in charge of *Illustrious* when the plan was finally put into practice. The raid itself had taken place only after the intense study of daily reconnaissance photos; and it had been postponed to a night when there would be a full moon to provide good visibility.

In contrast, our raid on the Tirso dam had been a pretty ad hoc affair. The pilots had been surprised by the heavy anti-aircraft defences, and the weather itself had been extremely unfriendly. We had flown in with weapons that had been designed to sink warships, not blow apart concrete walls, using a high level of guesswork about the most appropriate depth at which to hit the dam. Nevertheless, we had managed to drop four torpedoes and had lost only one aircraft. Later on in the war, when I heard about the attack on the three dams in Germany by the RAF, I couldn't help thinking that we had tried it first. That was a remarkable operation, by some very brave airmen, but flying low and steady over water towards the target was something that we knew all about – it was what we had to do to launch torpedoes – and if we had had something similar to the bouncing bomb that they had, we would have blown that dam at Tirso to pieces.

By the time the Swordfish had landed back on the *Ark*, it was 0900. I had woken up, flown my first reconnaissance patrol of the day and come back for breakfast. Before the lads had returned from the raid, the atmosphere was tense. It was bad form to say anything, of course, but it was impossible not to think about what might be happening to our colleagues 60 miles away over Sardinia, and not to wait, slightly apprehensively, to see when they would return, and how many. As I watched them land on, tired, their faces drawn, I was surprised and relieved that only one Swordfish had failed to come back. I thought, however, that the lost crew was the least experienced and might well have been me. Perhaps Tim Coode had made the right decision.

The raid on the dam completed, the plan was that we would now steam north and make our preparations for the attacks on Genoa and the other ports in northern Italy. We were scheduled for take-off later that evening, but the weather started to get rough, the seas became steeper and the ship was pitching a good deal. Flight operations were reduced to the bare minimum for safety.

Later that afternoon, the captain took the view that, given the rough seas, aircraft could not be flown off in the dark and only nine aircraft could be dealt with safely on the flight deck at any one time. Then we were reduced to a speed of 15 knots, and some of the destroyers escorting us were being damaged in the rough seas. There was also a forecast of low cloud over the targets. Two hours later, the operation was cancelled. It was inevitable, given the conditions, and the wiser, more experienced heads in the wardroom thought it was the right decision.

We made our way back to Gibraltar. On the way we practised torpedo drops, carried out live firing exercises, and I flew one of the squadron's planes back to the landing strip that had been built on the old racecourse at Gibraltar, so I had some time ashore.

There was a bit of an inquest into what our Swordfish crews had experienced when they flew over the Tirso dam.

There was some concern over the large discrepancy between the intelligence estimates of the anti-aircraft defences given to the squadrons and the quite formidable reality that had faced the attackers on the day. The captain cleared lower decks a few days later and addressed us, stressing the need for tighter security and greater awareness of the fact that Gibraltar, and La Linea in Spain where we sometimes went for meals, were hotbeds of spies and that we should be extremely careful of what we said. Evidently the senior officers believed that the Italians had got wind of our raid. I thought, however, that if our intelligence had been better we would have known about the increased gun emplacements.

A week later, on the afternoon of Thursday, 6 February, the *Ark* once more left Gibraltar, with *Renown*, *Malaya* and *Sheffield*. We were going to finish the operation that we had started with the attempt to breach the Tirso dam. I had been selected to take part this time, as part of a mine-laying attack on an Italian port. We steamed north-east, close to the French and Italian coasts, expecting to be attacked at any minute. There were several alarms as we were spotted by enemy planes on the way, and we had two accidents, one when a Skua pilot landed very heavily and collapsed his undercarriage, and the second when a Fulmar had to ditch with engine trouble.

Early on the morning of Sunday the 9th, I was woken and went to the briefing room. Our plans for the raid were little changed from the previous week, but it crossed my mind that, after the torpedoing of the dam, the Italian coastal defences might be more than normally alert. I put this to the back of my mind as we went through details of expected weather and flying times to the target. In its entirety, the operation was an attack on three separate targets. Force H was going to split up: the battleships *Renown* and *Malaya* were going north to steam 10 miles off the coast of Genoa to shell the port with their big guns. There had been reports of two battleships and a heavy cruiser in the docks at Genoa, one of them, *Duilio*, installed in a dry dock undergoing repairs to the damage she had suffered at Taranto. There was no confirmation of this, and various other important targets in the town had also been selected. Swordfish aircraft from the *Ark* would act as spotters to direct the gunfire and would no doubt discover if there were major warships moored up. Another section of Swordfish was going to bomb the town of Leghorn, just south of Pisa, while I and three other Swordfish were to drop mines in the harbour at La Spezia, farther north along the coast from Leghorn.

Renown and *Malaya* opened fire at about 0715. *Renown* hit the railway yards and factories on the banks of the Polceverra river, which entered the sea by the western part of the town. This started fires, and the battleship then moved her aim to the docks, which had been named by Mussolini after the East African countries Italy had invaded before the war, such as Abyssinia and Eritrea. Some merchant ships were hit, but no large warships were there. A salvo landed on the power station, causing a very big explosion – obviously the oil tanks had been hit, as the spotting aircraft saw the thick black smoke of an oil fire rising into the morning air. This started to make spotting difficult, but the guns shifted their aim again and began pouring shells on both the locomotive works of Ansaldo and another electrical factory.

Malaya concentrated on the dry docks and the factories and warehouses in the eastern part of the port, which had houses clustered around them. One of the pilots of the spotting Swordfish I spoke to said that he saw a single shell knock down a complete row of houses before it exploded. It must have been an incredible shock to the inhabitants of the town. Just one salvo from *Renown* would have been six 16in shells, landing within 50 yards of each other. Their explosive power would have been devastating and it would have been repeated every few minutes.

The firing continued for an hour, and I have heard estimates that it would have taken the Royal Air Force almost two weeks of bombing raids to have delivered the same amount of explosives as fell on Genoa in those sixty minutes. The attack was on a Sunday morning, so many of the factories and docks would have been empty of any workers; even so, there were 140 casualties, and most of those, of course, were civilians. Apart from the damage caused to the power station, and to the docks and factories, four merchant ships were sunk, a training ship was damaged and an oil tanker was hit by a 6in shell from *Sheffield*. One unexploded shell landed in the cathedral, where it is still kept on display in the nave. News of the bombardment must have caused some consternation amongst the Italian high command on that Sunday morning, but imagine what they must have felt when reports of other attacks started coming in.

Fourteen Swordfish were ranged up on the flight deck of the *Ark*, and at 0500 they started their engines. As each Bristol Pegasus engine burst into life, sparks and flashes were spat out of the exhaust that stuck out from the starboard side of the engine cowling. You felt that they could be seen from afar and must be signalling our position to every Italian ship and spotter aircraft for hundreds of miles around. We had come 700 miles from Gibraltar, hugging the coast of Corsica, but soon the bombardment would start and we felt that there would be no hiding place.

The Swordfish took off, heading for Leghorn. They were armed with 250lb bombs and incendiaries, and their intention was to attack the Azienda oil refinery in the port. They formed up over a flare dropped into the sea, then flew east to make a landfall north of their target, but lack of experience of night flying and the need for radio silence meant that two

Left: In our final prank at Greenwich before we went to our various squadrons, we hoisted this field gun onto the protective brick tower in the dead of night.

Right: This portrait was taken when I was eighty-five years old while we were filming the wreck of the *Ark Royal*.

Below: The Black Hand Gang poses for its last picture. *From left to right*: Eric Margetts, Robert Lawson, me, Buster May and Glan Evans.

Left: My Swordfish after the crash in Scotland. The lower wing is further back down the track, and it seems to have taken the top off a decent fir tree.

Left and below: HMS *Argus* was one of the ugliest carriers afloat, but she managed to survive the war. Her deck lifts were an odd shape and, even with their wings folded, the Swordfish were a tight fit.

Below: I was happier on the *Ark Royal,* which still had a squadron of Skuas on board. It was this aircraft that had made me think of flying Swordfish.

Above: This photo is of my first deck landing, which I did a few days after joining the *Ark*. There were plenty of spectators wanting to see me make a mess of it.

Right: The flight deck of the *Ark* could be a noisy and dangerous place. Here, two squadrons of Swordfish are ranged up, their engines starting as they prepare for take-off.

Above: This Swordfish has an 18in torpedo mounted underneath it. This was an exercise – if it had been a real mission an observer and air gunner would have been in the rear cockpit.

Right: Aircraft could be catapulted off the front of the flight deck, and here a Skua and a Swordfish are ready to be launched. Another Swordfish waits in the queue.

Left: A Fulmar, its tail hook down, makes a hash of landing. The unmistakable figure of Pat Stringer is running for safety.

Below: The ready rooms under the bridge were always a hive of activity. During the hunt for the German cruiser *Scharnhorst* we slept in here for several days.

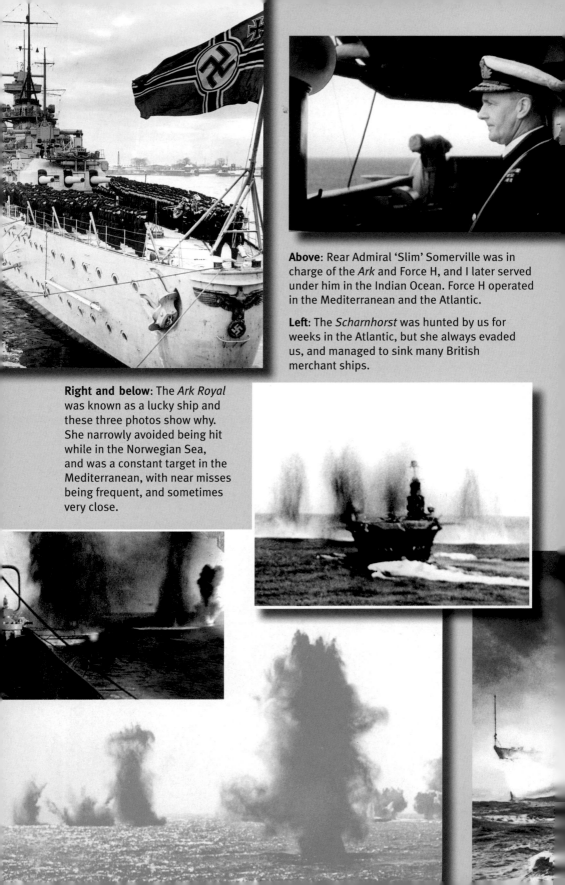

Above: Rear Admiral 'Slim' Somerville was in charge of the *Ark* and Force H, and I later served under him in the Indian Ocean. Force H operated in the Mediterranean and the Atlantic.

Left: The *Scharnhorst* was hunted by us for weeks in the Atlantic, but she always evaded us, and managed to sink many British merchant ships.

Right and below: The *Ark Royal* was known as a lucky ship and these three photos show why. She narrowly avoided being hit while in the Norwegian Sea, and was a constant target in the Mediterranean, with near misses being frequent, and sometimes very close.

Above: The war in the Mediterranean started with an attack on the French fleet at Oran, in an attempt to stop their warships being taken over by Germany.

Right: The most outstanding operation of 1940 was the attack on the Italian fleet at Taranto by Swordfish flying off HMS *Illustrious*. This picture (*right*) shows the warships smoking and leaking fuel after the attack.

Below: HMS *Hood* was the pride of the British fleet, and was famous throughout the world. She took part in the attack at Oran, but it was her destruction in the Denmark Strait that affected me most.

Right: When Hitler inspected the *Bismarck* in April 1941, she was thought to be the most powerful warship afloat. Her mission, with her sister ship *Prinz Eugen*, was to create mayhem among the allied convoys in the Atlantic.

Below: This photo was taken from *Prinz Eugen* at the start of the operation.

Left: *Bismarck*, now alone, was photographed from a Swordfish as she steamed for the safety of the French port of St-Nazaire and the protection of the German air force.

Bismarck silhouetted by the blast from her main guns on a night exercise. Outnumbered and out of control, this firepower would not prevent her destruction.

Desperate German sailors
struggle to save themselves
from the ice-cold Atlantic
and the choking fuel oil from
Bismarck's ruptured tanks.
This photo, taken from the
Dorsetshire, shows some
of the few survivors. Many
were left to drown.

Left: My next carrier was HMS
Formidable, a newer class of
ship than the *Ark*, and just back
from a major refit in the US. I
sailed into the Indian Ocean on
her to take on the Japanese.
I was now flying a more modern
version of the Swordfish, the
Albacore (*right*), but it was still
a biplane.

This portrait was taken when I went to take command of a unit at Cowdray Park in Sussex in 1943. It was here that I married, and finished my life in the services.

I was very pleased to attend a reception, hosted by the First Sea Lord Sir Jonathan Band, to commemorate the hundredth anniversary of the formation of the naval air force. I have always felt that our contribution in the war was never given the recognition it deserved.

Another photo of me taken with a group of former colleagues when we filmed the wreck of the *Ark Royal*, a memorable experience and an opportunity to recall all those great characters who fought with us but who are now no longer alive.

aircraft got lost and continued inland until they located a town. They had arrived over Pisa! I am not sure that they spent a lot of time looking for the Leaning Tower, but they made the best of a bad job and, circling low, with no anti-aircraft fire being hurled against them, they searched out two likely targets. One attacked the aerodrome, dropping his bombs on a hangar and office building, while the other found Pisa railway yards and dropped his bombs on that. Neither of them could tell what sort of damage they had done, but they clearly had done what they could and so headed back to pick up the *Ark*.

The other eleven aircraft managed to fly over Leghorn and started bombing the oil refinery. They had achieved almost complete surprise, with some slight anti-aircraft fire opening up at the sound of the first bombs, but in a few minutes tracer bullets were hosing up into the sky, and high-angle artillery was exploding around them. One Swordfish collided with the cable of one of the barrage balloons tethered all round the harbour; the plane was so badly damaged it spun and crashed into the harbour. The pilot, Sub-Lieutenant Attenborough, his observer, Sub-Lieutenant Foote, and the TAG, Leading Airman Halifax, were all killed.

I was one of the last to take off that morning – a member of a small force of four Swordfish armed with 'cucumbers', the long magnetic anti-ship mines we carried under the fuselage. We were headed to the naval base at La Spezia, which was about an hour away, and we flew low towards the coast.

At last I was flying on a mission to attack the enemy, but I was also extremely apprehensive about what I would find when I got there. Everybody had behaved as though this were just a normal anti-submarine patrol. My observer, Dusty Miller, had filled me in on the aiming points and the latest intelligence about the target in his usual laconic, matter-of-fact way; the rigger had bawled out his tuneless song about his mother's apple pie as he tightened my straps; and I too had been keen to appear organized and efficient. The engine fired first time, and we were on our way. As we formed up with the other three planes, the Swordfish seemed slightly heavier with the big mine strapped to it. I was nervous. I couldn't believe that I was going to fly over an enemy naval port without being challenged, shot at and attacked by enemy fighters. We were at war, after all, and this was the very first time that I had taken part in an attack on the enemy. I had been in the *Ark* for over two months now and it was high time I took part in operations of this sort, but my concern was not only what would happen, but that I would not make a mess of it.

La Spezia is at the head of a narrow gulf formed by the Italian mainland and a small peninsula to the west. The harbour is protected by a mole that cuts across the gulf, leaving entrances at the eastern and western ends, and inside this is a smaller harbour, which was the main haven for the Italian navy. Our targets were the gaps at either end of the outer mole. They were narrow and if we could block them with mines, the commercial harbour as well as the naval basin would be unusable until all the mines were cleared. If luck was on our side, the Italian navy would not succeed in clearing them all and one of our mines might blow up under a ship, with the wreck blocking the port for a considerable time.

I flew in to the coast south of the town, then headed north with the gulf to my left and the hills of the mainland to my right. It was just after 0600 and there was absolutely no activity. When we got to La Spezia, we noticed that the streetlights were all on. I went down to about 500 feet, then turned to fly over the town and head south to the mole. We didn't see any fishing boats or other small craft moving about in the harbour. I was surprised, and relieved. I heard Dusty saying to me when we crossed the lighted town, 'It must be to help them on their way to mass.' He was always one to say something to help break the tension. It was one of the reasons that I liked flying with him. I couldn't help smiling, and was settling in my seat to go lower down to 200 feet, feeling that this might be a piece of cake, when I heard in my ear, 'Holy Jesus, look to your left.' I looked across at the inner harbour, and there was the massive superstructure of a big warship.

No one had been absolutely sure where the remainder of the big battleships had gone after Taranto, but clearly at least one had ended up here. I kept straight and level now, flying at 100 feet and heading for the gap at the end of the mole, hoping and praying that nobody on watch on the battleship would raise the alarm. One minute, two minutes, and I pressed the button on the stick and the Swordfish rose up as the weight of the mine dropped away. Any conversation between us was superfluous. I kept the aircraft low, heading at full throttle out to sea. When we were 5 miles out, Dusty said that the guns of a battery had opened up and were probably targeting some of the other Swordfish, and also that some very bright flares that the Italians used, which we called flaming onions, had been fired and were slowly descending, looking from our distance like very impressive fireworks. In fact, when we returned and were debriefed we learned that some of our colleagues had faced low-level automatic cannon fire, which missed them, and some of the larger anti-aircraft guns had started firing blind into the air. None of our Swordfish was hit.

We landed on by 0845, the *Ark* rendezvoused with the rest of Force H and then we went west for safety. The return journey was equally tense, with several Italian aircraft that were attempting to shadow us intercepted and shot down by our Fulmars. There was also an attack by two bombers, but their bombs, dropped from around 3,000 feet, easily missed us. There was clearly a lot of activity as the Italians hunted for us. We could hear the sound of aircraft overhead as we skirted along the southern coast of France. There was a thick sea haze and this must have given us a protective cover, because they didn't find us. Intercepted signals indicated that Italian warships had also put to sea, but they too failed to pinpoint our location. When we got back to Gibraltar, there was a feeling that we had pulled off something pretty impressive that would be a real shock to Mussolini and the Italian armed forces. Their morale, already damaged after Taranto, must have taken another blow.

I could not help but think about that Italian warship in La Spezia and the fact that its presence had never been mentioned in any of the briefings. There was a real lack of reconnaissance carried out for Force H and I felt, and still do, that if we had had more support we could have achieved much more in the way of attacks on Italy and would have diverted Italian forces away from the Mediterranean Fleet in Alexandria. All we had were the Swordfish in our squadron on the *Ark*, and they would not have lasted long if they had been used for reconnaissance over the mainland.

Nevertheless, I had taken part in my first real aggressive mission, and I felt pleased that I had done as creditably as I could.

10
Hunting the *Scharnhorst*

I didn't want to take part in action through any bloodthirsty motive – far from it. I had a need, as a young man of twenty-one, to prove myself to more senior and experienced colleagues, and I felt that I ought to be engaged in the fight. It was akin to the feeling I had when I had looked up at the sky during that local village cricket match in the summer of 1940.

Whenever we went out into the Med, escorting a convoy to Malta or Alexandria, we knew that it was us on the *Ark* who were the target for the Italian bombers that came overhead. If they had their way, we would end up like *Illustrious* after being hit by the German Stukas – a smoking hulk; or worse, like the cruiser *Southampton*, which had been destroyed in the same bombing attack, with hundreds of her crew killed. We knew that London, Liverpool, Coventry and other cities in Britain were receiving a pounding from the Luftwaffe every night and thousands of civilians were being killed. I think it was natural for us to want to fight back, but we would all have been happy to see the war come to an end tomorrow if that had been possible.

An incident that involved one of my colleagues in 818 Squadron, Sub-Lieutenant Penrose, sums up the situation perfectly. He was an observer in a Swordfish and had been flying on a raid over Cagliari when his plane was attacked by a couple of Italian fighters, Fiat CR.32s. These were biplanes with an open cockpit, rather like the Swordfish itself. They were fitted with two forward-firing guns and were pretty obsolete. But one of them came in from the side and fired a few bursts at Penrose's Swordfish while the other made a stern attack. They seemed to make no impact, the Swordfish easily outmanoeuvring them. Both Italian pilots then throttled back and took up formation on either side of Penrose's aircraft, no doubt feeling that they had something in common with another biplane and obviously thinking that they were no threat to each other. One of the pilots seemed quite amused by the whole affair. Penrose carried a service revolver and drew it from its holster. Resting the barrel on the side of the cockpit, he took careful aim at the nose of the CR.32 on the starboard side and fired. The Italian fighter banked and, to the Swordfish crew's amazement, dived steeply and smashed into the sea. The chance of hitting the target with a service revolver must have been a thousand to one. The other fighter roared off and disappeared.

Penrose was congratulated for this act of bravery, but in fact he was distraught. He was convinced that his shot had killed the Italian pilot, for a single bullet would not have caused enough damage to the plane, and he felt that his behaviour had been utterly beyond the pale. Nothing I or anyone else could say would alleviate his remorse. In the wardroom he became a little like the Ancient Mariner and we all wished that he would snap out of it. He did eventually, but continued to feel guilty about taking someone else's life, as he felt, in an underhand way. Yet I am sure if he had managed to bring the fighter down in the heat of a battle, he would have felt completely different. This is how I believe it was for most, if not all, of us, particularly the hostilities-only pilots.

We were very exultant at our success in the attack on the Italian ports, but had little time to spend congratulating ourselves. No sooner had we put into Gibraltar than there was an urgent call to raise steam once more and prepare for sailing within two hours. We were called out to defend a homeward-bound convoy that had just left Gibraltar, because there had been a report that the German battlecruiser, or pocket battleship, *Admiral Hipper* had been observed in the eastern Atlantic. It turned out that an unescorted convoy of ships journeying from Freetown, in Sierra Leone, to the UK had come under attack from *Admiral Hipper* and had scattered. Seven merchant ships out of the nineteen in the convoy had been sunk or taken as prizes. We had to go and hunt for the German warship while rounding up the remains of the convoy and providing an escort. So once again I headed out into the Atlantic, carrying out long-range patrols from dawn to dusk. We managed to shepherd the freighters into some sort of order and they were taken off under the wing of the old battleship *Malaya*.

After ten days at sea, without any sign of *Hipper*, which had in fact reached its haven in Brest, the German-occupied port on the west coast of France, we once more returned to our home, Gibraltar. It was certainly about time for us, because long periods of patrol at sea were a strain on the aircraft and after several days there began to be fewer available for flying each morning. Some repairs and maintenance tasks either needed more time than the mechanics and riggers had or needed the space and equipment of the North Shore airfield in Gibraltar. We, the aircrew, also got tired and a period of leave in Gibraltar was always welcome. We could catch up on mail and the news from home. I had been sent a rugby ball by one of my teachers at Kelso High School and we often played a scratch game of rugby on the flight deck of the *Ark* when she was tied up. It was a great way of relieving a lot of the stress of operations. I still have that rugby ball today.

Ark Royal was a famous ship, and of course very imposing, so if any dignitaries were being entertained by Admiral Somerville a tour of the carrier would always be included in their visit. These would sometimes be leading Spanish politicians and military figures, or sometimes British officials and top brass passing through. I was in a party of five, which included Captain Holland, formed up to show two distinguished guests around the ship. To my surprise, one of them, a lady, turned out to be my opponent from the Greenwich College dinner. During wartime the ship's port-holes were kept closed while in harbour. Going below decks, the captain said that any further would take us into the ratings' quarters. The lady said that she would like to see where the men lived, and so the captain said to me, 'Open the hatch, Sub-Lieutenant.' I did so and immediately the lady grabbed a handkerchief from her handbag, saying, 'What a horrible smell of men!' – whereupon Captain Holland retorted, 'Have you any idea what it would smell like if the ship was manned by women?' I was so proud of the captain: he had paid her back for her rudeness.

Since I had been on the *Ark* as part of Force H, we hadn't seen any sign of the German air force that had moved into Sicily, punishing Admiral Cunningham in Alexandria with so many casualties. The German navy was, however, making its presence felt in the North Atlantic and it was this that occupied most of our time in February and March. Up until now it had been U-boat packs hunting in the Atlantic that had caused most of the British losses, but by March there were three German pocket battleships preying on the Atlantic convoys. *Admiral Hipper* had brought us into the Atlantic in February, and her two sister ships – we referred to them as 'the Ugly Sisters' – *Scharnhorst* and *Gneisenau*, which had sunk *Glorious* off Norway, had now resumed active service. Both ships had managed to take the northerly route past Greenland into the North Atlantic to attack UK-bound convoys leaving from Halifax in Newfoundland. They sank four ships here, then steamed rapidly east to rip into another one, part of a convoy from Sierra Leone to the UK. Here they were spotted by the crew of the battleship *Malaya*, which was the convoy's escort, and the German warships made off. *Malaya* had on board a catapult-launched Swordfish fitted with floats to act as a spotter and they launched it. If the aircraft could maintain contact, then other escort ships in the North Atlantic could be directed to them and convoys could be diverted. *Scharnhorst* and *Gneisenau* were fast ships, however, much faster than the old *Malaya*, and the Swordfish ran out of fuel attempting to stay in touch with the enemy. The ships disappeared, but this sighting was enough for us to be ordered to raise steam and leave Gibraltar, heading once more to the west.

We rendezvoused with the convoy, adding our strength to it as escort. We operated up to a very high state of alert for more than seven days as the convoy steamed north, so I was permanently on the lookout, not only for U-boats but also for the two German raiders on the loose.

We had at least six Swordfish in the air at all times and I was flying patrols to a depth of around 80–130 miles from the line of advance. In case we spotted *Scharnhorst* or *Gneisenau*, the Skua squadron was kept armed with 500lb semi-armour-piercing bombs, and a striking force of Swordfish armed with torpedoes was maintained in readiness as well. Three Swordfish were always on patrol, armed with two depth-charges each, and three were kept at readiness on the *Ark*, also 'bombed up' with depth-charges. If a submarine had been sighted on the surface then it would have been hit by six depth-charges from the patrolling aircraft and there would have been a follow-on attack of six more from the standby aircraft. At night the torpedo striking force stood armed and fuelled in the hangar, with another two aircraft carrying flares and flame floats. One of these last aircraft remained on the deck, as did another one armed with depth-charges, so that they could be flown or accelerated off with the minimum of delay.

So determined were we to maintain this state of preparedness that I never went below, but slept and ate in my kit in the briefing room underneath the navigating bridge. If I wasn't flying, eating or sleeping, I was in the ready room.

On 11 March there was quite severe weather and the carrier was pitching so badly that there was almost 30 feet of vertical movement on the end of the flight deck. It made for extremely hazardous landings and I thought we were flying at the very edge of our limits. Little did I know! In fact, the motion of the flight deck was a severe handicap. The anti-submarine patrols were loaded with two depth-charges, one under each wing, but this proved to be too heavy for landing in such conditions. Three Swordfish damaged their under-carriages and another broke its tail wheel, so the rest of the patrols were flown with just two 100lb bombs. On the 14th we had further news of *Scharnhorst* and *Gneisenau*, which were now again off the coast of Newfoundland, where they attacked a convoy of tankers, four of which they captured. *Scharnhorst* had put a German prize crew – a crew put in a captured vessel to operate her in place of her own – on each of these ships and they were heading, so it was assumed, back to Brest.

Next day another convoy was intercepted by the two raiders, with tragic consequences. Thirteen merchant ships were sunk, bringing the damage that they had inflicted on us in just this one single cruise to twenty-two vessels.

We didn't need any motivation to take the search for these

two battleships extremely seriously, but it was a gargantuan task. There were hundreds of thousands of square miles of ocean into which *Gneisenau* and *Scharnhorst* could disappear. It was like looking for a tiger in the jungle. It took its toll. On 15 March one of 818 Squadron's Swordfish, fitted with a long-range tank for extra endurance, failed to return. This was the aircraft of my cabin mate, Sub-Lieutenant Ferguson, whose loss I have already mentioned, and his fellow crewmember, Sub-Lieutenant Watt. Both had been fairly new arrivals on the *Ark* and I had hardly got to know them.

On the 19th, one of our patrolling Swordfish spotted a merchant ship flying Dutch colours, but the ship's name and her port of origin on the stern were painted over. There was a strong possibility that this was a supply ship for the *Scharnhorst*, as it was heading west at 270 degrees. On board the *Ark* we formed the opinion that it was *Wakama*, which we knew had left Brest for the Azores. We believed that in the waters of those neutral islands German U-boats were in the habit of resting up and rendezvousing with their depot ships. It was an important contact and a Swordfish was detailed off to maintain touch discreetly. Later that day, one of the final patrols before nightfall spotted a tanker that appeared to be running half empty, heading due east as though making for Brest. By the time the Swordfish had returned to the *Ark* with this information it was too dark to send out any further patrols, but the next morning I was one of nine Swordfish that took off at 0740 to comb the ocean for the two mysterious ships. There were plenty of unanswered questions. What were they doing in the vicinity? Were they a clue to the presence of the German battlecruisers? Had the tanker just left them after refuelling at sea? Were we going to take on these two powerful raiders? The German warships were fast modern ships and well armed. *Scharnhorst* had hit *Glorious* with a salvo from her nine 11in guns at a range of almost 25 miles – a

John Moffat

phenomenal performance. If we did make contact, *Renown*, our flagship, would have her work cut out against both the big cruisers and we would certainly attempt a torpedo strike.

At the briefing that morning I was given a bearing that should lead me to the tanker if she had kept to her course and speed overnight, and after an hour of flying we saw something on the horizon. We dived down to intercept it and flew low along the side of the ship, then around the bow at about 200 feet. We saw no movement on board at all. Flying round again, I could read *Bianca* painted on the bow. But there were no signals or any sign of the crew; neither was she flying any flag, which was a bit strange, as normally ships are keen to identify themselves as neutrals. Then Dusty realized that this was one of the tankers that had been captured by *Scharnhorst* several days ago – she was being operated by a prize crew. So the surmise that she was heading for Brest was correct.

At this point I was not in a position to do very much. I wanted the tanker to heave to so that a ship from Force H could recapture it, but all I had was my forward-firing machine gun. This was the .303in Vickers that was mounted in the fuselage on the right-hand side of the cockpit – a weapon that I had never fired before. I doubted for a moment whether I could remember how to use it at all. Then gradually the drill came back to me. Make sure the bolt is in the rest position. Pull up the high-pressure piston rod, then pull back the gun lever twice, ease the bolt forward and the gun should be ready to fire. So I went down to 50 feet to put some shots across the bows – a universal signal to heave to. Aiming about 50 feet in front of the ship, I pressed the button. The gun was fitted with an interrupter mechanism to prevent bullets hitting the propeller blades, so the rate of fire was extremely slow, rather like the chiming of Big Ben. I felt that I could have fired faster using a revolver. It was noisy, the fumes of cordite filled the cockpit, and every shot made the fuselage shake. There were splashes in the water as the bullets struck, but had the message got through? I flew round the ship and there was still no sign of any activity. I flew higher to see if I could see any of our ships in the vicinity and spotted *Renown* about 15 miles away.

Then Dusty shouted, 'Jock, look at the stern.' I went down again and *Bianca* was definitely lower in the water. Then a group of crewmen appeared and started to lower a lifeboat. I suddenly realized they had opened the sea cocks to scuttle the tanker and were now trying to abandon ship. The bastards! I was not going to get cheated like that, so I turned and made a low pass, firing the forward machine gun above the lifeboat. I had no intention of hitting the boat, or the sailors trying to get in to it, but it was not a very gallant action. They didn't seem to take any notice.

I shouted back to Hayman, my TAG, 'Can you shoot out that boat?' He had already seen what was happening and didn't need to be told. Four short bursts from his Lewis gun hit the lifeboat and splinters of wood flew off into the air. Hayman never missed! It did the trick. The German sailors clambered back on board and went to see if they could do something about the sea cocks. I then flew back to *Renown* and signalled them about the situation. They sent off a whaler with a boarding party to recover *Bianca* and take the German prize crew prisoner. The Germans, however, had not gone back to save the ship – they had instead started fires on board. The boarding party from *Renown* recaptured the ship and put out the fires. Eventually she was towed into port.

When I returned to the *Ark*, there was a general air of excitement in the briefing room because two more of the nine Swordfish that had taken off that morning had located another two of the tankers seized by *Scharnhorst* – *San Casimiro* and *Polykarp* – which were now also being sailed by

German prize crews. Shortly afterwards *San Casimiro* was retaken, but *Polykarp* eluded recapture. Three Fulmar fighter aircraft were dispatched later that day to search for her. They were much faster than the Swordfish, so it was hoped that this would allow them to make an interception while there was still some daylight left.

After nearly two hours one of the Fulmars returned and flew over the *Ark*, signalling by a hand-held Aldis lamp for an emergency landing. The *Ark* swung out of line into the wind and the Fulmar landed on. The crew were in no danger, but they had urgent news. They had flown north and seen two ships in the haze. They were not *Polykarp*, nor any other captured tanker, but the two German warships, *Scharnhorst* and *Gneisenau*, which had evaded us and the whole of the Royal Navy in the Atlantic for weeks! The crew of the Fulmar had been unable to report it immediately because their wireless had broken, so they had been forced to return at top speed to the *Ark* to pass the information on to Admiral Somerville in *Renown*. At last, the ships for which we had been carrying out an exhausting search over the last twelve days had been sighted. But this crucial failure in communications was serious. The information about the enemy warships was at least one hour old.

Nine Swordfish were ordered to be armed and prepared for a torpedo strike, but in the midst of the rapid preparations and briefings, the reality of the position started to sink in. The two battlecruisers were around 147 miles away and, when last seen, were on a course due north at around 20 knots. The light was already beginning to fade, visibility was no better than about 8 miles, and by the time the Swordfish flight had taken off and reached the last known position of the enemy ships, it would be dark, in addition to the fact that the co-ordinates they were heading for would be two and a half hours old. Moreover, if the Germans had realized that they had been spotted, they might well have increased speed and enacted a radical change of course.

The crew of the Fulmar that had made the original sighting took off once more to regain contact, but it was now a hopeless mission. They could not find the warships, completely darkened and running at high speed, hidden now by the blanket of the night and the black Atlantic.

We slept that night not knowing what would happen in the morning. Would we find the German warships again? If we did, we would undoubtedly attempt a torpedo strike, but we had been at sea so long that our serviceable Swordfish were dwindling. I took off the next day once again as both Swordfish and Fulmars from the *Ark* scoured the surface of the sea, but it was fruitless. *Scharnhorst* and *Gneisenau* had escaped. It's difficult to say what the outcome would have been if the radio on Lt Commander Tillard's Fulmar had been working. There would not necessarily have been an encounter between Force H and the warships, although the chances of a battle being fought the next day would have been much greater. As it was, my torpedo training at Abbotsinch had still not been put to any use, and *Scharnhorst* and *Gneisenau* had eluded us.

We changed course for Gibraltar at the end of the next day. We had been at sea for a fortnight and were at the end of our resources, in terms of fuel, food and energy. One disturbing event occurred shortly before this, however. A Swordfish from my squadron, 818, was being prepared for an anti-submarine patrol, with two depth-charges mounted under the wings, ready to be catapulted off the front of the flight deck. Each of these catapults was in essence a framework that could support the fuselage of an aircraft, mounted on a trolley that was secured to cables running along a groove in the deck. The aircraft's engine would be started and run up to full power, and at a signal the trolley would be accelerated forward by a hydraulic ram pulling the cable. The plane would automatically continue forward and detach itself from the struts holding it when the trolley smashed into its end-stop. It accelerated with considerable force and the crew had to brace themselves as the catapult was triggered. On this particular occasion, the artificer at the side released the catapult and it shot forward, but the Swordfish did not separate cleanly. It split in two, the rear fuselage and tail section remaining fixed in the catapult's struts. The forward section, however, including the cockpit and main planes, flew forward at take-off speed, hurled over the bows of the *Ark* and plunged into the sea. Within seconds the huge bow wave had engulfed the wreckage and the crew; then there was a deep, powerful thump and the hull of the great ship bounced upwards, kicking some people on board off their feet. The two depth-charges had exploded under the keel. There was clearly no hope for the three crewmen, Sub-Lieutenants Peter Opdell and Charlie Hearn, and Leading Airman 'Baron' Biggs, who now brought the total of deaths in 818 Squadron on this patrol to five. Opdell was a likeable young chap and once more I had to pack a co-pilot's belongings with great sadness. I wondered why I had to carry out this task, rather than the squadron CO or the ship's chaplain?

I had been in the *Ark* for almost four months now and I had started to fit in. We had largely to make our own entertainment, and my early experience with the amateur operatic society in Kelso came in useful, as did my ability to play the banjo and the violin, though most of my shipmates called it a 'fiddle'. On the days that we were in port we would organize concert parties, in which the more officious officers of the ship – not that there were many – were held up to ridicule, Hitler was lampooned, and our service life and difficulties were treated as jokes. We didn't venture much into Gibraltar or La Linea, where there was little nightlife and no women, apart from a female dance band that used to perform in one of the bars. Gibraltar was not a dangerous place, but there was something called the Gibraltar Dog, which was a particularly painful form of stomach bug. I have seen people writhing on the floor in agony with it, and the cure was a visit to the chief medical orderly and a roughly administered enema by a medical artificer. No thank you!

Nights in the wardroom after an operation could get very raucous as people let off steam, drank a great deal and started singing bawdy songs. It was at times like this, when the original pianist had passed out, that I was often hauled out of my bunk in my pyjamas, dragged to the wardroom and asked to play. I was not really a good piano-player, but I could follow a tune. I think most of the people in the wardroom by then were too far gone to tell whether I had hit the right note or not! Sometimes I would play the banjo instead. And so another few days in port would pass. Many of the people determinedly letting their hair down had seen a great deal more than I had. I was beginning to appreciate that constant flying, and the resultant losses, could take their toll.

I had seen more action in these few months than I had in the whole of the previous year of war. While most of the patrols were plainly boring, I had carried out my first of many deck landings, intercepted a captured ship, raided an Italian port and survived several attacks from the bombers of the Italian air force. I felt that I had been kept extremely busy and had been thrust into the thick of it. I had no idea just how intense the next two months were going to be.

11
The Thick of It

In April, following our unsuccessful pursuit of *Scharnhorst* and *Gneisenau*, we returned to the Atlantic twice more on receiving information that they had left their sanctuary in Brest, but both times that we steamed out through the Straits of Gibraltar were false alarms. We also sailed twice more into the Mediterranean, with Hurricane fighters on our flight deck. These aircraft were brought down from the UK by *Furious*, another aircraft carrier that, like *Glorious*, had been converted from a First World War cruiser, or by *Argus*. The *Ark* would moor up so that the stern end of *Furious*'s flight deck (*Argus* was the wrong height) could be connected by a wooden bridge to our round down and the Hurricanes would be pushed over from *Furious* on to our flight deck. They would remain there until, after three days at sea, somewhere in the Mediterranean they would start their engines and the pilots would make their first and last carrier take-off, form up and head for Malta. Even with auxiliary fuel tanks, the Hurricanes could easily get into the air at a point between the ship's island and the end of the flight deck. I often wondered what bureaucratic obstacles had stopped Hawker from producing a Hurricane with folding wings and a tail hook before the war had started in earnest. If the Fleet Air Arm had had fighters like them over Norway, it would have been a very different story and might have changed the course of the war.

The RAF pilots that I met had not had a great time on *Furious*; I gather they were not treated well at all. Later, I could appreciate why, but at the time it sounded as if their experience was similar to mine on the old *Argus*: very noisy, not very nice food and cramped accommodation, half of them having to sleep in hammocks. They were relieved to get on board the *Ark*, where they got a decent cabin and we went out of our way to make sure they felt welcome in the wardroom. They had a difficult job. The auxiliary drop tanks that were fitted under their wings to extend their range did not feed the engine directly; instead they were used to refill their main tanks. So they would wait until the point in their long flight when their fuel gauges showed empty, then flick a few switches and hope to see the needles start rising again. I imagine it could be quite a tense moment. The auxiliary tanks had been fitted while the aircraft were on *Furious*, and the only way the pilots could tell if they had been installed properly and were going to work when they were needed was to climb into the cockpit, press the fuel-transfer switches 'on', climb out again and stand close, with their ears to the tanks, to see if they could hear the faint whirr of the pumps. On a noisy ship this was not easy.

However, both our deliveries went off without any loss. No sooner had we got these out of the way than it was out into the Mediterranean again to escort another convoy of fast merchant ships. The aim this time was not just the resupply of Malta, but also to make deliveries to Egypt, where the Eighth Army was getting a battering from the German forces that had taken over from the Italian army in North Africa.

The convoy was going to deliver 307 tanks to the army in

Alexandria, as well as forty-three Hurricane fighter aircraft, in crates, to be assembled by the RAF in Egypt. HMS *Breconshire*, an auxiliary Royal Navy supply ship, would transport fuel and munitions to Malta, and the battleship HMS *Queen Elizabeth*, along with two cruisers, would also travel the length of the Mediterranean to reinforce Cunningham's fleet in the eastern Mediterranean.

By now all the Skuas that we had carried had been replaced by Fulmar fighters and there were two squadrons of these planes on board, numbers 803 and 807, but the Fulmars were not the most reliable of aircraft and only twelve in total were serviceable and fit to fly. The Mediterranean had got tougher in the few months I had been on the *Ark*. Not only had we lost *Illustrious* to the Luftwaffe, but our troops were on the retreat from Greece and the navy was suffering severe casualties. German dive-bombers attacked two destroyers, *Wryneck* and *Diamond*, as they evacuated British soldiers from Greece. Both of them were sunk and most of the crew and soldiers were killed.

We sailed on into the Mediterranean, carrying out our regular anti-submarine patrols, with a couple of Fulmars keeping a combat air patrol above us. On 8 May we were spotted by an Italian reconnaissance plane. We were very hard to miss, with *Queen Elizabeth*, our normal companions *Renown* and *Sheffield*, two other cruisers and eight destroyers, and in the midst of us the five mechanized transport ships. We must have left behind a wake of massive proportions. The cargo ships were capable of doing 14 knots, which was fast for civilian vessels, but they were still far slower than we would have liked. The Italian reconnaissance plane avoided being shot down, but even if it had been the damage was done. At this stage, however, three days into the voyage, we were close to the Italian bases in Sicily and Sardinia, so we were closed up ready to go to action stations very quickly.

When I wasn't flying, like most of the Swordfish crews I had been assigned an action station in the *Ark*. Mine was manning a quadruple 0.5in machine gun on a platform by the flight deck. The gun had shoulder rests with a large round sighting ring mounted above it. There were four of these platforms around the *Ark*, two at the bow and two at the stern, with two quadruple mountings on each. The four machine guns were mounted vertically above each other and were intended for short-range anti-aircraft fire. If the aircraft were as close as this we had probably already been hit, but this didn't stop me being pleased with my job, because it was marvellous to feel that I would be able to fire back with something when we were under attack.

And that is exactly what happened. Early in the afternoon we were attacked by a group of Italian bombers. They were flying low over the water, however, and I realized that they were not the normal high-altitude bombers, but that they were carrying torpedoes and were heading right for us. They were SM.79s, three-engined bombers that had been modified to carry two torpedoes. A squadron of these planes had been flying out of North Africa and had had some success against merchant ships. They had also managed to hit the cruisers HMS *Liverpool* and *Glasgow*, causing severe damage to both of them. Now we were the target!

I started pouring bullets at them, and the rest of the guns on the other ships also started firing. An 0.5in-calibre machine gun is a big gun – bigger than the machine guns mounted in the wings of fighters like Hurricanes and Spitfires. Firing four of these at a time was like holding the combined firepower of a fighter. I could feel the vibration through the deck plates and in the air itself, the concussion shaking my body and my internal organs. I was overwhelmed with the smell of cordite and the noise was indescribable. However, despite this, I was still able to notice how hard it was to fire accurately on the low-flying planes. Some of the main anti-aircraft guns could not be depressed low enough anyway, but even for those that could be, like my machine guns, it was harder to allow for sufficient deflection if they were really skimming the waves. With the aircraft below the horizon, silhouetted against the sea rather than the sky, it was not so easy to draw a bead on them.

The bombers dropped their torpedoes probably too far away to hit us, but they continued their low-level flight after they had dropped and they seemed to be heading straight for us. They were too big too turn away quickly like we did in the Swordfish; they had no choice but to bore on through the escorts and climb out above us. It seemed that one would go directly over my head. One of them had crashed before it dropped its torpedoes, hit by shells from the big-calibre guns on the destroyers, but two others dropped their 'kippers' before they also were hit, one smashing into the sea close by. For some strange reason there was a pause in the fighting and, as the bomber seemed to rear up, then flip over and hit the sea with an enormous impact, I could hear the strange noise of the wings and fuselage disintegrating, bits of wreckage breaking off and hurtling into the sky. At the same time a great cheer went up from everyone on the flight deck and in the gun positions. Then the *Ark* was twisting and turning to comb the tracks of the torpedoes that had been dropped. There were four torpedoes in the water altogether and two passed down the port side of the *Ark* – I could see the tracks in the water – while another two went past on the starboard. I waited tensely for the sound of an underwater explosion, but none came.

The noise of these engagements was beyond belief. My position was along from one of the 4.5in gun turrets and when they were firing I was completely deafened, my head ringing for hours afterwards. I wore a tin helmet, with an anti-flash hood, which at first I thought unnecessary, but as soon as the guns started firing there was a rain of pieces of shrapnel dropping out of the skies as the shells exploded. At the same time a running commentary on the battle was being broadcast over the ship's tannoy by the chaplain, of all people. Both the captains I served under in the *Ark*, Holland and Maund, believed it was good for morale to let everyone – in particular the men in the hangars and the engine spaces below decks – know what was happening, especially if there was action between the Fulmars and enemy aircraft some miles away. In a strange way it was comforting to feel part of what was going on and to be told that our fighters were getting stuck in.

The torpedo bombers had been accompanied by a squadron of CR.42 fighters, and their formation had been spotted by *Sheffield*'s radar ten minutes before they were seen from the *Ark*. The two Fulmars that were already in the air, flown by Lt Commander Rupert Tillard, CO of 808, and Lieutenant Hay, saw the fighters climbing to attack them. They were outnumbered three to one, but both pilots dived to make a head-on attack on the fighters, passing directly through their formation. The Fulmar flown by Lt Commander Tillard carried Mark Somerville, Admiral Somerville's nephew, as observer. They were the crew who had flown back to the *Ark* with news of a sighting of *Scharnhorst* in March. They went into the attack in a steep dive and were last seen trying to level out at 500 feet.

In the second Fulmar, Lieutenant Hay started to follow them down, but he was attacked in the dive by two CR.42 fighters and to evade them he turned into clouds, then dived down towards the fleet, where he was fired on by the destroyers in the anti-submarine screen. Fortunately, they scored no hits. A section of three Fulmars had been ranged on the flight deck when the enemy formation was identified and they had taken off. A group of six CR.42 fighters flew in to attack them, so they quickly became mixed up in a dogfight.

A confusing mêlée ensued, and Lieutenant Taylour shot the wing-tip off one of the Italian fighters, but before he could get in another burst he was himself shot up by an attacker closing in behind him. His plane was hit and his observer, Petty Officer Howard, was badly wounded by machine-gun fire.

The two other Fulmars, flown by Petty Officer Dubber and Lieutenant Guthrie, were both badly damaged in the dogfight, but Guthrie, after pulling out of a steep spin at a very low altitude, found one of the Italian torpedo bombers in his sights and attacked it twice before his guns failed.

The Fulmar flown by Lt Commander Tillard had disappeared and was never seen again. It had no doubt crashed into the sea, but none of the escort ships saw it go in; nor were they in a position to try to save the crew even if they had. The other four of the five Fulmars in the air when the torpedo bombers and CR.42 fighters struck were now all circling the carrier, waiting to land; all had been badly shot up and one man was wounded.

There was a lot of activity on the flight deck as the fire-fighting teams got ready, and there was a call for hands to the flight deck in case any of the planes crashed and needed man-handling over the side, but they all managed to land on. It was 1440: the torpedo attack and the battle in the air had lasted just one hour. The guns were now silent and the magazines of the rapid-firing cannon were restocked, ready for the next attack. The excitement and the adrenalin rush of action, the chaotic noise of every gun in the fleet hammering away, were gone, to be replaced by quiet. We were still at action stations, and there was a quick delivery of hot tea and sandwiches. We all knew that there would be another attack; it was just a question of when. I found this the worst sort of waiting. I would rather be firing away and not thinking about what was going to happen.

I knew what was happening down below. The warning bells on the lifts were ringing as planes were brought down from the flight deck; the fireproof curtains were raised; and the fitters and armourers were frantically trying to repair the Fulmars that had just returned in a damaged condition, I didn't know how bad. The already pathetically inadequate number of fighters on the *Ark* had just been reduced from twelve to seven; an observer was in the sickbay being operated on; and the CO of 808 Squadron, who had been in the *Ark* since November, just one month longer than me, and had several kills to his credit, was dead, as was his observer, Lieutenant Mark Somerville.

Another attack could occur at any minute and we were trying to keep four Fulmars in the air as a permanent combat air patrol. Aircraft landed and refuelled every hour to make sure that they would always have enough endurance to take on enemy aircraft. We also had to keep some Swordfish in the air for anti-submarine patrols, because we were approaching the area where submarines would lie in wait. One of the biggest handicaps we faced was that our route to Malta was inevitably predictable.

The next attack was not long in coming. *Sheffield*'s radar spotted a reconnaissance aircraft circling the fleet and two of the Fulmars in the combat air patrol were directed by radio to intercept and shoot it down. At the same time the patrol spotted an Italian SM.79 bomber. They all converged on it, shooting enough bullets into it to make it break up in the air. They then continued after the reconnaissance aircraft, but it escaped. When the Fulmars were returning to the fleet, one of them started to develop engine trouble. White smoke was pouring out from the cowling and the pilot decided he had no choice but to ditch in the sea, where the plane sank, though this time the crew were picked up by a vigilant destroyer.

Another half-hour went by before *Sheffield*'s radar plotter reported several formations of aircraft approaching from various points of the compass; two of them, we were told, appeared to be large ones. We quickly ranged the rest of our Fulmars and they were flown off, with instructions to climb to 8,000 feet and circle at 5 miles' distance. All the pilots had flown at least once that day and many of the Fulmars had already been damaged and repaired. Three Fulmars from 808 Squadron were sent to intercept the approaching enemy formations, but to emphasize how fragile some of them were, one was forced to return to the *Ark* when the pilot couldn't retract his undercarriage.

The other two Fulmars, flown by Lieutenants Kindersley and Hay, in the air for the second time that day, continued into the attack. Hay shot at a CR.42 from behind, causing it to turn away, and then took on three SM.79 bombers by flying directly at them in a head-on attack, firing his guns. They were forced to break up their bombing run and decided to jettison their bombs and seek shelter in cloud.

Meanwhile, Lieutenant Kindersley was manoeuvring to attack a group of bombers when he was ambushed by four CR.42 fighters. He decided to fly into the fleet's anti-aircraft barrage, where the enemy fighters refused to follow him. After this attack was broken up, the two Fulmars were then directed by the air control officer on the *Ark* to intercept another aircraft that had appeared on *Sheffield*'s radar. This was another SM.79 bomber and Lieutenant Hay shot it down in flames.

The third Fulmar in the air was flown by Petty Officer Johnson, who avoided three Italian fighters attempting to fire on him from the rear and then saw an SM.79 bomber which he pursued and eventually caught, firing all his remaining ammunition into it. By then he was 30 miles from the fleet and had to be directed home, not landing until almost 1700.

While Lieutenant Hay and Petty Officer Johnson were

making their attacks, three SM.79s had penetrated the anti-aircraft barrages and were heading for us, coming out of the sun, which was now low in the west, clearly hoping to drop their bombs down the centre line of the ship – the ideal approach for an air attack. This was the first time I had seen us targeted in this way, and I have to say it was alarming. All the guns opened up, including mine, although the bombers were at a height at which they were out of my range. The 4.5in anti-aircraft guns started blasting and the pom-poms were also hammering away, attempting to smash the aircraft out of the sky. One bomber did not survive the bullets and the high explosive that we were hurtling up into the sky; it turned away and jettisoned its bombs in a desperate hope to gain some height, but crashed into the sea. The other two turned to follow us.

It was new to me, but the *Ark*'s crew had had to deal with plenty of these attacks before. As the line of bombers approached, the captain threw the *Ark* into a very tight turn to port, with the ship vibrating at top speed and what seemed to be an enormous amount of heel. The two SM.79s released their bombs; I could see them in the air as they fell, exploding close to the bows on the starboard side with a sharp crack and an enormous gout of foam and seawater. Close, but not close enough, thank God.

Just before this attack, four more aircraft from 807 Squadron had taken to the air, flown by Lt Commander Douglas, Petty Officer Leggett, Lieutenant Gardner and Lieutenant Firth. As they climbed to reach another enemy formation, Gardner heard a sudden bang and his port wing dipped: he realized that the panel covering the four machine guns in his wing had been ripped off in the slipstream. He requested permission to land on the *Ark* again, but then realized that we were firing at the group of bombers approaching the ship. Clearly this was not the time to try to land on the carrier, so he climbed and attacked one of the planes in the formation, despite the poor air-flow over his wing, getting in several bursts before he lost his target in cloud. When Gardner gave up the chase and left the cloud he was fired at by the escort ships, so he too sought the shelter of the clouds and waited for fire to stop before landing on the carrier for his wing panels to be replaced.

The other three pilots also attacked the group of Italian bombers, firing at and chasing them for some distance, constantly hampered in their pursuit by the low speed of their Fulmars. They too eventually lost their prey in the clouds. They continued to maintain a patrol, occasionally being fired on by their own ships.

Throughout the day we had been getting closer to Sicily, and at 1918 the radar operators in *Sheffield* picked up echoes that they interpreted as large formations of aircraft approaching.

Was this the enemy we had yet to meet? Throughout the day, at the back of my mind had been the knowledge that the Luftwaffe had a large number of planes in Sicily. So far we had had to deal only with Italian aircraft, but surely the Luftwaffe was not going to stay out of it? *Illustrious* had been attacked by thirty-three Stukas, and we had just six or seven fighters left. Now we were facing another massive attack – this time it could easily be the Luftwaffe assembling over its airfields in Sicily.

I won't pretend that I was not apprehensive at that time. You didn't have to be in the squadron office to know what the situation was: we could all see the movements on the flight deck and knew which planes were taking off, which were returning and in what state. We did not have a great deal left to throw at the enemy, whether they were Germans or Italians.

The pilots still in the air, on that evening of 8 May, were joined by four others, all of whom had already seen combat earlier in the day. They took off from the flight deck, their Merlin engines hauling the heavy aircraft into the air. With the *Ark* going at 20 knots they could be airborne about halfway down the flight deck, less if the headwind was strong. Lieutenant Richard Gardner's Fulmar had been repaired and he was taking off for his fourth fighter patrol. Petty Officer Dubber, Lieutenant Taylour and Sub-Lieutenant Walker followed him. There were now seven fighters in the air, and these pilots, with their observers in the rear cockpit, were all that now stood between Force H and the German dive-bombers approaching – by this time that was what we believed them to be.

Our Fulmars went into the fight extremely aggressively, despite the overwhelming numbers of enemy aircraft that confronted them. The German aircraft had split up into different sections and the fighter direction officer in the *Ark* thought that they were preparing to make a concerted attack from three different directions, so that the *Ark* would always be presenting a perfect target to at least one section of dive-bombers, the preferred approach being along the centre line of the target ship, giving the pilot the maximum length of target.

The three fighters that were already on patrol at 8,000 feet were directed by the fighter direction officer to fly to the north of the fleet, where the radar operators in *Sheffield* had identified a number of aircraft circling above some stratus cloud. As they approached they saw that they were a group of fifteen Stuka dive-bombers under the protection of six Messerschmitt Me110s, twin-engined long-range fighters. The Luftwaffe really had arrived, and the news was radioed back to the *Ark*. Then Lt Commander Douglas in the lead Fulmar turned into the Me110 fighters and fired at two in turn, seeing the second one he hit go down into cloud. It was the first victory, but the reargunners of the Messerschmitts both returned the fire and

Douglas's Fulmar was hit in the leading edge of both his wings, his hydraulic system was damaged and fluid started pouring out into the slipstream.

Petty Officer Leggett, Douglas's wingman, dived straight on to the circling Stukas, but one of the German fighters attempted to intercept him. Leggett turned inside the Messerschmitt and fired a burst from his machine gun into its cockpit, putting the reargunner out of action. The German aircraft seemed to stall and turn, then dived into cloud with a trail of white smoke behind it. Lieutenant Firth was met by two of the German fighters climbing towards him and he made a head-on approach, firing into the leading aircraft. The pilot also turned away and dived into cloud, with smoke pouring from one engine. The second Messerschmitt was also fired on by Leggett, and it too manoeuvred away from the attack into cloud.

These three pilots had, in an incredibly brave and aggressive approach, driven off six Messerschmitt fighters, probably damaging at least three. The three Fulmar pilots continued to search for them under the cloud, but could not locate them and, running short of fuel and ammunition, they had to return to the *Ark* and land on the flight deck. It had been a stunning success. The Fulmar could fly at a maximum speed of only 230 knots and would have been outrun and outmanoeuvred by the single-engined Messerschmitt 109 fighters. The Me110s, however, were at more of a disadvantage, although they had some powerful machine guns and cannon in the nose, as well as a rear-firing machine gun.

The four other pilots that had taken off from *Ark Royal* to intercept the formation of German aircraft climbed to 9,000 feet and saw that, as well as the six escorting Messerschmitts, there was one group of sixteen Stukas and a second group of twelve. Lieutenant Taylour dived into the formation to break them up, carried out several attacks and pursued them into cloud for about 30 miles. His plane was hit, however, and the starboard undercarriage leg dropped down, forcing him to return to the *Ark*. Petty Officer Dubber, Taylour's wingman, made a head-on attack at a group of Stukas, then turned and started firing at them from the rear quarter. One of the escorting fighters then attempted to protect the dive-bombers and made a stern attack on Dubber's Fulmar, from which he escaped by diving into cloud.

Lieutenant Gardner had split off from Taylour's section and aggressively attacked another section of sixteen Stukas, pouring a burst of gunfire into the nearest one, which turned over and dived into the sea. Gardner hurled through the formation, firing at close range at several others. His own aircraft was hit, with bullets smashing the windscreen and punching holes in the engine radiator, but he broke up the formation and several of the Stukas started to jettison their bomb load. Psychologically, this was the point where the enemy was defeated. They made the decision that it was pointless to continue their attack, and so got rid of their load to give themselves more fuel and speed to escape. Gardner's aircraft, however, was badly damaged and he had to return to the *Ark*, but his number two, Lieutenant Firth, continued to attack a formation of three Messerschmitt 110s, which scattered into cloud. Searching for more targets, Firth flew on and attacked a formation of Stukas before becoming embroiled in a dogfight with an Me110, which broke off the action. Firth again launched his fighter at the Stukas, pursuing a straggler into cloud with smoke pouring from it. His air gunner, Leading Airman Shaw, saw at least one Stuka go down in flames.

At 2139 all the Fulmars had landed back on *Ark Royal*. Not one Stuka had succeeded in making an attack on the fleet, despite their overwhelming superiority. Yet the day wasn't over. At 2030, before all the Fulmars had returned, a separate attack was started. Sneaking in under the radar, while everyone was focused on the attack from the German dive-bombers, three low-level torpedo bombers flew both at *Renown* and at us on the *Ark*. One broke away after anti-aircraft fire started to hit it and bits of its fuselage were seen flying off, but the other two launched their torpedoes. For the second time that day we made a sharp turn to port after torpedo bombers roared overhead, and the torpedoes passed 50 metres away on the starboard side.

This was the final attack of a day that had seen us face an onslaught of more than fifty aircraft in total, defended by a maximum at the beginning of the day of just twelve service-able Fulmars out of two squadrons on board. I thought it was unbelievable. Some of us were puzzled that the German dive-bombers hadn't pursued their attack with more determination, and there were theories that the Luftwaffe pilots mistook the Fulmars for the more effective Hurricane fighters. Yet they had faced Fulmar aircraft when they had successfully dive-bombed *Illustrious*, so this seems unlikely.

The German attack was made late in the day, as it was growing dark, and the vigour and aggression of the Fulmar pilots may have been a nasty surprise. Several of the Stuka formations were broken up, and the German pilots may have become unhappy about continuing their attack, which was clearly going to be opposed, in the dwindling light.

Whatever the reason, the actions by the pilots, air gunners and observers of 807 and 808 Squadrons had saved both us and an extremely vital convoy. Captain Loben Maund, who had taken over from Captain 'Hooky' Holland, sent round a message to us all, saying, 'The immunity of the convoy and Fleet from damage due to air attack on this day is largely attributable to the work of this small force of fighters, made possible only by the exceptional efforts of the personnel of the flight deck and hangars.' We had been sorry to see Captain Holland go, but he had been in command since

Norway and needed the rest. Maund, however, had shown he could handle the *Ark* in a tight corner!

The only tragedy of the day had been the loss of Lt Commander Tillard, the commanding officer of 808 Squadron, and his observer, Lieutenant Somerville, Admiral Somerville's nephew. They had never returned to the *Ark*, and their plane was never found.

Two days later, the group of destroyers that had escorted the transport ships through the Skerki Channel to Malta were returning west when they were attacked by four bombers flying low and using broken cloud as cover. None of the ships had radar, or any air defence. Four sticks of bombs were dropped and the destroyer *Faulkner* was severely damaged by a cluster of four or five near misses very close to the stern. Her speed was cut in half, but she managed to limp back to meet Force H and eventually reach Gibraltar. It was a salutary reminder that the threat from the air never went away.

There was an enormous party in the wardroom when we got back to Gibraltar. The Fulmar pilots were naturally completely stressed, and in a bit of shock, after that day of action and they had needed more than one night's rest to overcome it. Despite the euphoria over seeing off the Luftwaffe, we felt that we had lived through an incredible battle. We must have thrown tons of metal into the sky; my ears were still ringing from the crash and blast of the anti-aircraft guns; and I have no idea of the number of enemy aircraft that were focused on destroying us. We drank as if there were no tomorrow.

12
Against All Odds

I was now part of a ship that was probably the best and most well-trained carrier in the navy. I am sure that a host of others will protest, but the ethos on board *Ark Royal* was one of practice and more practice. I have already said that my CO, Lt Commander Coode, was the sort of chap to inspire enormous confidence in us younger members of his squadron, and the leadership of Force H was similarly driven. Admiral Somerville was a stickler for training and practice, so, whenever the opportunity arose, at the end of a trip we would carry out exercises in torpedo attacks and dive-bombing, and would work on speeding up our flying on and off the flight deck. These exercises were not only for the benefit of us on board the *Ark*, but were also designed for the benefit of anti-aircraft gunners, to improve height-finding and aircraft-recognition in the escort vessels. We reckoned we had got our crews – and that meant everyone involved in ranging and striking down the aircraft, as well as the aircrew – worked up to a very high level of efficiency. Admiral Somerville was known to be very quick to ask questions if there was a delay in landing on or taking off, and we aimed for an average time between landings of thirty seconds. The slowest pilot landing on had to stand drinks in the wardroom to the rest of his squadron.

Despite this attention to detail, there was a real camaraderie. The admiral's flagship, *Renown*, had damaged part of her hull while going into a heavy sea. A forward section of the anti-torpedo bulge had been torn free. Some of our Swordfish had flown low over the ship to take a look at the damage before they landed on and Somerville had sent a signal saying, 'Why the interest? Is there something sticking out of Father's pants?' The reply had been sent back, 'You flatter yourself. It is only hanging out!' There were few squadrons in the navy, let alone in any foreign navy, where that sort of stuff would be signalled back and forth.

This *esprit de corps* sprang from self-confidence, a feeling that I have experienced in a rugby team when everybody knows that they are playing at the top of their game. Our efforts on the last operation added to that feeling. I was very pleased to be on the *Ark* and felt that I had achieved more than I had a right to. What else was there to do?

We made another trip to fly Hurricanes off to Malta, and returned, carrying out our usual programme of training exercises as we got closer to Gibraltar. We had been in Gibraltar for a day when, at around 0100 on 23 May, the *Ark* started to stir, tannoys sounded, hatches closed up with a bang, and the sound of feet running up the companionways and walkways signalled that we were going to put to sea. That meant that the morning flying schedule was probably changed and I might be woken early.

An hour later, when I was oblivious to the world, tugs pulled us from the side of the wall and we passed slowly along the detached mole to leave by the northern entrance. Then we headed south and into the Straits. If we were heading west, it was possible to see the lights of Tangier pass on the port side, and then in another hour we would be going at high speed, our bows biting into the big swells of the Atlantic Ocean. By 0500 Swordfish aircraft with folded wings would be brought up from the hangar decks on the lifts to start the first anti-submarine patrols of the day. I would be awake, and with other pilots and observers would be getting my briefing about the expected weather, the planned course of the ship over the next two or three hours and any latest intelligence about submarine sightings, the presence of convoys and any surface vessels in the vicinity, be they ours, the enemy's or neutrals.

I would expect that our job in the Atlantic was either to find and escort a convoy, on its way from Sierra Leone to Liverpool or vice versa, or to meet a small group of fast ships to escort them back into the Mediterranean, or I might be on the lookout for the two raiders still moored in Brest, *Scharnhorst* and *Gneisenau*. The *Ark*'s very first orders on 23 May were to provide an escort for a Sierra Leone convoy, but after a few more hours the word went round that a new threat was possibly entering the Atlantic – a new German battleship, *Bismarck*. I wouldn't say that we had much idea about this warship, but we quickly picked up what we could from the squadron office and the commander air staff. This was a true battleship, significantly bigger than *Scharnhorst* or *Gneisenau*; in fact, she was the biggest warship afloat, longer than *Ark Royal* and weighing 50,000 tons compared to the *Ark*'s 21,000. She seemed to be bristling with guns, with a main armament of eight 15in guns and a secondary battery of twelve 6in guns. She was well defended against attack from the air, with sixteen high-angle 4in guns to shoot down aircraft, numerous batteries of 20mm cannon and machine guns, so it was reported, and with very thick armour plating protecting her hull. She would be a tough nut to crack! However, as she was still some way away and was being hunted by the

Home Fleet, we did not think she was something we would have to worry about.

The more immediate problem was the presence of *Scharnhorst* and *Gneisenau* in Brest: if they chose to make a foray into the Atlantic at short notice, then we would have to try to stop them. With the fleet concentrating their efforts on *Bismarck*, now would be the perfect time for the two battle-cruisers to join the fight.

The impact that these German raiders in the Atlantic had was not just the damage to shipping or the loss of life that they could inflict, although that was extremely serious. No, it was the fact that, with up to six convoys in the Atlantic at any one time, it was very difficult for the navy to assign a battle-ship with the necessary anti-submarine escort to each one. To do so would drain resources from elsewhere, particularly from the Mediterranean, where the Germans were really stepping up their offensive in North Africa and had also begun the invasion of Crete. The threat from the U-boats was severe enough; Britain just could not afford to have powerful surface raiders loose in the Atlantic as well.

These considerations were of only passing interest to us, however. My task was to get into the cockpit, take off on a patrol and keep alert for two hours, then find the carrier to land on, where I would warm up and grab some food before embarking on another patrol before the day finished. On the 23rd, however, it got progressively harder. As the day wore on, the sea started to get rougher and the landings became more difficult. Fortunately, all twelve Swordfish that had flown patrols that day completed them without incident.

However, events had been developing rapidly 2,000 miles north of the *Ark*. *Bismarck* and a companion ship, the battle-cruiser *Prinz Eugen*, had left harbour in Germany on 19 May. They had sailed through the Kattegut, that belt of water between Denmark and Sweden, on the 20th and had then moored in a fjord south of Bergen so that *Prinz Eugen* could take on more fuel. The start of their mission into the Atlantic had already come to the notice of the Admiralty. Reports of their sailing through Danish waters had been passed on to the British naval attaché in Sweden, and by the time the two warships had moored in Norway a photo-reconnaissance Spitfire was able to fly over them at high altitude and take photographs. That night, unaware that they had been photographed, *Bismarck* and *Prinz Eugen*, her fuelling completed, continued on their journey. Later, on the 22nd, a Fleet Air Arm Maryland took off from Hatston in very bad weather on a reconnaissance of the Bergen area, and was able to alert the Admiralty that the two warships were no longer at anchor.

There were several routes that German warships could use to enter the Atlantic. There was the Denmark Strait, between Iceland and Greenland, which in May was reduced to a width of about 60 miles because of extensive pack ice; there was a passage between Iceland and the Faroe Islands about 240 miles wide; there was the gap between the Faroes and Shetland, which was about 140 miles wide; and there was the Fair Isle Channel between Shetland and the Orkneys. The most northerly was the most remote from any aerial reconnaissance flights, and this seemed to Admiral Tovey, who was in charge of the Home Fleet moored in Scapa Flow, the most likely. It was the same route that *Scharnhorst* and *Gneisenau* had taken for their own highly successful raid on merchant shipping at the start of the year, when they had been the subject of a long and unsuccessful hunt by the *Ark*. Nevertheless, the Admiralty took precautions to cover the other routes as well.

HMS *Suffolk* and *Norfolk*, two heavy County class cruisers armed with 8in guns, under the command of Rear Admiral Wake-Walker, were dispatched to monitor the Denmark Strait, while the sea between Iceland and the Faroes was patrolled by HMS *Arethusa*, *Birmingham* and *Manchester*, light cruisers mounting 6in guns as their main armament. These warships wouldn't have a hope against *Bismarck*, but their job was not to take her on; it was merely to report the presence of the German warship and continue to follow her until a larger force of battleships could arrive on the scene.

Two of the Home Fleet's big ships had been sent to Iceland from Scapa Flow in readiness to engage *Bismarck*: they were the battlecruiser *Hood* and *Prince of Wales*, a modern battleship recently handed over to the navy by Cammell Laird and still in the process of working up. They were to be joined by other ships from the Home Fleet after it was revealed that *Bismarck* had left Bergen. Late in the evening of 22 May, the battleship *King George V* and *Victorious*, the navy's newest aircraft carrier, put to sea from Scapa Flow. They were joined by the battlecruiser *Repulse*, accompanied by four cruisers and a group of destroyers. Also, HMS *Rodney*, a 16in-gun battleship, was diverted to join up with the ships of the Home Fleet.

Before sailing, Admiral John Tovey, commander of the Home Fleet, had paid a visit to *Victorious* and met the commanding officer of the Swordfish squadron, Lt Commander Esmonde. *Victorious* had been scheduled to steam to Gibraltar, then onwards to replace *Formidable* in the fleet at Alexandria. The voyage south would have given the carrier the opportunity to carry out exercises and train up the new crew. They would not now have time for that, and Tovey wanted to hear at first hand Esmonde's assessment of his squadron's abilities. Esmonde assured him that, although young and mostly inexperienced, his pilots knew what to do and would be utterly committed. Tovey left with as much reassurance as it was possible to get under the circumstances.

The stage was now set for a successful interception of *Bismarck*, the finest and most formidable product of German shipbuilding. Admiral Tovey had made his dispositions, his ships greatly outnumbered the German ones and there was, on the face of it, no reason why we on the *Ark*, several thousand miles away to the south, would need to become involved in this battle. His assessment of the likeliest route into the Atlantic was correct. *Bismarck* and her escort, *Prinz Eugen*, under the overall command of Admiral Günther Lutjens, were set on a course that would take them very close to the pack ice bordering the coast of Greenland. There were usually banks of sea mist swirling across the Strait that offered concealment, and Lutjens had received a weather forecast for the area that promised low clouds, snow and rain squalls, which would also cloak his presence. He believed too that his radar and sonar would help him avoid contact with our ships.

Bismarck edged along the pack ice, zigzagging to avoid ice floes, when a radar operator sounded the alarm. He had a contact on the port bow, which was confirmed almost immediately by a sonar trace on the same bearing. They had come into contact with *Suffolk*. *Suffolk* had also seen *Bismarck* and signalled at 1922 on 22 May, 'One battleship, one cruiser in sight at 20 degrees, range seven miles, course 240 degrees.'

An hour later, *Bismarck* spotted *Norfolk* and opened fire. *Norfolk* immediately withdrew into the mist, five 15in shells from *Bismarck*'s main battery crashing around her. Luckily none of them hit the ship, and *Norfolk* quickly put some distance between herself and the German battleship. She took up a position abeam of *Suffolk* and both ships started their work of tailing the battleship, sending regular reports back to the Admiralty, and to Admiral Tovey in *King George V*. *Bismarck*'s radar had been damaged by the salvo from her forward guns, which had been fired at *Norfolk*, and so *Prinz Eugen* had moved ahead of the battleship to probe for icebergs and other British warships. They drove ahead at high speed, through the murky twilight of the Arctic night, into squalls and fog banks, sometimes laying down a smokescreen to evade their pursuers. But the radar sets in *Suffolk* and *Norfolk* were working perfectly. These two cruisers stuck to the quarry's coat-tails, keeping on the very edge of *Bismarck*'s horizon, and it dawned on the German officers that, contrary to their intelligence reports, some of our warships did have radar on board.

In the middle of the night, Admiral Lutjens decided to confront his pursuers and ordered a 180-degree turn, but it was noticed by *Suffolk* and both cruisers avoided coming into close enough range. They had been waiting for this manoeuvre and were content to retreat, knowing that they would be able to re-establish contact in the very narrow waters that Lutjens had selected for his passage west.

The signals from *Suffolk* and *Norfolk* had, of course, galvanized the Home Fleet – *Hood* and *Prince of Wales*, and Admiral Tovey in *King George V*, with *Victorious* and *Repulse*. They had known for several hours where *Bismarck* was, and were rapidly steaming to intercept her. *Hood* and *Prince of Wales* were closest, so would be the first to make contact. On the morning of 23 May, at 0545, lookouts on *Bismarck* saw two plumes of smoke appear above the horizon, followed by the masts and upper works of two warships. The crews of *Bismarck* and *Prinz Eugen* went to action stations; the main guns were loaded and the gun directors started training them on the shifting positions of the targets as they got closer and closer.

Vice Admiral Lancelot Holland, in *Hood*, was also in command of *Prince of Wales* and had decided that he would not wait for the remainder of the Home Fleet under Admiral Tovey to support him. He steamed at full speed directly towards the German warships. His flagship, *Hood*, was an extremely well-known and highly regarded warship, which had toured the world flying the flag for Britain in the 1920s. She had once been considered the biggest and most powerful warship in the world, although technically she was a battle-cruiser. She was designed to carry very large guns at great speed in pursuit of an enemy. She was therefore comparatively lightly armoured, particularly on her main deck, and Admiral Holland knew that she was vulnerable to shells dropping from a height. It would be better for his ship to close the distance quickly so that *Bismarck*'s shells would have a flatter trajectory. Getting the targets into close range would also suit *Prince of Wales*, whose gunnery team had had little experience or training with their ship's systems. *Bismarck*, however, was built to stand and fight, with extremely thick armour covering her sides and decks, which even the 14in shells of *Prince of Wales* would find hard to penetrate. It might have been prudent for Admiral Holland to wait for Admiral Tovey's forces in order to overwhelm the German warships by sheer weight of numbers, but the Royal Navy has always expected its officers to join battle whenever the opportunity arises.

Hood was the first to open fire, but Admiral Holland mistook *Prinz Eugen*, which was in the lead and had a similar silhouette, for *Bismarck*, so both British ships directed their fire at the smaller German cruiser. Captain John Leach, in *Prince of Wales*, realized their error and directed his second salvo towards *Bismarck*, but *Hood* continued to fire on *Prinz Eugen*.

Admiral Lutjens did not make the same mistake: *Bismarck*'s guns were aimed squarely at *Hood*. With the third salvo, the shells found their target. *Bismarck*'s heavy guns split open the grey light of early dawn with a blinding flash, leaving a cloud of black smoke in her wake that rose as high as the mast before being snatched by the wind. After the firing had continued for a few minutes, the gunnery officer in *Bismarck* reported that he saw a fire on the deck of *Hood*. Four minutes later he saw another bright flash, larger than the previous ones, and then *Hood* exploded in an enormous fireball. A giant column of black smoke rose into the air. A ship 840 feet long and built by thousands of shipyard workers from 42,000 tons of iron and steel was torn apart in seconds. *Bismarck*'s navigator described the explosion as like being in a hurricane, with every nerve of his body feeling the pressure. A huge fireball blinded him. Enormous pieces of metal, some as large as a complete gun turret, were thrown through the air like toys. The navigator said afterwards that he never wanted his children to see a sight like it. Fourteen hundred men were killed in the blast, or drowned as the pieces of *Hood* sank beneath the sea. There were three survivors.

There was jubilation in *Bismarck*, but the officers quickly quietened the men. The ship was still being fired on by *Prince of Wales* and her 14in shells were finding their target.

Now *Bismarck* joined *Prinz Eugen* in targeting the last British warship still holding the field. *Prince of Wales* had been ordered to remain close to *Hood*, so it was relatively easy for the German gunnery officer to shift his aim. *Prince of Wales* was hit by four 15in shells from *Bismarck* and three 8in shells from *Prinz Eugen*. One of *Bismarck*'s shells hit the bridge; it didn't explode until it had passed through it, but it killed everyone except Captain Leach and the signals chief petty officer. Another hit her fire-control turret for the 4.5in guns, and a third exploded against her aircraft crane. The fourth penetrated the hull but did not explode. Two 8in shells from *Prinz Eugen* had hit the stern and caused flooding in some after compartments, while a third had penetrated a shell-handling room of one of *Prince of Wales*'s 4.5in guns, but had also miraculously failed to explode.

This major piece of good fortune was naturally over-shadowed by the greater disaster of the day. *Hood* had literally gone, just six minutes after opening fire on her German opponent. *Prince of Wales* was badly damaged, taking on water, with her main armament now proving to have some serious mechanical problems that prevented her from firing a full broadside. *Bismarck* had her range, as did *Prinz Eugen*. She could not survive for much longer, so, laying a thick smokescreen, Captain Leach ordered his ship to turn away.

Bismarck had not come out of the battle unscathed. The 14in guns of *Prince of Wales* had proved accurate before the turret mechanism started jamming, and *Bismarck* had received a hit through the bow, which passed completely through the ship just above the waterline, causing 2,000 tons of seawater to flood into the hull.

A second shell had hit below the waterline and flooded a generator room, buckling a bulkhead between that room and a boiler room on the port side. It also ruptured a fuel tank in the hull. The third shell hit a boat on the boat deck but did not explode. The damage caused by the shells had not threatened the integrity of the hull, but inspection by damage-control parties revealed the uncomfortable fact that 1,000 tons of fuel oil was leaking from the ruptured tank and could not be salvaged. The forward bulkhead next to the hole in the bow needed to be shored up and the speed of the ship needed to be reduced to a maximum of 28 knots to prevent it collapsing further.

Needless to say, I had known none of this on *Ark Royal*, but around eight o'clock next morning signals were picked up that the cruisers shadowing *Bismarck* had seen the battle between the German warships and *Hood* and *Prince of Wales*, and they had seen *Hood* blow up. As the news went round the ship the men were stunned. I was told about the loss of *Hood* when I returned from a patrol and saw how it affected some of my colleagues. Some knew sailors on board the battle-cruiser, or had once served on her. Percy North, the 818 Squadron writer, was a regular navy man from Portsmouth and the sight of the mighty *Hood* in harbour when he was a young boy had been one of the reasons why he had signed up. He was very shocked. We all accepted, I think, not only that the loss of *Hood* was a grave blow to the navy, but that there was now a very powerful enemy battleship on the loose, which might well prove invincible. The situation as it looked to us was that the two enemy ships were steaming at 25 knots into the North Atlantic. They were still being shadowed by the 8in cruisers *Norfolk* and *Suffolk*, while the commander in chief of the Home Fleet Admiral Tovey on board *King George V*, with *Rodney*, and the carrier *Victorious* were about 200 miles away. There was a large convoy steaming into trouble from the south, escorted by another 8in cruiser, HMS *Dorsetshire*.

The situation did not look hopeful. We had very little information about the scale of the battle and had no idea what efforts *Hood* had made before she was destroyed. Even if Admiral Tovey managed to intercept *Bismarck*, would his battleship, which we knew had smaller guns than *Hood*, be able to make any impression on this German behemoth? We talked about the situation in the wardroom, but I didn't personally think that we would get involved. It was serious, but we had lost ships before, and it was still some way away from us.

All through that day the wind was from the north-west, and it continued to strengthen; it looked as though a tough storm was brewing. The destroyers that had escorted us from Gibraltar started to take in seas over the bows. They could not keep up, so turned for Gibraltar. We continued to press ahead. That night, around 2200, we heard that *Victorious* had launched a Swordfish strike against *Bismarck*.

Victorious had been sent ahead by Admiral Tovey in the hope that her Swordfish might be able to do something to slow *Bismarck* down. He was still 200 miles from the German warships and unsure about their intentions. He was ignorant of the fact that *Prince of Wales* had inflicted enough damage on *Bismarck* to make Lutjens cut her speed and reduce her usable fuel supply. His overriding concern was to prevent *Bismarck* from continuing her course to the south-west and getting at the convoys. *Victorious* launched nine Swordfish from 825 Squadron when she was still 120 miles from the known position of the German battleship. The attack was lead by Lt Commander Esmonde, a civilian airline pilot in peacetime who had volunteered for the Fleet Air Arm at the outbreak of war. An experienced and mature pilot, he led a group of young men who for the most part were on their first combat mission. Their navigation was good and they had three Swordfish fitted with air-to-surface-vessel radar, which helped them locate their target. They made visual contact when *Bismarck* was 16 miles away, but unfortunately lost it again. However, they identified the cruisers that had been trailing the battleship for over twenty-four hours, and *Norfolk* sent a visual Morse signal to Esmonde's observer giving a heading and distance to their quarry.

They flew on for another 14 miles, descended from cloud and started their glide towards the target. *Bismarck* was still 6 miles distant and they had lost the element of surprise.

Admiral Lutjens in *Bismarck* had been faced with a number of decisions following his victory over *Hood*. *Bismarck* and *Prinz Eugen* could have pursued the damaged *Prince of Wales* and could probably have finished her off. However, Lutjens chose immediately not to do this. His mission, his personal orders from Hitler, had been to wreak havoc amongst the convoys crossing the Atlantic. While *Prince of Wales* might eventually have been sunk by his two ships, she had already inflicted some damage on *Bismarck* and might have created much more before any conflict was over. In the hours that followed, it had become clear to him that the two cruisers that had hung on to him like leaches throughout the course of the battle had very good radar and were not going to be shaken off. They had now been joined by *Prince of Wales*, which was keeping its distance on the horizon. *Bismarck* was down at the bows and Lutjens had finally accepted that the 1,000 tons of oil in the damaged tank could not be pumped to another one. Moreover, the oil was leaking into the sea and helping to reveal his position. The original mission was now in jeopardy and Lutjens had to decide what to do. He could retrace his steps, returning to Norway via the Greenland Straits or, like *Scharnhorst* and *Gneisenau*, head for a French port, Brest or St-Nazaire, where his ship could be repaired. It must have been clear to him that the Admiralty would be mobilizing all its resources to catch and sink him, but he was ignorant of the exact disposition of our ships. The safest course was to head to the west coast of France, where he could get some support from German U-boats that might be sent out to meet him, and he would be within range of German aircraft.

Lutjens decided that *Bismarck* and *Prinz Eugen* should separate, allowing *Prinz Eugen* to continue the mission to attack the British convoys in the Atlantic. He hoped that this separation would also allow him the opportunity to confuse his pursuers and break contact with them. At three in the afternoon of 24 May, when the German ships entered a fog bank, Lutjens gave the order to separate and *Bismarck* executed a 360-degree turn to starboard, bringing her on to a heading towards *Suffolk*. The massive 15in guns of her two forward turrets belched fire and smoke, and *Suffolk* sheered away, laying a thick smokescreen. *Prince of Wales* now also opened fire, and *Bismarck* shifted her aim to the British battleship. Both ships were firing at the limits of their range and neither scored any hits, but the ploy had served its purpose. *Prinz Eugen* slipped away unnoticed. *Bismarck* completed her wide turn and continued on her course to the south.

When Lutjens had signalled his intentions to his superiors, they had replied acknowledging that both St-Nazaire and Brest were being made ready to receive him. In addition, six U-boats were being positioned on his route to the French ports. There was little more to do except wait for nightfall and attempt once more to throw off the pursuing cruisers and *Prince of Wales*.

Then, in the quasi-twilight of a northern night, the lookouts in *Bismarck* reported approaching aircraft. They had spotted the Swordfish from *Victorious*. Apart from the 15in-calibre main armament, every gun on *Bismarck* opened fire. Esmonde's plane was hit when he was still 4 miles from the target. The barrage was so heavy that the second and third flights of three aircraft broke away and turned to port. Re-forming, each flight attacked from three different angles on the port side, with a lone aircraft coming in from starboard. *Bismarck* was being steered from her open bridge and manoeuvred to avoid the torpedoes that seemed to be coming from all directions.

Some Swordfish flights turned round and made a second approach, some of them only 2–3 metres above the sea. All the torpedoes were dropped at close range. Only one torpedo hit the target, however, and it sent up a huge column of water, followed by thick black smoke. Unfortunately, it exploded against the thickest part of *Bismarck*'s belt armour, at the waterline, and caused no structural damage to the ship at all. A seaman in the compartment next to the detonation, however, was thrown against a bulkhead and killed by the impact. This was the first casualty to be suffered by *Bismarck*'s crew. All the Swordfish survived the attack and made for their carrier. But it was a long way back and the dark had now finally descended. *Victorious* shone a searchlight vertically into the sky as a beacon for her returning aircraft and they all managed to land on safely. It was a gallant attack made by a squadron that had barely completed its training, but they had not succeeded in their aim of slowing *Bismarck* so that Tovey could catch her. The great battleship was unscathed.

At this point, it seemed that it must only be a matter of time before *Bismarck* succumbed to the superior numbers of the Royal Navy. Warships were diverted from their escort duties all over the North Atlantic and were converging on *Bismarck*'s position, which was being continually updated by reports from *Suffolk*. Individually, none of the battleships or battlecruisers was a match for *Bismarck*, and there was no doubt that one or two would be severely damaged, if not sunk, but it would be impossible for *Bismarck* to defeat all the ships that were descending on her. Later that night, however, fortune confounded Admiral Tovey and the Admiralty in London.

Admiral Wake-Walker had allowed his three ships, *Suffolk*, *Norfolk* and *Prince of Wales*, to take up a position to the east of *Bismarck*, so that as she headed south they were on her port quarter. They were sailing in a zigzag pattern as a defence against any U-boat attacks, and every now and then *Suffolk* would lose radar contact with *Bismarck*, but establish it again on the next leg of the zigzag. Two hours after midnight, Lutjens ordered an increase in speed and turned the giant battleship on a new course to the west. Gradually, over a period of an hour, *Bismarck* completed a circle, moving behind *Suffolk* and *Norfolk*, then set a new course of 130 degrees, heading south-east for St-Nazaire. On board *Suffolk* there must have been the assumption that *Bismarck* would shortly appear again on their radar screens, but this time there was no trace. *Suffolk* continued on her course for some time, but there was still no sign. An hour after *Bismarck* started her manoeuvre, *Suffolk* radioed that she had lost contact with the enemy. The error was compounded when Rear Admiral Wake-Walker continued on his course to the south-west, assuming that that was the direction that Lutjens had taken. *Prince of Wales* continued to head south, under orders to join forces with Admiral Tovey, and she too sailed away from *Bismarck*.

On board *Ark Royal*, as dawn broke on 25 May, we heard that contact had been lost. It was not going to be easy to locate her again. Visibility was decreasing and a gale was blowing. *Renown* was taking seas solidly over her forecastle and speed had to be reduced to 21 knots. Anti-submarine patrols took off when it seemed that visibility would be lifting and the crews would be able to see something. Twice during the day Swordfish had to be recalled because of low visibility. I didn't fly that day: my scheduled patrols were both cancelled because of the weather. Heavy rain clouds came down at a speed of 50 miles an hour, blotting out the horizon over wide arcs. At times the rain squalls were so bad that returning Swordfish could not see the flight deck and had to circle, hoping for a break in the weather for a few minutes so that they could put down. It was an outstanding test of endurance and skill on the part of the pilots.

There was increasing speculation over where the German battleship had got to. Underneath the chart room in the island a briefing room was in almost permanent session as people wandered in to find out the latest news, and there was an active discussion about when, and if, we would be asked to go into action. In the absence of any hard information, specu-lation filled the vacuum; people even wondered if *Bismarck* would try to head, not for St-Nazaire, but for the Mediterranean to strengthen the Italian navy. While Force H was at sea in the Atlantic there would be little to stop her from bombarding Gibraltar.

I have to say that, while I was aware that all this speculation was going on, like most of the Swordfish pilots I was largely concerned about the prospect of flying while the weather was as bad as it was. Take-off and landing called for good judgement and strong nerves, and flying the planes through such strong winds and thick clouds was arduous. The observers had to be spot on with their navigation as well. Flying through rain and wind in the open cockpits of the Swordfish was also tough. I saw many pilots and observers helped out of their cockpits by the deck crew because they were so stiff from the cold. But without question the possibility of flying against *Bismarck* was also at the back of my mind and I knew that it was going to be no picnic.

Since the manoeuvre to throw off *Suffolk* and *Norfolk* had been perfectly executed, Admiral Lutjens ought to have been feeling extremely confident. Yet this was not the case. Remarkably, he had no idea that he had managed to shake off his pursuers and so continued eastwards in ignorance of his increasing safety. Because of this, he then made an exceptional error of judgement. Three hours after *Suffolk* signalled that she had lost contact with *Bismarck*, Lutjens signalled to his superiors that two cruisers and a battleship continued to maintain contact. No one knows why this message was sent, or what led Lutjens to believe that his turn to the east had not succeeded in fooling *Suffolk*.

His error was compounded two hours later when he sent another, much longer message, lasting 36 minutes, that gave a brief history of events since his first contact with the cruisers in the Denmark Strait. He stressed that the British ships were fitted with very good radar (he was so impressed with it that he overestimated its range by 20 per cent) and that his own had failed with the first salvoes from his main gun turrets. The signal concluded with the fact that he had detached *Prinz Eugen* to continue the mission on her own.

The German navy had its own listening posts in France and had been able to pick up and decode the enormous amount of signal traffic between British ships and the Admiralty since the first sighting of *Bismarck*. They knew a great deal – more than Lutjens did, in fact – about the positions of the warships hunting him. After his first signal to them they advised him that he had in fact lost his pursuers. They knew this because there had been no more signals from *Suffolk* after she communicated that she had lost contact. It remains a mystery why the wireless room in *Bismarck* had not also noticed this and reported it. In addition, Lutjens and everyone on board *Bismarck* believed that they had been exchanging fire with *King George V*, but the German navy HQ was aware that it was *George V*'s sister ship, the newly commissioned *Prince of Wales*.

Tragically for Lutjens, the information that he had lost them was not received until after his second message and the damage was done. It was these signals that enabled the Admiralty and the ships at sea to work out where *Bismarck* was. Again, those in *Bismarck* were ignorant of this. Why Lutjens sent the signals will never be known, but it is even more perplexing why he felt the need to send such a long signal, describing the previous day's events in such detail. He must have been aware that the German navy was intercepting British signals and would thus have a very good idea of the state of play. It is possible that Lutjens had suffered some sort of emotional collapse.

From the British point of view, he had sunk *Hood*, damaged *Prince of Wales* and now we had lost contact with his ship. I don't think anyone in either the navy or the Admiralty in London was feeling very happy, or very confident. Admiral Tovey had even taken the Home Fleet in the wrong direction, mistakenly calculating the coordinates from the results of the direction-finding stations. Error was being compounded by error.

Admiral Lutjens, however, must have seen it differently. This victory over the Royal Navy was not his main mission. Given command by Hitler of the biggest and finest ship in the German navy specifically in order to bring carnage to the Atlantic, his battle with *Hood* and *Prince of Wales* was a failure on his part because its consequences were that he now had to abandon his mission and beat it back to port. Even though we would see it as a huge propaganda success for the Germans, the latest public sign that the Royal Navy was losing its grip, for Lutjens his arrival in St-Nazaire for repairs would be nothing short of a humiliating retreat. Perhaps his long signal was motivated by a desire to smooth the path for himself on his return.

This is the only reasonable explanation for his actions, and I think it is borne out by accounts of the speech that he made to the crew of *Bismarck* at midday on the 25th. He wanted to sum up the situation and confirm officially what most of them already informally knew: that they were heading for a French port. It was an opportunity to tell the truth about the situation and give a real boost to the crew's morale. Those young men in *Bismarck* really needed some leadership at that moment; they needed officers like our Captain Maund in the *Ark*, or Rear Admiral Somerville, who could send some slightly rude signals to each other at the drop of a hat. Sadly for them, Lutjens was not in the same mould. Instead, he predicted that they would face yet another battle and that they would fight until the gun barrels grew red and the last shell had been fired. He then ended by saying that the question for them as sailors now was victory or death. As a young man in wartime, seeing colleagues and friends disappear on a mission, I knew that I never thanked anybody for reminding me that I too might die. The situation was made bearable only by ignoring that uncomfortable fact as much as possible, and by concentrating on the here and now. It was useless to worry about the future, so you just didn't think about it. I can sympathize with the young crew of *Bismarck*, many of whom had come straight out of training school. Listening to their admiral talk about death or glory must have been intensely depressing. Their morale plummeted, as did everybody's on the ship. Even the officers started walking about with unbuttoned lifejackets.

Something was clearly going wrong on the bridge of *Bismarck* that day, because an hour later Captain Ernst Lindemann made a second broadcast, in which he tried to repair the damage done by Lutjens. Lindemann wanted to lift the crew, so he told them that they would put one over on the enemy and soon reach a French port. This helped slightly, and confirmation that *Bismarck* had lost her pursuers also had a positive effect. As the day continued, optimism increased. *Bismarck* had seen no sign of any of our planes or warships for the whole day: it must have seemed that her chances of making it to safety were increasing hour by hour, as in fact they were.

There was other good news. Divers had managed to enter the flooded part of the bow section and manually open some valves so that 100 tons more fuel oil were available. Also, engineers had carried out some remedial work to the machinery affected by the flooding of one of the port boiler rooms so that an adequate supply of distilled water was available to all the high-pressure boilers. These measures did not fundamentally change the situation, but they alleviated problems that might have slowed *Bismarck* even further. They also helped boost morale, serving to reaffirm to the crew that their fate was still in their own hands. The day ended without further incident.

Early in the morning of 26 May the captain made another announcement. 'We have now passed most of Ireland on our way to St-Nazaire,' he said. 'Around noon we will be in the

U-boats' operational area and within range of German aircraft. We can count on the appearance of Condor aircraft after that.' This message seemed to confirm the captain's original upbeat broadcast and cheers were heard around the ship. The crew could have been forgiven for thinking that they had outrun the British navy.

Then, later on in the morning of the 26th, as *Bismarck* steamed ahead towards safety, her alarm claxons started rattling and the tannoy announced that there was an aircraft on the port beam. Flying in and out of the clouds was a Catalina flying boat. The noise of the anti-aircraft guns firing once more was a rude shock to all on board – they knew instantly that they had again been discovered by their enemy. Their thirty-one hours of hope had finished. The radio room picked up the signal that the Catalina was even now transmitting, then half an hour later another aircraft came into view. This was a more ominous sight. The aircraft had wheels, not floats, which indicated that there was an aircraft carrier within flying range. If there was a carrier, then there would be other surface units also. Where were they – ahead or behind? And would they be able to make an interception before the Luftwaffe appeared in the skies above them? *Bismarck* was now just 700 nautical miles from St-Nazaire – fewer than twelve hours from safety.

Back on *Ark Royal*, the information that several direction-finding stations in the UK had picked up a radio signal from *Bismarck* and the position lines they had established were broadcast to the fleet. This was not an ideal fix, because the lines were almost parallel to each other, but it did confirm that the battleship had changed course to the south-east and neither returned to Greenland nor continued into the middle of the Atlantic.

At midday on the 25th I was informed that plans were

being prepared to search for *Bismarck* the next day, starting at daybreak. The air staff started looking at three patterns that would cover a range of options depending on *Bismarck*'s estimated speed, from a top speed of 25 knots to as slow as 16 knots; the plans would also take into account the possibility that the ship would make a wide detour to the south before finally heading for St-Nazaire. At that time we had no idea that she was damaged, or suffering a fuel problem, and were still not aware that *Bismarck* and *Prinz Eugen* had separated.

The flight schedules and crew rosters were pinned up outside the wardroom and in the squadron offices later that afternoon, and from them I deduced that we were going to make our first search at 0700 the next day, over an area of 140 miles by 90, and it was expected that we ought to have made contact by 0800. If we drew a blank there would be a second search at 1300, then a third later in the afternoon if that also failed. I would learn my particular search area at the briefing in the morning.

The stormy weather, however, did not abate. By the end of the day we were punching into a north-westerly gale and also running into a strong southerly current. Our speed was cut to 17 knots and it seemed that we wouldn't reach our desired flying-off position by 0700. Would *Bismarck* slip ahead of us? Our chances of intercepting her seemed to be diminishing.

Next morning, 26 May, *Ark Royal* was running into very high seas and wisps of spray were reaching as high as the bridge. The first dawn anti-submarine patrol was cancelled. The navigation officer was sent to measure the movement of the flight deck and he reported that it was 56 feet. This seemed impossible. No aircraft had ever been flown from the deck of a carrier in such weather. No pilot would jump at the chance to land on a runway that was rising and falling over 50 feet just as the aircraft touched down, but that was what we were being asked to do. The conditions were noted in the ship's report of proceedings, the daily diary of events on board, as 'extremely severe and entailing a great hazard to aircraft.' I think that says it all.

Ten Swordfish were going to make the first search and they were brought up on the lifts from the hangar decks. We had to get extra ratings to help the normal deck crew hold the aircraft down in the gale-force winds, which were gusting at Force 7. Combined with our speed into it, the fitters and the riggers were struggling with winds of 50 miles an hour over the flight deck. The whole ship was covered in spray and the *Ark* was digging into the Atlantic waves, which were beginning to break green over the flight deck, 63 feet up from the waterline.

Taking off from the plunging deck I formed up, then flew off to my assigned search area. Radiating from the *Ark,* each Swordfish would patrol a small segment of a rectangular area that would cover the whole 180 degrees to the west for a depth of 70 miles. I would be in the air for around three and a half hours. On the northern boundary of the search area there was some overlap, with searches being carried out by two Catalinas from Coastal Command – long-range twin-engined flying boats that were operating out of Northern Ireland.

At about 1050, the wireless office in the *Ark* intercepted a signal from one of the Catalinas saying that they had spotted *Bismarck* about 50 miles to the west, within the area being searched by the Swordfish. There was enormous excitement at this news, and this increased when, twenty minutes later, one of our Swordfish reported that she too had a battleship in sight, giving the same position as that of the Catalina. There was almost no doubt now, although the observer of the Swordfish, Sub-Lieutenant Elias from 810 Squadron, was careful to say 'battleship' – he was still not certain it was *Bismarck*. He was aware that *Bismarck* and *Prinz Eugen*, and *Scharnhorst* as well, actually had very similar silhouettes, so he was still uncertain which ship he had spotted. He was quite right: you must report back only what you can be sure of.

We still did not know that *Prinz Eugen* had separated from *Bismarck*, or indeed that *Scharnhorst* had not secretly put to sea. The standard drill in this situation was that, once a sighting had been made, the Swordfish in the adjacent search area would also attempt to respond to the signal and make contact. We now had two Swordfish identifying the target and there was no doubt in most people's minds that we had finally located *Bismarck* again, though it was yet to be confirmed. I continued to patrol my area until it was time to head back to the *Ark* to make an extremely difficult landing on the plunging deck. Surely, I thought, it cannot get worse than this. I found, of course, that the *Ark* was in full swing as a result of the sighting of *Bismarck*.

We could not afford to lose her this time. Six more Swordfish had already been fitted with long-range tanks to take over the job of shadowing as soon as the target had been found. Two of these now took off to relieve the crew that had found her and the other one that had joined them as back-up. They were having a hard job of it, as they were being fired on by the ship whenever they popped out of cloud, and the fire was accurate and concentrated. It made the job of identification that much harder. Meanwhile, the other Swordfish that had been searching were returning to the *Ark* to land on. It was a hazardous business, as the deck was still pitching wildly, and one aircraft was caught by the rising stern and swatted like a fly, its undercarriage crushed beneath it and its lower wing buckled. Fortunately, although the crew were shaken and stirred, they were not badly hurt. The broken plane caused a big hold-up until the wreckage could be pushed overboard so that the rest of the patrol could land, some of them probably flying on their last teaspoonful of petrol because of the delay.

The two Swordfish that had actually spotted the brute we were hunting arrived back, finally relieved by the two long-range Swordfish, and their pilots and observers were hustled into the bridge to be interrogated by the senior officers. They were still not prepared to say categorically that the ship they had seen was *Bismarck*.

'Did you see more than one ship?' they were asked.

'No, there was just the one.'

'Could you say what it was?'

'I think it was *Bismarck*, but her silhouette was more like *Prinz Eugen*.'

'Was there a gap between the funnel and the bridge?'

'No, there was not.'

It was never going to be anything more than inconclusive, but Rear Admiral Somerville was pressing for answers, as was everyone else in the Home Fleet and the Admiralty. The captain of *Ark Royal* sent a message back to Somerville in *Renown*: 'There is only one enemy ship. The evidence favours her being the *Prinz Eugen*. I am sure, however, she is the *Bismarck*.'

So the die was cast. It was a gamble with very high stakes, and I am glad that I did not have to commit myself.

At this point, it became clear to everybody in the *Ark*, and in Force H, from Admiral Somerville down to the engineers in the *Ark*'s boiler room, that unless aircraft from *Ark Royal* could reduce the enemy's speed, *Bismarck* could not be over-hauled by our battleships until she was well within the range of bombers from the French coast, which would be around midday the following day. An extra complication, of which we were unaware at the time but which was causing added anxiety, was that Admiral Tovey, pursuing *Bismarck* in his flagship *King George V*, was running very low on fuel.

This problem had been compounded by the navigation officer in *King George V* having made an error in his calculations. He had arrived at a position, based on the radio fixes supplied to him by the Admiralty, which seemed to show that *Bismarck* was heading north. Admiral Tovey took this as evidence that Lutjens was going to try to make it back through the Norwegian Sea and signalled all the ships under his command to turn north. The Admiralty, in the meantime, had carried out their own calculations and come to the correct conclusion. It took some time to persuade Tovey that he was wrong, and by the time he realized his error and changed course yet again to the east, he was 150 nautical miles astern of *Bismarck* and incapable of making up the distance. In truth, it was the *Ark* or nothing.

I certainly didn't know about Admiral Tovey's mistake. I was getting some food and a hot drink, but it was clear to me that we were preparing to make a torpedo attack. It didn't really matter what the target was or how important: the same urgency and anticipation spread throughout the ship. Even in the engine room, the stokers and engineers would be told that they needed to be ready to manoeuvre the ship for flying operations. They would be told through the intercom what was happening, and even on a ship as big as the *Ark* news spreads very quickly. Aircraft were being overhauled and refuelled in the hangar deck. Torpedoes on their trolleys were wheeled forward, ready to be fastened underneath the fuselage once the Swordfish were brought up to the flight deck and ranged aft. Extra ratings were mobilized to assist on the careering flight deck. Then a briefing about the expected attack on *Bismarck* got under way in the observers' office. Pilots were hastily informed of the orders for the mission by their squadron writers and told their aircraft and their order in the take-off.

I was not selected for flying on this mission, which was being led by Lt Commander Stewart-Moore, the CO of 820 Squadron. The attack, for some reason, was being made up from 820 and 810 Squadrons – I don't know why, but it meant that, as a member of 818, I was not included in the plans. It was pointless to protest, as the operation clearly had a momentum of its own and had been put into preparation while I was still on patrol.

Meanwhile, *Bismarck* was still heading east, 30 miles south of *Ark Royal* and the rest of Force H. Admiral Somerville on *Renown* ordered *Sheffield* to steam towards *Bismarck* and make contact, then to continue shadowing her. The signal was sent to *Sheffield* via Morse code using an Aldis signal lamp. The Admiralty was also informed of the order, in a coded radio signal that was simultaneously copied to *Ark Royal*.

The prevailing wind was from the west, and every time aircraft were landed on or took off, the *Ark* had to change course and steam westwards. Each time this occurred, *Bismarck*, steaming east at around 22 knots, would increase the distance between them, and the *Ark* had to race to catch up. It was a long time since the *Ark* had had a major refit and she had steamed over 100,000 miles in the interim. At full speed the centre propeller shaft vibrated badly and hatch screws regularly had to be retightened as they shook loose. But we believed that the *Ark* would never let us down.

By 1400 the Swordfish that were going to make the strike against *Bismarck* were ready, but the weather was no better. The wind was still high, there was a lot of rain and visibility was low. Thick cloud started at 800 feet and the frequent rain squalls reduced the poor visibility to almost zero. But there were occasional clear patches, and at 1415 the aircraft were brought up on the lifts and the torpedoes were run aft along the flight deck to them to be hoisted up into the cradles underneath the fuselage. The engines were started and at 1445 the flight deck officer reported all ready. The flagship made an executive signal and the first of the Swordfish, with the CO of 820 Squadron in command, started its run down the deck. By 1500 they were all in the air, formed up in their sub-flights and turning south to meet the enemy. I was merely watching from the sidelines, standing near the bridge, with nothing to do but wait.

13
The Attack

I saw fifteen Swordfish aircraft take off from the deck of *Ark Royal*, still not certain whether they were heading for *Bismarck* or *Prinz Eugen*, but within a few minutes one of them, flown by Nigel Gardner, had to return to make an emergency landing, its torpedo still fastened under the fuselage. The plane was heavy, with a full load of fuel as well as the torpedo, but its Pegasus engine was failing and there was no time to wait to jettison the weapon safely. It landed without any damage to the undercarriage and was quickly taken down in the lift for work to be done on the engine. There were still fourteen planes flying towards the target, however. It had been part of the original plan of attack to fly off a section of Fulmar fighters to create a diversion and confuse the anti-aircraft-gun controllers in *Bismarck*, but the weather conditions had been so foul that this had been abandoned. The weather was still very bad over the target, and the rain squalls that continually engulfed the Swordfish cut visibility to almost zero.

A Swordfish in the lead section was equipped with air-to-surface radar, capable of informing the observer of the presence of a ship and its bearing from the aircraft. Twenty miles from the expected position of *Bismarck*, the airborne radar indicated a substantial target. The flight leader signalled to the rest of the Swordfish that they were going to descend through the cloud and make an attack. Down they went, exiting the cloud layer to find the warship practically dead ahead. They flew lower and sought out their prearranged bearings from which to drop their torpedoes. There was no anti-aircraft fire, and the guns of the warship continued to remain silent as the first and then the second section dropped their torpedoes. The ship was travelling fast, the hot exhaust gases and hints of smoke whipping away from her twin funnels as she steamed in an easterly direction. As the torpedoes entered the water, the ship rapidly went to full speed ahead, seeming almost to leap forward in the water, and at the same time she turned her bows in an attempt to comb the tracks of the torpedoes heading towards her. There were two explosions at a distance as two of the unreliable Duplex warheads exploded harmlessly in the water.

Several torpedo tracks seemed to travel underneath the ship, but there was no explosion. Three more explosions came in her wake and then, as the last section came into the attack, the observer in the lead aircraft saw that a signal light was flashing from the bridge. It was repeating the pennant number for HMS *Sheffield*. Captain Larcom, the cruiser's captain, successfully conned *Sheffield* through the tracks of the remaining torpedoes without suffering any injury and resumed his course to make contact with *Bismarck*, as he had been ordered to do by Rear Admiral Somerville two hours earlier. The final section of Swordfish pulled away and, as they flew over *Sheffield*, a ship that had been a constant companion of *Ark Royal* since the Norwegian campaign and should have been easily recognized, the TAG in the last Swordfish signalled, 'Sorry for the kipper.' I don't know what went on in the minds of the Swordfish crews as they flew back. They must have had a sense of utter failure, tempered by relief that they had not sunk *Sheffield*. The emotions of the crew on board *Sheffield* also do not bear thinking about. The language was probably strong enough to melt the deck head.

The fourteen Swordfish returned to *Ark Royal*. The three torpedoes that remained slung under the fuselages of the last section of aircraft had to be jettisoned before it was safe for them to land on the pitching flight deck. One of them failed to release – I remember how, when the Swordfish carrying it landed on, this particular torpedo finally came free from the fuselage and careered up and down the deck with sparks flying off it. In a moment the flight deck was deserted. I looked up from where I was standing in the deck level on the starboard side at the stern to watch the torpedo rolling from side to side. The commander air literally screamed over the tannoy: 'Torpedo party report on deck and catch that bloody torpedo!' It was one time when we all thanked God that the Duplex pistols in the warheads were so unreliable.

There were naturally some rather hard questions asked of the flight leader and the other pilots as they squeezed into the briefing room. Their attack had almost proved an utter disaster, at a time when the *Ark* and her Swordfish were in such a crucial position in the action against *Bismarck*. Feelings were running very high, and one observer reported to the operations officer, 'It was a perfect attack: right height, right range, right cloud cover, right speed and the wrong fucking ship!'

In their defence, the flight had not been told about *Sheffield*'s presence. Somerville's signal to her and to the Admiralty sending her forward to trail *Bismarck*, which had been merely copied to the *Ark*, had not been deciphered in time. None the less, it was extremely worrying that eleven of the pilots had mistaken a very familiar 9,000-ton cruiser with two funnels for a 50,000-ton battleship with one. Force H's report to Admiral Tovey about the success of the attack made no mention at all of the near destruction of a British cruiser, stating merely that *Bismarck* had received no hits.

Time was now running out and we had to get a second strike in if we were to have any chance of stopping *Bismarck* or salvaging our reputations. There was a serious concern that we didn't make a mess of this again. By now we were under no illusions about how important this was to the navy, and to Churchill, and we felt under enormous pressure to pull it off. But we knew that if we did find the right target it would not be like attacking *Sheffield* again. *Bismarck* was a powerful and well-defended battleship. The previous attack by 825 Squadron from *Victorious* had shown that she could just shrug off direct hits, and the anti-aircraft fire would be very hot indeed.

I knew that we would be making another strike that day – I had been expecting it even if the first one had managed to attack *Bismarck*. We were short of available aircraft, so many of those that had just returned would have to be used again. This time the attack was to be led by Tim Coode, my CO in 818, and I was to fly; in fact, I was second aircraft in his section. Amidst all the tumult, I felt quietly proud. While the Swordfish were being refuelled and re-armed, we met and had a final briefing about the mission. I was told that the *Ark* would be moving closer to *Bismarck*. We would need to find *Sheffield* first and she would give us a bearing on to the target. By the time we were in the air above her, it was expected that she would be in visual touch with *Bismarck*. In fact, she saw her on her radar at about 1745. There would also be some of our destroyers between the *Ark* and *Sheffield*, and we had to be aware of them. *Sheffield* would be making her call sign on the radio to help us in direction-finding, but we would also have some of the Swordfish fitted with radar with us.

The CO told us that he wanted to change the fuses on our torpedo warheads from the magnetic Duplex ones to contact pistols. Eleven torpedoes had been fired at *Sheffield* and not a single one had scored a hit. In particular, some of them had exploded when they hit the water, and Coode was responding to the general feeling that these magnetic pistols were too unreliable. In fact, I learned that both he and Stewart-Moore went to see the captain of the *Ark* and insisted that they be allowed to fit the old-fashioned contact pistols instead of the magnetic ones. Obviously the captain had agreed, because the contact pistols were fitted. This meant that we had to get direct hits against the hull in order for them to be effective, and we had to set the running depth of the torpedoes for a ship the size of *Bismarck*, which ought to have been 22 feet. There was some disagreement about this because of the weather, which had started to deteriorate again. If the battleship was pitching as severely as the *Ark* was, then a torpedo set to run as deep as her keel might pass underneath. In the end a decision was taken to set the running depth at a shallow 10 feet.

The Swordfish were brought up to the flight deck and I went out via the side ladder on the starboard side. The weather was atrocious. On the flight deck, out of any shelter from the side gallery, or by the bridge, the wind hit you like a hammer, threatening to knock you down. The flight deck was still heaving and visibility was very bad. The deck crews were really struggling with the aircraft, spray was coming over the side and waves were breaking over the front of the flight deck. The CO had decided that the first three aircraft would be from 818 Squadron: he would lead and I and another pilot, Sub-Lieutenant Eric Dixon-Childe, would be his wingmen. Dixon-Childe and I had gone through training school together; he was a quiet lad, more of an introvert while I was the gregarious type. By picking us, Lt Commander Coode had picked two hostilities-only recruits, each with less than 250 hours' flying time. Why he did this I cannot say, but it was his call. I was second to take off, so climbed up into the cockpit, with Dusty Miller and Hayman settling in behind me. They had been briefed as well, and it was a simple procedure. We were to stay close and watch for hand signals after contact with *Sheffield*.

The rigger was not quite as boisterous as he normally was. A lot of stokers and other deck hands had been gathered round the planes to make sure the aircraft didn't slide about, particularly as the *Ark* headed into the wind. As she turned broadside on to the waves, there was a real danger that she would heel and Swordfish could slide sideways. Standing close to the propeller and turning that heavy starting handle was going to be a tough job on a day like this. The flight deck officer, Commander Pat Stringer, had a rope round his waist and was lashed to the flight deck so that he wouldn't get blown overboard. He was 6 foot 4 inches tall and in a very exposed position, but a lot of the deck crew had the same trouble with the wind and the pitching deck but had to be able to move about.

Stringer was a lifesaver that day. He would signal to start the take-off when he sensed that the ship was at the bottom of a big wave, so that even if I thought that I was taking off downhill, the bows would swing up at the last moment and I would be flying above the big Atlantic swell rather than into it. I felt that I was thrown into the air, rather than lifting off, and I was struggling to control the aircraft while the wheels were still on the deck, watching for a sideways gust that might push me into the bridge, praying that we would clear the tops of the mountainous waves.

It was hard work in the air as well: the winds were gusting and there was very low cloud, as low as 600 feet, with some strong updrafts. We were thrown about, and I fought the plane through the turbulence. It was cold, the wind was fierce, but we had no need to worry about the drift because we did not have far to fly. I was fighting the wind all the time, circling was like riding a roller coaster, hitting a sudden headwind, then blown sideways, then thrown forward by a tailwind.

Eventually we formed up over *Renown* and headed off south into a heavy cloud of rain, looking for *Sheffield*. *Bismarck* was just 38 miles distant, on a bearing of 125 degrees. All my training – at Abbotsinch, in the practices we had carried out from the *Ark* as we approached Gibraltar, and in the interminable hours that I had been ploughing the air above the oceans – was now focused on an attack on the biggest, most heavily armed warship at sea.

I was in the thick of it now, well aware of how important a mission this was. For the last two days every single person in the *Ark* had known what was up – and that it was down to us to somehow stop *Bismarck*. I would not say that responsibility weighed heavily on me. I was concentrating on staying close to my CO, keeping an eye on my instruments and suppressing the butterflies in my stomach.

We found *Sheffield* and this time we recognized her. I followed Coode round her and she signalled by lamp that *Bismarck* was 12 miles further on. Dusty Miller relayed the heading to me. We were at low altitude, about 500 feet, and Commander Coode signalled us to start our climb, passing through thick cloud. It was difficult to keep in touch with each other. At 6,000 feet we broke cloud, there was a big drop in temperature and in about six minutes ice was forming on the leading edges of the wings and the main struts, causing us to lose power and stability. This was worrying, because we could not allow too much ice to build up. I wondered how long we could go before needing to descend to some warmer air. Even though I was in clear sky with blanket cloud beneath, after ten minutes shells burst all around us with black clouds of smoke. We knew then that *Bismarck* was nearby and we assumed she had found us on her radar.

Commander Coode signalled to form a line astern, then he dived down through the cloud. We tried to go down together, but the cloud density was such that it was impossible to maintain formation. Watching the altimeter, I knew that I should be clear at 600 feet. We were gaining speed and I was worried that my plane, with a ton of torpedo slung underneath, would not stand the strain when levelling out. The altimeter unwound – 600, 400, how low was this cloud? – then, suddenly breaking out of it at 300 feet, I realized we were diving at the sea, but I managed to pull out perfectly, the struts and frames taking the pressure. There on my starboard beam was *Bismarck*. I had overshot to the west so she was about 2 miles away, and I turned right towards her. Even at this distance the brute seemed enormous to me – this was a huge ship, much bigger than the *Ark*.

I realized then that I was on my own. There was no sign of the other two, who must have come out of the cloud well ahead of me. I did not have a lot of time to take in the scene because the guns started firing at me almost immediately I popped into sight, and there was a red glow in the clouds ahead of me, about 100 yards away, as the anti-aircraft shells exploded. As I left the cloud, the gunfire was repeated, two bursts at a time but always ahead of me, throwing up walls of water. As I descended, there were two explosions to my right and below, which shook the aircraft severely and knocked us violently 90 degrees off our course. I struggled to turn us back towards the target, looking anxiously for any signs that we had been hit or that the engine had been damaged. The two boys in the back seemed OK and we continued flying, the Pegasus roaring away, the Swordfish still responding to the controls – but it was getting decidedly unhealthy.

The Germans in their big battleship were trying to kill me,

and it was not pleasant. I continued to drop height, with *Bismarck* looming bigger, some of her guns flashing from amidships with vivid orange flames now aimed at us. The big explosions that had blown us about did not follow us down to this height, but the smaller cannon and machine-gun fire, with their red tracer bullets, were now coming towards us in a torrent. I thought about what I had noticed when I had been firing from the machine-gun platforms on the *Ark* at the Italian torpedo bombers: the lower the target, the harder it was to hold in your sights, particularly if it was below the horizon. I went down as close to wave-top height as I dared. The sea was rough and I did not want to be caught by a wave, so I levelled out at around 50 feet, probably just a tad lower. I was not sure how effective this was going to be because the tracer seemed to be very focused.

In our briefing in the *Ark* we had discussed coordinating our attack, the first three flights coming in on the port beam from various bearings, with the second wave doing the same on the starboard side. This would help to confuse the anti-aircraft fire and would also make it difficult for *Bismarck* to manoeuvre into the torpedo tracks. But it seemed that we had got badly separated in the high cloud; it was utter confusion. I felt that every gun on the ship was aiming at me. It was heading towards us, the lazily spinning tracer from scores of guns coming at us like hail. I do not know how I managed to keep flying into it: every instinct was screaming at me to duck, turn away, do anything – an impulse that it was hard to fight off. But I held on and we got closer and closer. I went down, as low as I dared, though even that took an act of will to overcome my fear of hitting the rough sea. At training school I had been taught to assess the speed of the ship and lay off my aim by using a simple marked rod mounted horizontally along the top of the cockpit. But the nearer I got the larger the target became, so I decided to aim for the bow.

Then I heard Dusty Miller shouting in my ear, 'Not yet, not yet!' and I thought, 'Has he gone mad? What is he doing?' I turned and realized that he was leaning out of the cockpit, looking down at the sea, trying to prevent me from dropping the torpedo on to the crest of a wave, where it would bounce off or dive deep, either way knocked off any course that I might have fired it on.

We were getting closer and closer, the ship was getting bigger and bigger, and I thought, 'Bloody hell, what are you waiting for?'

Then he said, 'Let her go, Jock,' and I pressed the button on the throttle. Dusty yelled, 'I think we have got a runner.'

When a Swordfish is suddenly relieved of the weight of a torpedo, it naturally rises in the air, but above us was a stream of bullets and shells. I did what I could to hold the plane down, avoiding the temptation to bank into a sharp turn, which would give the gunners in *Bismarck* a bigger silhouette to aim at.

I held the aircraft down and went in to a full left-rudder turn at full throttle, thinking, 'Let's get out of here.' The gun-fire pursued us, but I kept low for 3,000 yards, praying that nothing would hit us, desperately wanting to get into the clouds but knowing that it would be fatal to climb too early. Finally I thought it would be OK to try to find some height. As we rose above 300 feet two bigger shells again exploded, this time to our rear, but that was all.

I shouted to Dusty to give me a course back to the *Ark*, but I think it was beyond him. 'Find one of those radar Swordfish and follow him,' he said. I spotted one from 810 Squadron, flown by Godfrey-Faussett, and got into line astern with him. Visibility was getting very poor now and the *Ark* was sending out a radio beacon signal. When we came round to make our final approach the deck was still heaving up and down – sometimes it looked like a steel wall in front of you, then all you could see were the quarterdeck and the propellers churning away. Commander Stringer was still secured by a line tied to a stanchion, ready to wave me away at the last moment, but I made it back, and there was nothing more welcoming than the thump of the wheels on the deck and the clatter of the hook catching on the arrestor wire. Miraculously, we had all returned, but one of the Swordfish from 820 Squadron, flown by Sub-Lieutenant Swanton, had 175 splinter holes in it from a close shellburst. The pilot and the TAG also had wounds, fortunately not very serious, from the shell splinters. A few other aircraft had some minor damage from shellbursts.

When we had landed and the rigger clambered up to the cockpit, making notes of any maintenance or repairs that needed doing, we eased ourselves out of the cockpit. I was stiff and sore, as though I had been flying for a day, and I was completely exhausted, almost light-headed from fatigue and adrenalin. We assembled in the bridge for debriefing and it was obvious that the attack had become broken up and disorganized by the weather. It was difficult to piece together the various accounts from the pilots and the observers into anything that made sense. Very few of us were willing to make any claims. I for one knew that I had not lingered over *Bismarck* for the one and a half minutes it would have taken for my torpedo to hit her and to allow Dusty to follow its track, and I suspect that most of the other pilots behaved in the same way. I had no idea if my torpedo had found its target or not. The only thing I could remember through the stress of the attack was that *Bismarck* had seemed to me to be turning away from my attack, rather than towards it. We told our debriefing officers what we could and left it to the air staff.

We went below, where the cooks had made us a special hot meal, but we couldn't eat it – the strain and tension had robbed us of any appetite. Fear inevitably leaves its mark. We all sat around and wondered how it was that we had survived, even those who had received hits. A cigarette and several pink gins were what we craved, then the oblivion of sleep. We were told that visibility was too poor for another attack that night, but that there would be another mission the next morning, led again by Coode, me and Dixon-Childe. If this was calculated to ensure we got a good night's sleep, it failed. Someone remarked that the Light Brigade had only been asked to do it once.

By the time we had finished our debriefing, two signals had been sent to Rear Admiral Somerville in *Renown* and forwarded to Admiral Tovey, struggling to reach *Bismarck* in *King George V*. The first signal said that one torpedo had definitely hit *Bismarck* amidships, and then the second one, sent twenty minutes later after more planes had landed, stated that another hit had been obtained aft. It was very hard to be certain of anything, and the narrative report that was put together was written in the order in which the attack had been planned, not in the sequence in which it had probably actually taken place. Many flights had been split up in the very thick cloud over *Bismarck* and had attacked in ones and twos over a period of thirty minutes.

What was eventually pieced together was that my flight, led by Lt Commander Coode, probably went in first, joined by another aircraft that had become separated from no. 3 sub-flight. I think we went into the final run-in towards the target with all of us separated, but all attacking the port side, and as we made a getaway a hit was observed from the cockpit of the Swordfish of the third sub-flight, flown by Lieutenant Stanley Keane, who had found himself behind us and had decided to follow us in. According to him the hit was on the port side, about two thirds of the way down from the bows. It could have been mine, but there was no way to tell.

The second sub-flight had also got disorientated in the

cloud and had climbed to 9,000 feet, where they started to get ice forming. Two aircraft got a bearing on *Bismarck* with their radar and went into the attack from the starboard side. They came under concentrated fire from all the guns on that side of the ship, but managed to get away. The third Swordfish of that flight remained in the cloud for some time, then actually returned to *Sheffield* for another bearing. He then came back towards *Bismarck* and made an attack on the port bow, and his crew saw a strike amidships. This must have been the last attack that night because of the time it would have taken him to fly to *Sheffield* and return. The fourth sub-flight and the other aircraft of the third sub-flight met up as they flew out of the cloud, and they saw *Bismarck* firing heavily at the second sub-flight. All four aircraft made an attack from the port side. They came under very heavy, intense shellfire and it was in this attack that Sub-Lieutenant Swanton's aircraft was riddled with shell splinters and he was wounded in the arm. The gunfire followed them for almost 7 miles before they escaped.

The fifth sub-flight, another made up of just two aircraft, lost each other and also started to suffer from icing. They descended and found that they had come out of the cloud upwind of *Bismarck*. One of the pilots decided to fly forward to make his approach from the bow, and while he did so he saw a torpedo strike amidships on the starboard side. He reached a position on *Bismarck*'s starboard bow, then flew out for about 5 miles, made a very low-level approach and dropped at about 1,000 yards. The second pilot of the fifth flight tried to make an approach on the starboard quarter, but came under such intense fire that he jettisoned his torpedo. The final flight of the attack, the sixth one, also got lost in the cloud. They too returned to *Sheffield* for a fresh bearing, but on their return opted to remain out of the cloud and flew low to *Bismarck*, attacking on the starboard beam. They were spotted at long range and came under heavy fire. One pilot dropped his torpedo at 2,000 yards, while the other abandoned his attack and returned to the *Ark*, jettisoning his torpedo before landing on.

This, then, was the official narrative – as I say, not really written up in the sequence that the attacks occurred. There had been sighting of two, possibly three, hits, but very little firm confirmation of the exact number. The *Ark* was prepared only to claim two. And it was this that was communicated to Rear Admiral Somerville and the Admiralty. Yet hits were not enough. *Bismarck*'s armour was extremely thick. The Swordfish from 825 Squadron on *Victorious* had seen a hit amidships on *Bismarck*, but she had brushed it off. It wasn't enough to hit her: we needed to cause some serious damage and it seemed that in that aim we had failed.

There were still two long-range Swordfish circling over *Bismarck* when our attack left and they were asked by the *Ark* to stay on station as long as possible to direct a small group of four destroyers on to *Bismarck*. Then indications started to come in that *Bismarck* was in trouble. *Sheffield* reported that the German battleship had slowed down, then that she had changed course and was heading back towards Admiral Tovey's *King George V*, still in hot pursuit 80 miles away. It was hard to ascertain whether this was deliberate, because during this turn *Bismarck* had fired a salvo of her 15in guns at *Sheffield* from a range of 9 miles, and although *Sheffield* did not suffer a direct hit, three ratings were killed by shell splinters, with eight others wounded. *Sheffield* broke off the contact and raced away under cover of a smokescreen. Then, an hour and a half later, the two Swordfish that had been trailing *Bismarck* at last, in total darkness, landed on the *Ark* and made their final report. *Bismarck*, they said, after being torpedoed, had made two complete circles and reduced speed. Somerville passed this information on to Admiral Tovey at half past midnight on 27 May.

The attack had worked. For reasons that we still did not know, *Bismarck* had been prevented from running at speed to St-Nazaire. Instead she appeared to be slowing and her course was uncertain. Unless she regained speed and course quickly, Tovey with the two big battleships *Rodney* and *King George V* would still have a chance to catch her. Final confirmation of the crisis that had overwhelmed *Bismarck* was given in a signal by one of the four destroyers, HMS *Zulu*, that had arrived on the scene a little earlier. She signalled that *Bismarck*'s course was fluctuating wildly through 60 degrees to 340. We had got her. It was not a moment too soon. We were just 500 miles from the German air force's French bases and the submarine pens of L'Orient.

I cannot imagine what it must have been like on *Bismarck* that night, and I thank God that I never had a similar experience. A torpedo had hit the ship in the after section on the port side. Some floor plates in the engine room buckled upwards and water started pouring in through the port shaft tunnel. Damage-control parties rushed to the port side to discover that the hole in the side was so big that all the steering rooms had been flooded and the crews had abandoned them. The water in them was rhythmically splashing up and down with the movement of the ship. Seawater was leaking through to the main deck and watertight seals on cable tubes had been damaged, causing water to flood into the upper and lower passageways on the port side of the hull just aft of the rear main gun turret. But these leaks were of minor importance compared to the damage that had been caused to the steering control rooms. The rudders had been jammed at 12 degrees to port, so the ship could not be steered. The room that contained the electric rudder motors and gearing was open to the sea, under the waterline, and when an emergency access hatch was opened, water shot out of it as the stern rose and sank in the rough seas. It was clearly impossible to send men into the room to decouple the motors or carry out any sort of repairs.

Ratings from one of the port gun turrets were ordered to try to seal the hole with a collision mat, but the sea was too rough. The captain tried to overcome the influence of the jammed rudders by varying the speed and direction of the propellers, but *Bismarck* was too long and unwieldy for this to be effective: the strong wind always turned the ship's head back. As the impossibility of repairing the damage dawned on her crew, they also started to absorb the fact that they could no longer hope to avoid another battle with the Royal Navy, this time with the odds very much against them.

They were heading inexorably back over the course that they had just covered, straight towards Admiral Tovey and his flagship, *King George V*, with her eight 14in guns, and *Rodney*, a battleship that, when she was launched in the 1920s, was considered, along with her sister ship *Nelson*, to be the most powerful on the high seas. *Rodney* was armed with nine 16in guns, all mounted on the huge foredeck that stretched out from her armoured bridge. In addition, other warships were steaming to join Tovey's forces. There was little point in *Bismarck* rushing to her fate, so now her speed was reduced to 6 or 7 knots. After midnight, work on repairing the rudder was abandoned and the ship sailed towards the superior forces that were intent on destroying her.

During the night the four destroyers that had been directed to *Bismarck* by *Sheffield* – the three Tribal class, *Cossack*, *Zulu* and *Sikh*, and the Polish *Piorun* – attempted to attack *Bismarck* with torpedoes. They were frustrated by the heavy seas and the still accurate fire of *Bismarck*'s guns. Yet time after time they steamed closer, only to be forced to retreat. At around 0200 they launched star shells to illuminate the target, to indicate the position of the enemy to Admiral Tovey. These and the continual attacks, however, kept *Bismarck*'s crew awake throughout the night, increasing their fatigue and no doubt their despair. They were on board one of the most powerful and modern battleships in the world, yet despite all the technology, the highly advanced gun control, the massive armour plating and the powerful turbines, all had come to nothing. They had set out just a few days ago, the pride of the German navy, with Hitler's blessing. Now, because of a slow, single-engined biplane launched from an aircraft carrier, they were almost impotent.

At 0600 on 27 May, as dawn broke, the destroyers realized that they were dangerously close to *Bismarck* and retreated into the cover of a rain squall. The men in *Bismarck* now waited for our battleships to arrive, but it was not until 0843 that the alarm claxons went off. *King George V* and *Rodney* had arrived, and at 0847 *Rodney* fired a salvo of her massive guns, to be followed a minute later by *King George V*. Within a few minutes, *Rodney* had scored a hit on the forward part of *Bismarck*. Captain Lindemann could neither choose his course nor evade the fire from the British ships, while Tovey could manoeuvre both his battleships and the cruiser *Dorsetshire*, which had joined him, and close the range until even shells from *Rodney*'s secondary armament were exploding on the superstructure of the helpless German warship. The casualties and deaths started to mount. Soon *Norfolk*, whose captain had trailed *Bismarck* from the Greenland Strait only to lose her again the next day, arrived on the scene and started to add her 8in guns to the fusillade that was ripping into the stricken ship.

At 0931 *Bismarck*'s main guns fired their last shells. She started to list to port and fires had broken out along her length, but still the salvoes from *Rodney* and the other ships continued.

I had a disturbed night on the *Ark,* still vividly alert after the fears of the day and anticipating another run into

Bismarck's concentrated anti-aircraft fire. I did not get much sleep and was not particularly hungry at breakfast. The weather was obviously still bad and I did not know what was worse – attempting another hazardous take-off and landing or the prospect of another flight into a storm of tracer. We had been extremely lucky the day before, but surely we could not make another attack and expect to escape without any casualties.

I was scheduled for take-off at 0700 but was up much earlier. Two reconnaissance Swordfish had taken off at 0430, apparently with a great deal of difficulty. The wind had increased again, the night was as black as the inside of a flying boot and spray was washing over the length of the flying deck. The wind was almost a constant 50 knots and when the Swordfish took off into it they rose into the air as if they were on a lift. They were brought forward abreast of the island. If they had taken off from their normal position at the end of the flight deck they would have been airborne so quickly that there was the chance that in the dark they would collide with the bridge or the funnel as the carrier pitched and rolled.

Admiral Tovey's battleships, the destroyers and the cruiser were now known to be in the vicinity, but visibility was so poor that identification was difficult. I hoped that it would be sufficiently improved by the time we arrived over the target. We were told at our briefing about the attacks on *Bismarck* during the night, but that our big warships had not yet made contact with her. Clearly thanks to the damage that we had inflicted yesterday, the battleship would be in no condition to carry out any fast evasive manoeuvres when we attacked, but this might allow her gunnery directors more time to range their fire. That was a very worrying prospect. Lt Commander Coode's plan was that we would attack in groups of three, from whatever direction seemed the most propitious. There were only twelve Swordfish available this morning to mount the attack and they were brought up on deck, but the wind was so strong it was impossible to open the wings and start up the engines. The captain decided that the attack would have to be delayed, so the aircraft were taken down again in the lifts, their wings still folded.

Now it was a question of waiting, and I dozed in a chair until daylight had fully arrived. But the wind and the seas did not abate, so we were told that the Swordfish would be ranged and their engines started while the *Ark* was stern on to the wind, then she would turn her flight deck into the wind for take-off. The Swordfish were lined up and I sat in the cockpit, the engine thundering away in front of me, while I waited for the ship to make its manoeuvre. The Swordfish were temporarily lashed to the deck and more men were brought up from the other squadrons to hold the aircraft. After a particularly steep wave, the captain ordered the helm down. I watched as the flight deck turned to starboard across the fetch of the waves and felt three or four heavy rolls. I saw one Swordfish skitter sideways like a spooked horse, but fortunately it didn't collide with anything, or anyone. I have never seen or heard of a similar manoeuvre carried out by a carrier, before or since. Looking back, the prospects of a disaster were quite high, but the captain pulled it off, and I think it took some marvellous seamanship.

Then the *Ark* slowed, it was my turn to advance the throttle and I was airborne in next to no time. We formed up over *Ark Royal* and, flying at 300 feet, set off. We could see that the battle was now taking place; flashes, and plumes of water and thick black smoke were becoming visible. It was our understanding that Admiral Tovey knew about our planned attack, but with shells flying through the air and the gouts of water from exploding near misses reaching 150 feet into the air, we could not make a sensible torpedo run on to the target. As it was, *Bismarck* was a shocking sight – black and smoking, with crewmen lying or milling around on her decks. We could see pieces of twisted wreckage, a huge gun turret, now all silent, the guns awry, one barrel of a 15in gun pointed almost vertically. There were great holes in her super-structure and a fire blazing amidships where a seaplane crane hung over the rails, blasted from its mounting. She had almost come to a stop, and was rising and falling in the sea like a giant blackened dead thing.

We flew close to *King George V* and the squadron CO signalled by an Aldis lamp to ask for orders. I wanted the shelling to be stopped so that we could go in and launch our torpedoes, to finish the job that we had started the day before – I believe that that is what we all wanted. *Bismarck* was ours if she was anybody's. We circled, waiting for a reply, then Dusty shouted at me, 'Bugger me, Jock, they're shooting at us!'

The flashes of the guns from the 4.5in turrets on the side of *King George V*, which we had all observed, resulted in some shellbursts not on *Bismarck* but in the air around us. God knows what those halfwits were thinking. Dusty said, 'They're flashing a signal telling us to keep away.'

There was no more fire against us and we circled over *Bismarck*, smouldering and smoking, listing to port, pitching in the heavy seas, oil covering the surface of the water around her. I saw that both our battleships had finally stopped firing and were now steaming on a course north, away from *Bismarck*. Tovey's flagship, *King George V,* had finally reached the limit of her available fuel and had to make urgently for port. *Rodney* went with her. In retrospect, I believe it was a strange thing to do while *Bismarck* was still afloat. A heavy cruiser – I now know it was *Dorsetshire* – manoeuvred close to *Bismarck* and fired a couple of torpedoes at her starboard side, then circled and fired another at her port beam.

Our CO led us down to see, I suspect, if we could finally sink this giant beast. We got to a range of about 1,000 yards, flying low with what was now the hulk of *Bismarck* in front of us, and then I saw a sight that has remained etched in my mind ever since. This enormous vessel, over 800 feet long, her gun turrets smashed, her bridge and upper works like a jagged ruin, slowly, frighteningly toppled over, smashing down into the sea, and her great hull was revealed, the plates and bilge keels glistening dark red as the oily sea covered her. Still leaping from her were men, sailors, and there were hundreds more in the sea, some desperately struggling for their lives, some already inert, tossed by the waves as they floated face down. I saw these hundreds of desperate human beings in the water and I was immediately pierced by the knowledge that they had no hope, and that as I flew just 100 feet above them there was nothing that I could do to save even a single one.

We flew back to the *Ark*, and no word was exchanged between me or Dusty or Hayman.

We went into the circuit and waited for the signal to land on. The flight deck was heaving and pitching even more than the previous day, but we all got in without any more aircraft being damaged. As I had just completed my landing and was unbuckling my harness the air-raid rattler went off. A Heinkel bomber appeared out of the clouds and a stick of bombs crashed into the sea about 500 yards from us. We got the Swordfish down in very quick order, because several Heinkel and long-range four-engined Focke Wulf 'Condor' bombers had been seen in the area. We were pretty defenceless. *Sheffield*'s radar had been damaged by the near miss from *Bismarck* and it would have taken some time to get the Fulmar fighters ranged, if it had been possible at all in such weather. It was a real demonstration, if one were needed, of how close *Bismarck* was to the protection of the Luftwaffe and how critical our attack had been. We quickly got the

Swordfish lashed down in the hangar, once more the carrier turned beam on to the sea and we headed south-east back to Gibraltar.

By the afternoon we had found better weather and sunshine broke through on to the flight deck for the first time in days. The next day, the 28th, I was once again flying my Swordfish over the Atlantic, this time on a routine anti-submarine patrol. It was back to normal for me, if that was possible.

Admiral Somerville gave the order for *Ark Royal* to precede the rest of Force H into harbour when we arrived at Gibraltar. As we closed the northern entrance the garrison came out to meet us, in small rowing boats, sailing boats and launches. The merchant ships in the harbour signalled their greetings with sirens and the crews on their decks cheered as we passed slowly down the detached mole to our regular mooring. A band of the Black Watch was playing and there was an almost carnival atmosphere. That night the cooks made a very special effort and served up what they called a 'Swordfish Surprise' – fresh swordfish steaks, purchased straight from one of the fishing boats in La Linea I am sure. I told the CO that in my view they had little alternative: it was either that or 'Bismarck Kippers'. The party in the wardroom that night was truly staggering.

On board the *Ark* there was a great deal of satisfaction about what we had accomplished, and a general feeling that if the squadrons on *Illustrious* could pull off the great attack on Taranto, then we in the *Ark* had shown what we could do with *Bismarck*. We had, so the stories in the newspapers and newsreels had it, avenged *Hood* and saved the honour of the Royal Navy. There was also a feeling, held privately, that we in the Fleet Air Arm had been robbed of our rightful victory by the sailors in their battleships and that Admiral Tovey had deliberately not wanted us to take any further share of the triumph over *Bismarck*.

I don't know that there is any truth in that last assertion, but it was true that our intervention at the eleventh hour had been the one thing that stopped *Bismarck* reaching the haven of St-Nazaire. Another few hours and it is clear that the Heinkel and Focke Wulf that we saw would have been joined by other aircraft and we would have had a serious fight with the Luftwaffe on our hands.

However, on the day that we had returned from watching the end of *Bismarck*, none of us who had seen all those men in the water felt any joy or elation at all. We sat in the ward-room, not talking, a stiff drink in our hands, thinking our own thoughts. Sadly, none of the other people in the cockpits of those twelve Swordfish that flew over *Bismarck* when she capsized and sank is still alive. It is, after all, something that happened almost seventy years ago. All I know is that there has not been a single day of my life when the image of those poor men struggling in the freezing oily water has not entered my mind, and I do not expect to see a day when it doesn't.

14

After the *Bismarck*

Back in Gibraltar we had a few days' rest before embarking on another mission into the Mediterranean. The navy had been suffering some terrible losses. Germany had invaded Greece at the beginning of 1941; the British army had retreated to Crete. In May German paratroopers had landed there and attempted to send troop ships in support of them. There were very heavy casualties on both sides, with most of the German troop ships sunk by the Royal Navy, but the Germans managed to capture the airfield on Crete and from that moment the battle was lost. Reinforcements arrived by air and, at about the same time that we had been flying over *Bismarck*, Admiral Cunningham in Alexandria was told to organize the evacuation of British troops from the beaches on Crete.

We had almost no air cover and the Luftwaffe really went for the warships, whose only defence was the anti-aircraft guns on the cruisers and battleships. The carrier that had been sent to replace *Illustrious*, HMS *Formidable*, suffered damage from several bombs at the beginning of the German campaign and, like *Illustrious* before her, had to leave for repairs in a US shipyard. I had seen *Formidable* in the fitting-out yards at Harland and Wolff in Belfast when I had learned to fly solo.

She had not been in service for long. These armoured carriers carried so few planes, and their supply was so erratic, that when she was under attack *Formidable* was able to launch just six serviceable Fulmars. There were at times almost four hundred German aircraft based in Sicily and Italy, so it was no surprise to learn that the evacuation of the British and New Zealand armies from Crete had cost Cunningham dearly. It was a real trial of strength between the Royal Navy and the German air force. Unfortunately, we lost. Two battleships, *Barham* and *Warspite*, were put out of action for months, as was *Formidable*. Seven cruisers were either sunk or badly damaged, six destroyers were sunk and around two thousand sailors were killed. But seventeen thousand soldiers were evacuated from Crete.

When not bombing ships, the Luftwaffe was bombing Malta, and keeping that island defended and alive occupied *Ark Royal*'s time after our return to Gibraltar.

Most of June was spent on anti-submarine patrols in combination with convoys. The major effort was to keep supplying Malta with Hurricane fighter aircraft, which were brought down from the UK either in *Argus* or in *Furious*. The latter, like her sister ship *Glorious*, which sank off Norway in 1940, was a conversion of a First World War battlecruiser with a flying deck built over the hull and the bows projecting a fair way forward of the flight deck. She had a small island located in the same place as that on a modern carrier – that is, on the starboard side amidships – but there was another small bridge on the port side that was used for navigating and directing the flying operations.

We must have delivered about 130 Hurricanes to Malta in a month, with only one serious incident. The Swordfish could be launched from the *Ark* using the forward catapults, so we still carried out our early-morning anti-submarine patrols just as dawn was breaking, and then the first Hurricane would roll down the flight deck. It was important to get the Hurricanes off the *Ark* quickly, because if we were attacked by the Italian or German air force, we would want to start operating the Fulmars. On one mission in June *Furious* started launching her own Hurricanes, but the second plane that went down the flight deck veered sharply to port, smashing into the navigating position. One of the Hurricane's long-range fuel tanks was ripped off and the plane crashed into the sea. The fuel spilled out, caught fire and started spreading along the port side. The carrier had to turn quickly out of the wind and come to a stop while the fire was dealt with. Nine people were killed, and as the smoke rose up into the sky we realized it was not a very healthy position to be in: in full daylight the chances of the column of smoke being spotted by an Italian reconnaissance aircraft were quite high. However, the fire was put out, and the flying off continued.

At the end of the month my squadron, 818, was due to be rotated back to the UK and replaced by 825 Squadron. I was eager to get back home, but I was told by the CO that another pilot and I from 818 were going to be assigned to *Furious*. I was not pleased. Leaving *Ark Royal* to go home was one thing; leaving to go and fly off a converted battlecruiser was something else entirely. However, there was little I could do, except look forward to an endless round of flying anti-submarine patrols as the old *Furious* plugged her way through the Bay of Biscay on her return to the Clyde.

The accommodation in *Furious* was not up to the standard of the *Ark*, but more important to me was that there was not the same sense of purpose and camaraderie on board. There was no feeling that the ship was run for the benefit of the air group, rather than vice versa. I came in for some special attention because I had served in the *Ark* and also, I suspect, because I had taken part in the *Bismarck* attack, although I did not make a big thing out of it.

The exhaust from the boilers on *Furious* was not vented through a vertical funnel, but was instead channelled along large ducts that ran down both sides of the hangar deck and poured out a stream of hot gases at the rear of the flight deck. This sometimes caused a bit of turbulence when aircraft were landing on and I was always cautious with it. There were instructions about how to land on and the atmosphere on the carrier made me feel that I should play by the book, so I was meticulous in my landing-on procedures. One day, however, I was summoned to see the captain, who complained to me about the time I was taking to land and how long he had to remain out of line while I did so. He ended the meeting with the remark, 'I thought you *Ark* pilots were meant to be the best!' and dismissed me.

I thought, 'How dare he!' and was determined that I would show him. At the end of my next patrol, instead of landing on in the normal way and following the directions of the deck landing officer, I flew through the convoy, approaching along the side of the carrier from the bow, level with the flight deck. I saw everybody, including the deck landing officer, looking at me with their mouths open, then as I reached the round down I pulled back on the stick, went vertically up and executed a stall turn. I rolled the plane through 360 degrees and then, with a blip of the throttle, settled her down gently to land squarely on the flight deck, catching the second arrestor wire. Nobody said a word while I unbuckled and climbed out, but the tannoy bellowed out a message: 'Sub-Lieutenant Moffat to report to the captain.'

He could have thrown the book at me, and looking back it was a very stupid thing for me to have attempted, but curiously all he said to me was, 'Moffat, I haven't seen flying like that since the last time I was at the Hendon flying display. Don't repeat it,' and he walked off. 'And **** you too,' I thought.

That was the last I heard of it, and it was the last time that I heard any comments about either *Ark Royal* or my ability as a flyer.

We were escorting a 10-knot convoy of slow merchant ships from Gibraltar to the Clyde. It was dreadfully monotonous, carrying out patrol after patrol, and the only consolation was that I was heading home. It seemed an age since I had journeyed in the reverse direction, to Gibraltar, a young man fresh out of training without even a single deck landing to my credit. Now, just a few months later, I had recorded eighty deck landings, seven catapult take-offs and four hundred hours of flying time in my logbook. Plus one torpedo attack.

Furious came to anchor, finally, in the Clyde and I was posted back to my old squadron, 818, which had in my absence taken up residence in Arbroath. We had a new CO, a Lt Commander Terence Shaw, who was known as 'Shaggy' because of his beard. We had got to know each other in the *Ark*, where he had been an observer with 820 Squadron. Although he was a likeable enough sort, for me he did not have the charisma of Lt Commander Coode.

While I was at Arbroath I took every opportunity to fly to HMS Sanderling at Abbotsinch so that I could pursue my courtship of my dear Marjorie, the girl to whom I had proposed so impetuously after that Sunday afternoon tea party. We had corresponded all the time that I was away, and her letters had been extremely important to me – a reminder that there was another life, separate from the broad expanse of ocean and the routine of existence on board the carrier. She lived about 10 miles south-west of Glasgow at a place called Shilford.

I would take the tram to Barrhead, where she would meet me in her Morris 8. She ran a hairdressing business on the south side of Glasgow and one of the strange vagaries of wartime regulations was that this was considered an essential occupation. I can't think why, unless it was thought vital to the maintenance of civilian morale, but it meant that Marjorie could not join any of the women's services and was given a petrol ration for her car for her daily business use. It was a real joy to go for a spin in the countryside. I had not seen Marjorie since I had left to join *Ark Royal* and a great deal had happened in the intervening months. Much of what I had seen and felt had affected me deeply, but I was loath to unburden myself on to her. I knew that I would most likely have to leave for another tour of duty soon and I did not want her to worry unduly about what might be happening to me.

Also, I wanted to enjoy the peace and calm of her company without disturbing it by talk of bombing raids. It was an abrupt transition between life in the *Ark* and my relatively tranquil days in Scotland, and I wanted to keep them separate. I was becoming extremely attached to Marjorie, and I hoped I could see a long-term future with her, stretching way past the end of the war, if I managed to survive it. I wasn't that keen to go away again, so my next posting with 818 Squadron suited me down to the ground. It would have been marvellous to stay in Arbroath, or even better Abbotsinch, but at least we were still almost in Scotland, although in a place with the unfortunate name of Twatt, in the Orkneys.

Twatt was only half finished during our stay, so we were billeted in half-finished sheds nearby and were driven into the base by lorry every day. The place was awful, a sea of mud. We had a lot of new members in the squadron and spent a great deal of time trying to get them into shape, with dive-bombing practice and various other exercises. We also started to carry out joint manoeuvres with the army. This lasted for a few weeks at Twatt and then we moved yet again, this time to Machrihanish, at Campbeltown in Kintyre. This was particularly disliked by the southerners in the squadron, who hated the weather and couldn't pronounce the name. It was always Machri-bloody-Hanish to them. Here our joint exercises with the army were part of the development of planning for amphibious operations.

Like most pilots everywhere, we were constantly on the lookout for ways to brighten up the day and have a little fun, particularly if we could play a practical joke on the pongos – our not very complimentary nickname for soldiers. On one of these exercises four of our Swordfish were to play the role of enemy aircraft. The army was going to be storming the beach from landing craft and at a crucial moment we were going to dive-bomb the troops. They would then be expected to get into their positions to set up what anti-aircraft defences they had and deal with casualties. Having been briefed on the exercise the day before, we decided that we would make it a little more realistic for them. We spent the next few hours raiding the cookhouse and the sickbay. From the cookhouse we took sacks of flour, which we divided up into smaller paper bags. We debated taking potatoes, but someone pointed out that they could cause serious injury if they were dropped from any height. In the sickbay we liberated a large number of condoms and filled them with water.

Next morning we took to the air, with the observers carrying haversackloads of flour-and-water bombs to launch at the poor lads struggling up the beach. We arrived over the exercise area and there below us were the landing craft, just grinding through the breakers, their ramps crashing down and the army charging out of them. Thunder flashes were going off and there was the noise of gunfire – blanks, fortunately – from some of the machine guns that had been set up. We were to commence our dive-bombing attack five minutes into the landing. To our surprise, the army was accompanied by a naval officer in his blue uniform with shiny black gaiters. He was obviously acting as the beachmaster, the officer in charge of the landing area, responsible for the unloading and organization of immediate supplies and ammunition stocks. Without any communication between us at all, we immediately realized that we had the perfect target, and in turn we took our Swordfish down into a dive directly at him. In an instant his lovely uniform was covered in sticky white flour, while he stood impotently shaking his fists at us.

Extremely well pleased with ourselves, we formatted on to Shaggy, the CO, to return to Machrihanish. As we turned over the harbour at Campbeltown to make our approach, his engine started faltering and he began to lose height. I continued to follow him, with Shaggy standing up in the observer's position waving desperately at me to shear off. I would have none of it, thinking I would do the decent thing and keep him company, when I realized that his Swordfish was going to land in Campbeltown harbour and I was going to follow him. He had run out of petrol. He went down and down and down. I pulled up as his Swordfish hit the sea with a splash. I flew on, landed at Machrihanish and couldn't wait to tell everyone the news: 'The CO has landed in the water at Campbeltown. Drinks all round – Shaggy is buying.' He got his own back the next day, however, because I was ordered to go to the diving school established by the navy in Campbeltown, where I had to assist with the recovery of the aircraft. All day I stood on a pontoon as the divers secured ropes and buoys to the Swordfish, which was stuck in the mud 30 feet below the water. By the time the main plane appeared out of the murk, I was absolutely chilled through and through.

There were no official repercussions from our attack on the beachmaster, although we never tried it again. The exercises continued throughout the time I was in Machrihanish and I was to learn later that they were preparations for landings at

Diego Suarez in Madagascar. The art of amphibious landings was in its infancy. All the landing craft, with their ramps or with big bows that opened to unload troops or tanks, were quite new inventions and were still being developed.

In September I was taken out of 818 Squadron yet again and drafted on to that old floating shoebox, *Argus* – although this time I got on board without having to resort to a fast motor-boat as the carrier steamed out to sea. I was one of two Swordfish crews escorting a convoy bound for Gibraltar. When I got aboard I was astonished to find that there were also Wrens on the carrier. They were all of petty officer rank. This must have been the first time that Wrens had been allowed on board a warship at sea and they had the best accommodation, because all the officers in *Argus*, including the captain, had given over their cabins to them. They were the finest bunch of young ladies that you could imagine and as the voyage progressed they naturally became even more attractive. I struck up conversation with them as soon as I could and discovered that they were special cipher clerks on their way to work in the signals and radio listening stations on Gibraltar. They had been rushed aboard *Argus* because they were replacements for an original detachment of Wrens who had been killed when their passenger boat was torpedoed in the Bay of Biscay. The fate of their predecessors cannot have been a very comforting thought to them, but they seemed to cope with it admirably and they were marvellous company on the two-week voyage. If I hadn't had to go out on patrol in the Swordfish, the whole cruise would have been just marvellous.

There was no let-up in the hunt for enemy submarines. I tried to point out to one of the Wrens, to whom I had taken a particular liking, that I was in the front line in defending them from harm and I had no doubt that, if I had been around then, their former colleagues would have arrived safe and sound in Gibraltar. As it was, I was risking life and limb every time I took off.

Unfortunately, this line turned out to have more truth to it than I cared for. One day during the voyage we had had an uneventful patrol quartering the sea for 10 miles in front of the convoy, keeping our eyes peeled for the track of a periscope in the water, the most obvious sign of a U-boat shadowing the convoy, or for any other disturbance that might reveal a submerged wake or a fuel leak. However, as usual we had seen nothing.

As we approached the carrier to land on, my observer received a signal asking us to drop our depth-charges astern of the convoy. They gave no reason, but we assumed that an asdic operator on one of the escort vessels had picked up some echoes that suggested a U-boat might be following us. We had no indication of where the target might be, but I turned round and made a wide circuit to do as I had been instructed.

I flew across the combined wakes of the carrier and the merchantmen about 1 mile astern of the convoy, flying at about 50 feet above the sea, with the intention of dropping my two depth-charges in a line. It might not sink a U-boat, but the explosions might persuade the captain to stay submerged for a while longer, where his speed was reduced, or further slow him down by making him take some evasive manoeuvres.

I pressed the button and no sooner had the depth-charges released from the racks under the wings than there was an almighty explosion and I was physically pummelled by a massive blast, the Swordfish being flung into the air from 50 feet to a height of 300 feet. A wave of very hot air engulfed us and the smell of burned explosives filled my nostrils. For some strange reason, the depth-charges had exploded on the surface of the sea, rather than at what should have been their pre-set depth in the water. The equivalent of 500lb of TNT had exploded directly underneath us with an enormous force.

The Swordfish was wallowing around and I immediately struggled to get it under control. To my alarm, I saw that the bottom main planes had been torn open by the blast, revealing the ribs and stringers over which the canvas was stretched. There was no floor left in the cockpit and I could see down past my flying boots to the sea below.

I had lost communication with my crew so had no idea what condition they were in. There was a good chance that they had received more of the blast than I had, but I was preoccupied with the effort to keep the Swordfish in the air. With the control column pushed as far forward as possible I could just manage to keep her level, but it took an enormous force to hold the stick forward and I had to use my feet as well as my hands. I shouted down the Gosport tube that connected me with the rear cockpit to anyone who might be listening to fire a red emergency flare. I do not know whether anyone did or not. I managed to steer a course to *Argus*, adjusting the height to a degree by using the throttle. As we headed for the flight deck I saw the deck landing officer vainly waving his bats, but I was in no position to respond. We were sinking fast: I thought I had misjudged my height and I was going to crash straight into the open quarterdeck beneath the flight deck at the stern. I saw some ratings start to run from their gun stations as they realized I was heading directly for them, but I managed to lift my Swordfish nose up with a blip of maximum power on the throttle. This was not a time to worry about elegance – we were yawing from side to side, and as soon as I saw that the round down was underneath us I cut the engine and we smashed down on to the metal plates of the flight deck in the heaviest landing I have ever made.

To my relief, my observer and TAG were unharmed, although probably pretty shaken up and confused by now.

They were able to drop straight out of the bottom of the fuselage on to the flight deck, for they had been hanging on in their harnesses with their feet and legs exposed to the slipstream. The bottom part of the fuselage had been completely blasted away. Later that evening my rigger and fitter asked me to meet them in the hangar. I was told to look up under my rudder bar at the bottom of the petrol tank and there, sticking into the tank, was a large piece of shrapnel from the depth-charge casing. I was told that I was very lucky because the metal would have been red hot from the explosion. The rigger turned to me and said, 'Well, at least you know that a self-sealing petrol tank does work!'

There was, however, some consolation to this almost fatal disaster. The Wren, who had become somewhat blasé about my line-spinning of the dangers I faced every day, had witnessed the whole incident. That evening she went out of her way to be extremely comforting. I was very sad to see her go when we got to Gibraltar.

We escorted the next convoy back from Gibraltar to the Clyde with more anti-submarine patrols, then I was back once more with 818 Squadron, to be told that we were changing over to a new aircraft called the Albacore. This was a modernized version of the Swordfish and had an enclosed cockpit, but it did not have the handling ability of the old Stringbag. The engine, a Taurus radial, was not as reliable as the Pegasus and I don't think you would find a Swordfish pilot who preferred it.

In November 1941 came the news that *Ark Royal* had been sunk coming back from another Malta supply mission. She was torpedoed just outside Gibraltar. I was extremely sad to hear this news. It was a minor miracle that all bar one man had been rescued, but I felt the loss personally. My experience of the Fleet Air Arm so far was that the *Ark* was a remarkable ship, not just because she was more modern than any other carrier I had served on, and more comfortable, but because I thought she was superbly well run. Someone remarked to me that on the *Ark* food was ready when you wanted it, not when the galley said it was. This seems a petty thing to say, but if you were a mechanic or armourer, struggling through the night to get sufficient planes ready to range on the flight deck by first light, it made a big difference if you knew that food would be available no matter how late you finished your work. The *Ark* had been my home for nine months, and it was on her that I felt I had won my spurs and found a maturity and pride that up to then my life had been lacking. I looked back to the time when we had turned round in a gale to launch our attack on *Bismarck*, superb manoeuvres as bombs and torpedoes narrowly missed us, the riggers and fitters who never gave me a duff aircraft, and I didn't think I would ever again serve on a ship that had the same easy pride in her abilities. Subsequently, talking to other former crewmembers, I knew that I wasn't the only one to think this.

In January 1942 we were, I think, the only front-line Fleet Air Arm squadron in Britain. At the end of the month we received a signal in the duty office at Machrihanish to mobilize and head to Hatston in the Orkneys. The German battleship *Tirpitz*, the sister ship of *Bismarck*, had been moored in the German port of Kiel and reconnaissance indicated that she was no longer there. The possibility that she was trying to break out into the Atlantic like *Bismarck* was alarming. After Pearl Harbor, we were now fighting a war in the Pacific against the Japanese and the surface fleet was even more stretched. *Prince of Wales*, one of our most modern battleships, which had been part of the initial engagement with *Bismarck*, had been sunk by Japanese bombers along with the battlecruiser *Repulse*, the sister ship of *Renown*, our old companion in Force H.

We flew up the Great Glen, the big glacial valley that cuts through the Highlands and carries Loch Ness, heading northeast. We encountered snow all the way up, then the weather followed us towards Wick. We eventually landed at Hatston that night. The squadron arrived in one piece, despite the poor conditions, but half the aircraft could get no hangar space. The Met office had issued a gale warning and it seemed every aircraft for miles around had landed for shelter. Eight of us ended up in perimeter bays, where we covered and tied down our aircraft as best we could.

The gale hit Orkney that night while we were still eating in the wardroom. The temperature plummeted as the wind whistled round the buildings. We could not get to our bunks in a Nissen hut, as the snow was blowing horizontal and there was a white-out. Anyone going outside would barely be able to stand up and would inevitably get lost, with fatal consequences. So we stayed that night in the wardroom, keeping the fire going and sleeping in our uniforms on the leather-covered chairs and settees.

Next morning the blizzard had abated, but the snowfall had been very heavy. We had to dig ourselves out of the snowdrifts that had heaped up against the doors and then trudge through 2 feet of snow down to our aircraft. We got an enormous shock, because the bays where we had left our Albacores the night before were completely empty. These aircraft, weighing over 3 tons each, had been picked up by the gale-force winds and blown for hundreds of yards, some of them as far as the waters of the bay next to the aerodrome. None of them was flyable without major repairs. There was nothing left for us to do except wait for replacement planes.

We were stuck there for over two weeks, kicking our heels, and while I was there I heard not about *Tirpitz*, which had moved north to anchor again at Trondheim in Norway, but about the awful tragedy surrounding the escape of the two

German battlecruisers *Scharnhorst* and *Gneisenau*. I had searched for these two raiders over thousands of square miles of Atlantic Ocean, until an aircraft from *Ark Royal* had finally found them, but it was too late – there was not enough daylight left to mount an attack. So they had escaped us and had made it safely to the French harbour at Brest. A month or so later they were joined by *Prinz Eugen*, the heavy cruiser that had accompanied *Bismarck*.

There these three ships had remained, with *Prinz Eugen* in dry dock undergoing lengthy repairs. Late in 1941 photo reconnaissance carried out by the RAF showed that *Prinz Eugen* was now afloat, and that the two battlecruisers had also left the dockside and were moored in the harbour. A build-up of smaller warships, including destroyers and motor torpedo boats, had been observed at Brest. Germany had to do something with these ships – the question was what? Would they make another foray into the Atlantic, to be joined by *Tirpitz*, and hope to pursue the mission that *Bismarck* set out to do? Or would they make an effort to return to port in Germany? The Admiralty had even considered the possibility, now that the *Ark* had been sunk, that these heavy units of the German navy might make a run through the Straits of Gibraltar into the Med to operate out of Genoa.

British intelligence took the view that a return to a German port was most likely, but that still left open the route they would take. Over the month of January the ports all along the coast of France and Holland were the scene of increased movements by motor torpedo boats and minesweepers, and it looked as though the Germans would try to get their three big warships back home via the English Channel. This was not as absurd as it might seem, because this route would give the German navy the best air cover they could hope for during the day, and it was assumed that they would attempt passage through the Straits of Dover at night. All that remained to discover about their intentions was the date that these ships were going to put to sea. The main striking force against them, if they attempted to pass up the Channel, was going to be some twin-engined Bristol Beaufort torpedo bombers operated by the RAF, but the Fleet Air Arm's 825 Squadron of Swordfish aircraft was sent to Manston airfield in Kent to take part in the attack. Under Lt Commander Esmonde, 825 had of course flown off *Victorious* to attack *Bismarck* and had then subsequently replaced 820 Squadron on *Ark Royal*. We had had a fine old party when they joined us in Gibraltar, and I vaguely remember winning a wrestling contest with one of their pilots, Percy Gick, later that night. When the *Ark* was sunk most of the squadron on board were temporarily disbanded, so 825 had only just been re-formed. With just six Swordfish, it was placed on standby, ready to intercept the German warships. The RAF constantly carried out reconnaissance patrols of the approaches to Brest harbour, so it seemed that we were ready to deal with any breakout by *Scharnhorst*, *Gneisenau* and *Prinz Eugen*.

On the night of 11 February four radar-equipped RAF Hudson aircraft were patrolling the approaches to Brest, but two of them suffered an equipment failure. In one of those horrible coincidences, the three large German warships slipped out to sea at the same time, accompanied by a fleet of almost thirty destroyers and fast torpedo boats. This nighttime move took us completely by surprise. The assumption had always been that the Germans would seek the cover of night to negotiate the Straits of Dover, and in order to obtain this they would have to leave Brest and sail up the western approaches in daylight, giving the Royal Navy and the RAF ample time to intercept them. Leaving Brest when they did meant that they would be in the Channel at Dover in broad daylight, but their departure had given them an advantage of secrecy which they were now able to continue to exploit. The large number of ships steaming around the Cape of Ushant and up the Channel was observed twice by us. The first time they were spotted by two reconnaissance Spitfires, but their pilots assumed it was just one of our large convoys; and the second time the RAF pilots who saw the ships recognized them for what they were but did not report their sighting until they had landed for fear of breaking radio silence! All the forces that had been mobilized to stop the German warships were now caught on the back foot and were desperately struggling to regain the initiative. There was still snow on the ground when at 1055 on the 12th, 825 Squadron at the RAF base in Manston received news of the German ships' approach up the Channel.

Esmonde quickly got most of his crews together, although one of the six Swordfish was carrying out some practice torpedo drops in Pegwell Bay, and the armourers and ground crew started loading torpedoes and topping off the fuel tanks of the five at Manston. A joint attack with the Beaufort torpedo bombers from Thorney Island near Chichester, part of the original plan, now seemed very difficult to execute. There was just not enough time to coordinate the routes, radio frequencies and rendezvous times.

The German warships were already close to the Straits of Dover, so Esmonde elected to take off as soon as the squadron's Swordfish were ready; it was expected that they could be in the air at 1220, with an attack on the enemy ships commencing just fifteen minutes later. The Swordfish that was in the air, flown by Sub-Lieutenant Rose, had been recalled and the other crews had already moved out to their aircraft on their hard standings when he landed. Esmonde briefed Rose while he was waiting in the duty office for a telephone call that would confirm the enemy's position and tell him what air cover he could expect from the RAF.

A group of Royal Navy motor torpedo boats had been

mobilized. They had made contact with the German warships and called in with the latest position. Esmonde hoped they would be able to mount an attack at the same time as the Swordfish were going into their dive. The RAF was going to put five squadrons of fighters into the air to defend the Swordfish, three from Biggin Hill and two from Hornchurch. They were scheduled to rendezvous with 825 Squadron over Manston, but again the pressure of time prevented proper coordination. Only one fighter squadron of ten Spitfires had arrived over the airfield when Esmonde ordered his Swordfish to take off. He felt that there was no more time to waste, because the ships had already passed thought the Straits and were steaming away at 28 knots.

Another two squadrons of Spitfires, however, did fly straight to the target area, where they were met by German fighters, but the aircraft from Hornchurch never managed to navigate to the scene of the action. Esmonde had briefed his squadron to form into two sub-flights of three planes each and to make an approach to their targets in line astern, to keep their profile as small as possible. German fighters pounced on them when they were still over the English coast and their Spitfire escort of just ten planes was utterly over-whelmed. The Luftwaffe had not only put Messerschmitt 109s into the air, but the new, faster Focke Wulf 190 fighters were also deployed and were the equal of, if not better than, the Spitfire mark Vs that were then used by the RAF.

The six Swordfish continued their approach to *Scharnhorst*, *Gneisenau* and *Prinz Eugen*. By now they had been joined by other German warships and were defended by a screen of eight destroyers, E-boats and flak ships. It was an absurdly small number of planes to send against two battlecruisers, a cruiser and their attendant fleet, which now totalled forty ships. When we attacked *Bismarck* we sent fifteen aircraft against just one battleship and scored at most three hits. The concentrated anti-aircraft fire that the Swordfish crews would have to confront does not bear thinking about. In addition, the German air force had more than two hundred aircraft on standby and they dominated the air above their warships. The Swordfish were hit by machine-gun and cannon fire from the Focke Wulf fighters that swarmed around them long before they could get within dropping range of their targets.

Lt Commander Esmonde was leading his flight in at 50 feet when he was hit. His aircraft's right lower wing started to disintegrate. Then another fighter manoeuvred behind him and started pouring bullets into his aircraft. The fuselage caught fire and one of the Spitfire pilots saw the TAG climb half out of the cockpit to extinguish it, but at this point Esmonde was killed and his Swordfish crashed into the sea.

The second Swordfish in the sub-flight, piloted by Sub-Lieutenant Rose, was also attacked. Rose was wounded in the back by a shell splinter and his air gunner was killed; the same burst of fire ruptured his fuel tank as well. He had lined up on *Scharnhorst*, but he lost control when the cannon shells ripped through his fuselage and found he was flying at *Prinz Eugen*. He managed to launch his torpedo, however, at a range of 1,200 yards, but the cruiser manoeuvred out of its way. Rose tried to gain height, but with fuel pouring from his ruptured tank he realized that he was going to have to ditch. They hit the sea, and he and his observer managed to clamber out of their cockpit, released their dinghy and lay floating in it until they were rescued one and a half hours later by one of our motor torpedo boats.

The third Swordfish in Esmonde's flight, flown by Sub-Lieutenant Kingsmill, had also been hit by cannon shells, losing two cylinders out of their Pegasus engine, but it still kept running. However, the signal flares in the dinghy had been ignited by tracer bullets and the centre section of his upper wing was on fire. He too was struggling for control of

254

his aircraft, which had been hit by shrapnel, and so he launched at the target that immediately presented itself, which also happened to be *Prinz Eugen*. His torpedo failed to hit and Kingsmill crashed in his Swordfish just after turning away. He and his crew had only their lifejackets to keep them afloat, but fortunately they were picked up by a British fishing boat that had been engulfed by the battle.

The second flight had for some unknown reason flown into the attack at a higher altitude, and as they approached over the destroyer screen they were met head on by a section of Messerschmitt fighters and were all shot down. Only five men survived the attack out of eighteen who had set off from Manston.

We were all shocked by the news: 825 Squadron had been wiped out and many brave men had lost their lives. There were also very heavy casualties in the Spitfire squadrons, who had been badly briefed on what to expect. I could not help reflecting on how, a few months earlier, so much time had been spent searching for these ships, and now they had escaped after being barely 10 miles from Dover Castle. It was a sad, frustrating incident and my mood, and that of my squadron, was exacerbated by being stuck, helpless, 500 miles away in the Orkneys. Esmonde received a posthumous Victoria Cross for his part in the raid, but I feel that every single one of the men who flew that day deserved it. Like us in our attack on *Bismarck*, 825 Squadron was thrown into action as a last resort when everything else had gone wrong. We survived, they didn't.

15
Another Carrier

In wartime events could quickly lead to a radical change in circumstances, sometimes overnight. Within three or four days of our replacement aircraft arriving at Hatston we were instructed to fly to Machrihanish and then on to Belfast, where I had completed my first solo flight. Once there we loaded on to *Formidable*. The 'Formy', as we called her, had, like me, seen plenty of action since that day in early 1940 when I had flown over her at Harland and Wolff. She was a more modern aircraft carrier than *Ark Royal*, similar to *Illustrious* and *Victorious*. Like them, she had been built with an armoured flight deck and this extra weight meant that there was only one hangar deck, not two as there were in the *Ark*. This reduced the number of aircraft that could be carried. An advantage she did have over the *Ark* was that her deck-lifts were wider, so she could carry Sea Hurricanes, although at the time these were in incredibly short supply.

Formidable had been sent into the Mediterranean in January 1941 to take the place of her sister carrier *Illustrious* after the latter had been hit and badly damaged by German dive-bombers. *Formidable* had taken part in the Battle of Matapan, where her Swordfish had torpedoed two Italian cruisers and her fighters had shot down two Junkers 88 bombers. The 'Formy' took part in the fleet bombardment of Tripoli, but these armoured carriers always had to contend with the problem of keeping enough fighter aircraft operational, and sailing to attack Scarpanto airfield she was damaged by near misses from two 1,000lb bombs. Fragments from the blasts penetrated the boiler rooms and her speed was reduced. So, like *Illustrious* before her, she was withdrawn to Alexandria and then made the journey to the United States for major repairs. Once these had been completed she had returned to Belfast to have new radar equipment fitted and to work up before going into active service.

My feelings were mixed. Going to sea for another tour of duty would tear me away from Marjorie. I knew that after another few months I would be desperate for the sight of dry land, and the hills and fields of Scotland. Also, there was the feeling at the back of my mind that ever since I had survived the bomb blast at Worthy Down I had been quite fortunate, and I wondered how long my luck would last.

Our arrival on board was peculiar, I remember, because we flew to Sydenham airfield in Belfast then taxied our Albacore aircraft, with their wings folded, down a narrow Belfast street to the dockside, where they were then hoisted aboard by crane.

Britain faced a very difficult situation at this time. The Japanese navy had successfully launched a major attack on the US fleet at Pearl Harbor in Hawaii on 7 December, showing that they had learned the lesson of Taranto and that they understood the importance of naval aviation. Three days later their carrier-borne bombers had successfully sunk two British warships, *Prince of Wales* and *Repulse*, which had been sent out to reinforce the British fleet at Singapore. The Japanese army had quickly fought their way down through Burma and Malaya, and at about the same time as we were getting our aircraft on to *Formidable*, the order was given to the army in Singapore to surrender to the Japanese.

We had our hands full with getting the squadron and stores and administration embarked on the carrier, so we probably paid less attention to events in the Far East than we did to the German warships escaping down the Channel. Also, the German Afrika Corps under Field Marshal Erwin Rommel was advancing in North Africa and it was clear that things were not going very well for us all round. Now we were going into a part of the world that was unfamiliar to most of us, to face an enemy that was unknown. There was a lot of talk in the papers about the inferiority of the Japanese and their poor ability as fighting men, but the latest events seemed to prove otherwise. When we had an odd moment, we pored over the charts to get some idea of where we would be going, and we tried to locate identification charts of Japanese warships and aircraft, but information was sparse.

Formidable had spent six months in the United States and her crew had become used to what we gathered was generous hospitality, with food and nightlife that it was impossible to find any more in Britain. The Fleet Air Arm squadrons that were now ensconcing themselves in the hitherto empty hangar deck and ready rooms were for the most part just out of training school and still had a lot to learn. However, there was no time to work up the ship and carry out the range of exercises needed to make sure that we would hold our own in combat. Our job was to get out to the Far East as quickly as possible to reinforce what resources we still had out there. What training there was going to be would have to take place during the journey round the Cape.

One pleasant surprise was the discovery that Admiral 'Slim' Somerville, who had commanded Force H when I was in the *Ark*, was going to be in charge of the Eastern Fleet, as we were to be known, and he was going to hoist his flag on

Formidable until we got to Ceylon (Sri Lanka today). He was, of course, a stickler for training and maintaining high standards – it was partly due to his influence that *Ark Royal* had been so efficiently run – and he took a real interest in our flying-off times and how quickly we could land on, refuel and range up again. That, after all, is what an aircraft carrier is all about: the effectiveness of the entire fleet can hang on the efficiency of the carrier's flight deck.

Sure enough, as we sailed down the Irish Sea and set out on the first leg of our journey to Sierra Leone, there was a whole programme of exercises – in navigation, direction-finding, torpedo attacks – and anti-aircraft-gunnery practice for the gun crews on *Formidable* and our escorts.

Sadly, I took little part in any of this. The medical staff had inoculated us against yellow fever and other tropical infections, and I had been badly affected by some of the after-effects of these injections. I was confined to the sickbay with a very high fever for several days and then forbidden to fly until I was fully recovered. I did not return to flying duties until we docked in Sierra Leone, but on the way down we had lost four Albacores through accidents, and it was clear that Somerville was not happy with the way the ship was working.

The Indian Ocean was second in importance only to the North Atlantic at that time in the war. It carried cargo and troop traffic not only from India, New Zealand and Australia to Europe, but also, with the near impossibility of getting any-thing through the Mediterranean safely, the western edge of the Indian Ocean saw all the traffic supplying the British Eighth Army in Egypt and North Africa. The Japanese advance to Singapore posed a serious threat to this and we were on a heightened alert for enemy submarines gathering around the Cape of Good Hope, so the flying programme became very intense. We were now called upon to practise nighttime operations as well. The potential strength in the air of the Japanese fleet led Somerville to think that our only chance of carrying out a successful torpedo attack on units of their navy was to do so under cover of darkness. At the time we didn't know whether the Japanese ships were equipped with radar – we thought that they weren't – so it might have given us an advantage. The radar that had been fitted to some of our Swordfish had proved very useful in the search for *Bismarck*, but there was more to a night attack than finding and fixing the position of the enemy. Judging the speed and distance to the target, the sea conditions and, crucially, one's height over it could all affect the success of a mission and required a lot of experience and nerve.

On any one day the flying programme would start at dawn with the standard reconnaissance patrols and anti-submarine sweeps. Then our Fulmar fighters would take to the air for practice in radar direction and deck landings. *Formidable*'s single Swordfish would then tow a target sleeve over the fleet for firing practice and then a torpedo-attack exercise was conducted in the afternoon. Often Somerville would be a passenger in one of the Albacores and this certainly helped him gauge not only the expertise of his squadrons, but also their morale and general level of self-confidence. His willingness to get stuck in like this, and his general disregard for formality, extended his excellent reputation to those who had not already served under him. It did not endear him, though, to some of the regular navy types, who had not been brought up to get their hands dirty.

On one particular night-flying exercise, carried out by the Albacores of 820 and 818 Squadrons, several pilots found it hard to make a deck landing; four or five had to go round more than once without catching the arrestor wire. One pilot in particular found it hard and the deck landing officer remarked that if he didn't make it on the next attempt he would have to be shot down. He did finally land, but then, to everyone's growing alarm, the bridge realized that another aircraft had failed to return from the exercise. It was Mike Lithgow from 820 Squadron, who had been a friend of mine on the *Ark* and one of my colleagues when I flew against *Bismarck*. Most officers would have sailed on and started writing letters to the next-of-kin, but Somerville ordered his destroyer escort to continue while *Formidable* turned round and went back on her course. At slow speed, with our four 32in searchlights flickering over the surface of the ocean, we hunted for our lost airmen. I always remember the strong beam from the lights playing across the waves; wherever it stopped for a minute or two the sea would boil as huge shoals of fish flocked to the intense light. I wondered what good we could do, and thought that Mike was going to be another casualty of the war. Then a lookout suddenly shouted. He had heard the sound of a distress whistle in the darkness and a few minutes later there was the Albacore's crew, in their liferaft, the yellow lifejackets reflected in the searchlight's beam. They had ditched their aircraft because of engine failure. That night I think if Somerville had ordered us to fly to Tokyo we would have had a crack at it. He was later to do something similar on a grander scale, which again illustrated what we all thought was real humanity.

The pilot who was rescued that night, Mike Lithgow, later became a test pilot for Vickers and captured the world's absolute speed record in a Swift jet fighter. Sadly, in 1963 he was flying the prototype BAC 1-11 passenger aircraft when it stalled and crashed, killing him and his crew. But that night in the Indian Ocean he had all the luck in the world.

The intense working-up continued until we reached Cape Town, where at last we experienced the largesse of which the sailors had had their fill in the United States. We anchored at the foot of Adderley Street, the road that runs down to the dockside and seems to guide the eye up the steep sides of Table Mountain at its end. On our first run ashore we stood open-mouthed at the food and merchandise for sale. Piles of fresh fruit – oranges and bananas, which we hadn't seen for ages – shirts, tailored suits and clothing in the windows: it was a rather grim reminder of just how much rationing and austerity had affected us back in the UK. However, we were here now and we were going to enjoy it as much as we could. We found a restaurant, the name of which I can still recall – The Blue Lagoon; and then floating on a sea of good food and alcohol we continued up that wide street, our eyes peeled for any girls who wanted to make the acquaintance of a group of heroic pilots. We had only gone 100 yards when some of us found a large store selling a huge variety of musical instruments. The owner was very friendly and was happy to let us try out the instruments, and in no time at all we were putting together a small band, with me on the banjo, performing to a crowd that had gathered in the street. God knows what they made of us.

We received some remarkable hospitality. A regular RN friend from Glasgow, 'Jock' Stewart, and I were chauffeured everywhere by a couple of friendly, attractive women. We were met in the morning and driven out to the country for a picnic, then back in the evening to a night club called the Bohemian, and everywhere we went it was on the house.

Needless to say we were not keen to leave, but there was a war on and we once more put to sea for exercises and patrols. There were also plenty of games. A good ship will make sure there are plenty of competitive sports for people to take part in. In the *Ark* we had played deck rugby and soccer, and *Formidable* had a well-supported deck hockey league. Played by teams of seven a side, with various departments in the ship competing against each other, this could be quite hazardous. The rules were made up more or less as we went along, the puck was made of a rope's end, and the hockey sticks were any piece of bent metal or wood that could be pressed into service. The victors were not necessarily the most skilful, but the toughest.

We steamed on across the Indian Ocean, heading for Colombo in Ceylon. There was an important naval base on the island at Trincomalee, and Ceylon itself was the source of most of our supplies of raw rubber. With Singapore now in Japanese hands, holding on to Ceylon was absolutely vital if we wanted to keep control of the Indian Ocean. We expected the Japanese to make a move on the island at some time, but nobody knew when. Somerville had moved his flag on to the battleship *Warspite*, and with the rest of the Eastern Fleet – a First World War vintage cruiser, HMS *Enterprise*; a modern County class cruiser, HMS *Cornwall*; and a few destroyers – *Formidable* docked in Colombo.

Our air group flew off and landed at Ratmalana, which was south of the capital, and we carried out maintenance, swung our compasses and flew operations from there until *Formidable* put to sea again. We made regular long-range patrols, alert for any signs of the Japanese fleet. Looking back, I am very glad I did not come across any sign of them, because I don't think we would have lasted long.

When we left Colombo we met up with a much larger and strengthened fleet. Our sister carrier HMS *Indomitable* had joined us, and we also had three more battleships, *Revenge*, *Resolution* and *Royal Sovereign*, and eleven cruisers. The fleet patrolled to the south of Ceylon, with patrols taking up to three and a half hours at a time. On one of these I got caught in a tropical storm, which blew up extremely quickly. We could not, of course, get above the weather, so it became extremely hairy. There was an enormous amount of lightning and we were struck several times. Each time the compass gyrated violently, there was a strong smell of ozone, and I felt as though I had actually been shocked, although the plane was not in contact with the ground and so could not transmit a current.

More alarming was the presence of enormous thunder heads, with extremely violent turbulence underneath them. I feared for the plane's structure, as we suddenly rose in the air, then descended like a stone for several hundred feet. We fought our way through the driving rain, struggling with the controls to keep an even keel, being hurled about in the cock-pit just praying that the compass had not been permanently affected. After an hour of this I felt as though I had been flying in a giant washing machine. I was utterly exhausted, and anxious, not sure that we would get out alive. However, we plugged on and eventually reached some calmer weather. Was I glad to see the flight deck of the 'Formy' after that, and the pink gins were lined up in the wardroom for me that night!

It seemed that the top brass were so certain that Ceylon would fall to the Japanese that we had set up a secret refuelling base at a remote island group called Addu Atoll in the Maldives. The southernmost island later became known as Gan, and was an RAF base after the war. It is apparently a tourist destination now, but then it was a godforsaken spot and very unpleasant. Almost on the Equator, a runway had been built for our aircraft out of crushed coral and large oil-storage tanks had been erected. It didn't have the spares and servicing facilities of a normal shore-based dockyard and there was absolutely no reason to seek shore leave!

We flew our patrols as we journeyed there as well, and I remember one particular incident that makes me wonder if the heat and long, monotonous patrols didn't send us all more than a little crazy. I was flying along the Equator on an extremely hot day with the sun bouncing off a flat, calm ocean. I was trying to concentrate on the compass and maintain my visual search of the horizon. The fatigue level was building up. I had my cockpit open, otherwise it became absolutely stifling in the hot sun, and I felt a tap on my head. The Albacore was different from the Swordfish not only because the cockpit was enclosed, but because my seat was entirely separate from the observer's and TAG's position. There was a fuel tank between us, and we could communicate only via our headsets. Then there came another, more insistent tap on my head, so I turned. I saw a hand holding a bar of chocolate level with my eyes. I looked up and there was my observer, Midshipman Woodward. He had left his seat and climbed out in order to give me this piece of 'nutty' as we called navy-issue chocolate. I grabbed it and he gave a thumbs-up, then clambered back to his own cockpit. It was some time after we had landed that it suddenly struck me how absurdly dangerous it had been. He had become either so bored or so blasé that he had completely ignored the risks of falling to his death in the Indian Ocean.

We had berthed at Addu Atoll and were in the process of refuelling, and loading any stores available, when we were ordered to be ready to put to sea as soon as we finished oiling. Reconnaissance aircraft had signalled the presence of Japanese warships 200 miles to the east of us, and they were heading north-west. At midnight we set off to find them. We would not be able to stop them from attacking Ceylon, which we were certain was their target, but might be able to launch an attack on them as they retreated. The information about them was patchy. Two Catalina aircraft that had approached the enemy fleet had been shot down before they could pass on much more than their course and position. In fact, as we found out later, the Japanese fleet was commanded by Admiral Nagumo, who had taken part in the attack on Pearl Harbor, and he had five aircraft carriers, with 350 aircraft, and they had an escort of four battleships and three cruisers.

We had never before confronted an enemy that had its own carrier fleet. The Germans and Italians had never possessed carriers; the big threat we had faced in both Norway and the Mediterranean was land-based fighters and bombers, particularly those of the Luftwaffe. The Japanese, however, had invested heavily in their fleet's air arm. Their carriers were designed for large numbers of modern aircraft, and they had tremendous endurance. They were able to operate the fast Zero fighter from their flight decks – the same aircraft that was on front-line duty in the Japanese air force – and their torpedo aircraft, like the 'Mabel' and 'Kate', were modern single-engined planes able to carry a torpedo or 1,600lb of bombs on a 700-mile mission. Like the Swordfish and Albacore, they had a pilot, an observer and a reargunner, but they were almost 100 knots faster. They also had another dive-bomber, the 'Val', which could carry an 800lb bomb and reach 260 knots. What was to prove most decisive, though, was that the Japanese fleet could put these aircraft to sea in great numbers.

On 5 April, the Japanese bombed Colombo, causing considerable damage. They lost seven aircraft, but twenty-five of our Fulmars and Hurricanes were shot down by the Zero fighters escorting the bomber force. They were outclassed and overwhelmed.

However, as serious as this attack was, there was worse to follow. Not all the ships in the Eastern Fleet had made it to Addu Atoll with us on our refuelling trip. HMS *Hermes*, a small aircraft carrier built at the end of the First World War, had been permanently on station in the Far East. *Hermes* was modern in appearance, really the first purpose-built aircraft carrier, but she was only able to carry a maximum of twenty planes and was not very stable in any kind of poor weather. These were the reasons she had never been moved out of the

Indian Ocean to take part in operations in the Atlantic or the Mediterranean. She was in dock in Trincomalee undergoing repairs, and two heavy cruisers, *Dorsetshire* and *Cornwall*, were also in port in Colombo. *Cornwall* had just escorted a troop convoy, and *Dorsetshire* was carrying out repairs to her engine room. I had last seen her at sea almost a year earlier, when I had flown over *Bismarck* as *Dorsetshire* fired three torpedoes into her hull. All three ships had put to sea at the end of March, when the first indications that an attack on Ceylon was about to take place were received. When this seemed to be a false alarm, they had returned to port.

Now, a week later, when Somerville received the signals that warned him of the Japanese fleet's presence, both *Dorsetshire* and *Cornwall* were once again ordered to put to sea and make a rendezvous with us on our course from the Atoll. The admiral's estimate was that, once they had made their attack, the Japanese would head for home. We still, of course, had no accurate idea of the size of their carrier force. Most of the units that our reconnaissance had located were battleships, they were still about 320 miles away and it was expected that if we maintained our present course for the next twenty-four hours a combined force of torpedo-armed Albacore from us and from *Indomitable* might have a crack at them. *Dorsetshire* and *Cornwall* were thought to be 120 miles south of the Japanese and moving away from them. Radio silence was being strictly adhered to, so we did not expect to hear from them until one of our reconnaissance patrols spotted them. Then later that afternoon a signal was received saying that the two cruisers had seen a shadower. Nothing further was heard, but they must have been perfectly sure that they had been located by the enemy, otherwise they would not have broadcast the signal and given away their position.

Around 1600 hours we were preparing for a briefing to

make our first night attack on the Japanese. The galley had put on a decent grilled supper, although many of us didn't seem to be very hungry.

Shortly before we sat down to eat, at around 1530, a patrolling aircraft saw some wreckage floating in the sea, with some survivors in the water. Another reconnaissance patrol spotted the Japanese fleet again, this time 100 miles to the north of us, and it included carriers and battleships. The Japanese carriers put up a section of Zero fighters to attack the reconnaissance patrol, which managed to make a successful run back to *Formidable*, and it was now clear to us that a large Japanese force was in the Indian Ocean and was not planning on going home. It was probably searching for us, and Somerville decided at that point that he was in danger of meeting up with a far superior enemy. He made a decision to cancel our planned attack and attempt to preserve his fleet.

The Japanese had seen our reconnaissance aircraft and had to assume that we were aware of their presence and their position. Somerville calculated that they would expect us to retreat to the west. This we did under cover of darkness, but we then turned and headed east again. We did not know what had happened to *Dorsetshire* and *Cornwall*, but it was obvious the Japanese had either sunk them or badly damaged them. Somerville was determined to save as many of their crews as he could and sent a cruiser and two destroyers ahead of the main fleet. It was a very tense time. Throughout the early morning our patrols went out and there were radar traces of patrolling enemy reconnaissance aircraft, but miraculously the Japanese never found us. It was a nasty situation though. This was utterly typical of Somerville, and it must have taken strong nerves to believe that his reading of the Japanese intentions was correct. If he had got it wrong, we would all have paid the price.

We found the wreckage of both ships, with hundreds of

men in the water, and we learned that they had been attacked by between forty and sixty dive-bombers. Each cruiser had been hit at least eight times. They had sunk within fifteen minutes of the first bomb being dropped. The Japanese pilots were clearly well trained and determined. It was another grim lesson for us, but there was a plus side: we had managed to save twelve hundred sailors and there was a feeling throughout the carrier similar to that when Somerville had retraced our course to find Mike Lithgow. We had an admiral in command who was going to look after us.

Admiral Nagumo had not finished with us yet, though. He steamed north-east, then north-west, and on 9 April bombed the port of Trincomalee on the north-east coast of Ceylon, again causing a lot of damage to the dockyard and to the China Bay airstrip. *Hermes* was also caught at sea: she was attacked by seventy dive-bombers and hit forty times. Her escorts, the Australian destroyer HMAS *Vampire* and the corvette *Hollyhock*, and two oil tankers were also sunk.

In the space of a few days we had lost two heavy cruisers, and a carrier, several escorts and around twenty-five merchant ships had been either sunk or damaged in the attacks on the harbours. We retreated once more to Addu Atoll to refuel, the heavier battleships with us having an endurance of only four days at sea at high speed. Around this time, *Formidable* suffered a mechanical problem when one of the large gears driving the central propeller stripped its teeth and we were reduced to 8 knots. It was said on board that the two near misses that she had suffered in the Mediterranean had twisted her frame and her central propeller shaft was permanently misaligned but, whatever the reason for the failure, we were clearly of no use until it was fixed, so we sailed slowly for the docks in Bombay.

The repairs took ten days, and when we returned to Colombo I was sorry to learn that a good friend of mine

'Bagshot' Thompson, whose father was the provost of Edinburgh, had died on the *Hermes*. 818 Squadron was disbanded and I was attached to 820 Squadron. In company with *Indomitable* we headed south and moored at the beautiful harbour of Mahé in the Seychelles. There was clearly a senior officer's conference, and the next day we were informed that we were going to assist in the landings on Madagascar, which was controlled by the Vichy government. We feared that the island would be offered as a refuelling base for both German and Japanese submarines, which would then be able to attack shipping using the southern route via the Cape of Good Hope. The Japanese had some large and very long-range submarines in their fleet, and intelligence had been received that they were planning to take up station in the channel between Madagascar and Mozambique. Our landings were to be made from landing craft, supported by *Illustrious* and *Indomitable*, and the battleship HMS *Ramillies*. *Formidable* would be further out at sea, providing air patrols and a combat air patrol from our Fulmars and the new American fighter bombers that we had on board, the Grumman Wildcats. The amphibious force, composed of infantry and Royal Marines, landed in the bay at Diego Suarez in the north of the island. They met stiff resistance from the Vichy forces and the fighting went on for several days, with our forces suffering around five hundred casualties. My contribution to this was to fly two long-range patrols a day for around three days – eighteen hours in all. The French army retreated to the south and we secured the port on 7 May, but it took several months of sporadic fighting before all the French forces had surrendered.

At the end of the month, surprisingly, the Japanese did show themselves. Two corvettes patrolling the bay picked up a sonar contact and started depth-charging the area. It was a Japanese midget submarine and, despite the fact that it was under attack, it fired two torpedoes, one of which hit *Ramillies*, while the other hit an oil tanker, *British Loyalty*. There were, in fact, two midget submarines, which had been ferried to Madagascar by two of the large long-range ocean-going submarines in the Japanese fleet. The second ran aground without being able to make an attack and the crew were killed.

By then, however, we had left and sailed to Mombasa, on the Kenyan coast, mooring in the Kilindini river. On the way there a strange thing happened one night. Sailing in the tropics, we got permission to use a campbed on the quarter-deck, which was open at the rear. You were more or less above the propellers, but got used to the noise – there was nowhere quiet on a big warship anyway. One night I awoke to hear a faint shout for help. I could not fathom where it was coming from and crawled forward to the guard rail on my hands and knees to listen.

Again I heard this faint call for help, so I crawled further to my right and could just see a pair of hands hanging on to the deck edge. I grabbed a wrist and shouted for assistance, and eventually managed to haul a young officer on board. I have no idea how he got there and neither, he claimed, did he. He was lucky to be alive. The doctor arranged for him to be locked in his cabin and he was discharged when we got to harbour. A ship is no place for a sleepwalker.

When we arrived at Mombasa, I was sent to assist in the building of an airstrip about 50 miles inland. The RAF already had a base in Mombasa at Port Reitz, which was to become Mombasa airport, but apparently another one was needed at a small railway halt called Mackinnon Road, on the main line from Mombasa to Nairobi. It was in the middle of nowhere, with absolutely nothing on the horizon, just a rail sign. I was the only officer with two petty officers and about thirty men. We lived in tents and all our supplies, including water, were brought to us by train. There was one train in the morning heading to Mombasa and another in the evening making the return journey to Nairobi. The airstrip was a pre-fabricated one, made of sections of metal mesh that we laid down and joined together. The construction was completely dependent on the irregular delivery of the metal sections by train.

It was a very unpleasant and unhealthy place. The one saving grace was that I had a Swordfish aircraft, so I managed to fly to Tanga and Nairobi for a regular supply of quinine tablets and other medication. I also had to ferry quite a few cases of malaria to Mombasa hospital. There was a waterhole a mile away which was regularly visited by wild animals at night. In the dusk we could hear the lions making their loud grunting roars and I managed to get some rifles to guard against any attacks. It was an extremely debilitating task and after a few weeks of intense heat, an infestation of scorpions and large black spiders, I was very glad when I was recalled back on board.

During the time that I was at Mackinnon Road, my first visitor was an amazing female pilot flying a twin-engined de Havilland Rapide. She was dressed in RAF battledress with no rank or insignia, just RAF wings. Her name was Evelyn and I enjoyed flying with her – and she was able to secure quinine tablets more easily than I could. Evelyn had been a commercial pilot in Kenya before the war and had answered a call for volunteers in 1939. Her story was that the recruiters had assumed she was male, so by the time she arrived at the airbase in Nairobi she had been assigned a service number and it was too late. She was not allowed to take part in combat, but as far as I was concerned she was a damned good pilot.

Mackinnon Road eventually became a town with a mosque, all from a few bricks at the rail side and a metal runway. Ironically, Tim Coode, my old CO of 818 Squadron from the *Bismarck* attack, died there in January 1943 when a Grumman Martlet he was flying crashed as he was taking off.

Back in *Formidable*, heading to Addu Atoll, I was made deck landing officer to replace Lt Commander Cubitt, who had had an unfortunate accident when he fell off the flight deck trying to avoid an aircraft that had attempted to land on. I found it a great relief, as the patrols in the Albacore were beginning to get me down, although I had to be on duty early, making sure that the aircraft for the dawn patrols were ranged properly and that the flying schedule was organized and properly notified to the squadrons.

So we went back to Colombo, in the company of *Illustrious* and *Indomitable*, patrolling the Indian Ocean, crisscrossing the Equator, escorting convoys to India, training and exercising but never coming across the Japanese who, after their carrier fleet had made airborne attacks on Colombo and Calcutta, and their submarine foray to Madagascar, had abandoned any expeditions into the Indian Ocean. With a full programme of flying, coordinating with two other carriers, there were plenty of accidents, and one stands out in my mind as being as dreadful as any I had witnessed.

We were towing a target buoy behind us for a dive-bombing exercise and a Swordfish from *Illustrious* was taking part. The plane was at 1,000 feet when the pilot rolled and went into his dive, and suddenly the wings on his plane folded back. I had heard stories of occasions when the bolts holding the wings straight had started to loosen, but I had never experienced it, nor did I know anyone else who had. The bolts were checked by the rigger each time the wings were straightened after coming up from the hangar deck.

But now there was nothing to be done. The Swordfish continued uncontrollably in its dive: it went straight down vertically, hitting the sea at 200 miles an hour. There was no wreckage and no survivors, of course, despite the fact that a destroyer circled the area for some time. I think it was the most heart-wrenching accident that I ever saw, and I have seen a few.

By August we learned that we were scheduled to return to the UK via Cape Town – a move which I had wished for for some time.

Shortly before this we left Colombo for Mombasa and then were due to sail on and call at Durban. One evening, Brok Brokensha knocked on my cabin door and asked me to play a tune for him on my fiddle. Brok was an old colleague, originally a Skua pilot on *Ark Royal*; he was also one of my South African friends at Arbroath. In fact, he was one of the three I had left at the hotel in Princes Street in Edinburgh on my way to visit my parents on my last leave before joining the *Ark* myself. We had met up again on the 'Formy', where he was flying Grumman Wildcats. He was a great pilot and had shot down several enemy aircraft, being awarded the Distinguished Flying Cross. He had married a girl he met in Scotland, a real stunning beauty, and I liked him a great deal. He had the cabin opposite mine and we often spent time in each other's company.

We sat and talked that night and I played, at his request, 'Smoke Gets In Your Eyes' on my violin. Then we turned in, as I had to be on deck first thing, and I knew Brok was on the first combat air patrol to be launched the next morning.

Next morning, Brok's Martlet was ranged up and was scheduled to be the first for take-off, but there was no sign of him. Despite repeated calls on the tannoy for Lieutenant Brokensha to report to the flight deck, he still didn't turn up, so eventually I climbed into the cockpit of his plane and taxied it out of the way so that the rest of the section could take off. When the flying off was finished I went down to Brok's cabin. His bunk had not been slept in. We never found him. The carrier was searched from keel to flight deck, but there was not a trace of him. Brok came from Durban, and when we docked there we had a difficult visit from his parents, who were naturally distraught, but couldn't offer any reason for his disappearance. I was the last person to see him alive and continually went over in my mind that last evening that I saw him, when he had come to my cabin, but his behaviour had seemed perfectly normal. It was a complete mystery, and a very sad one.

So we left Durban, made a halt at Cape Town and Sierra Leone, and eventually docked at Greenock. After a couple of weeks' leave I was sent as an instructor to 824 Squadron to assist in deck-landing training.

I had been there a few weeks when I collapsed with a very high fever. At first I imagined that I had suddenly started a bout of malaria, although I had not suffered from it at all during my sometimes arduous postings in the Eastern Fleet. I had been extremely nervous of getting it while I was based at Mackinnon Road, but unlike many others there I had escaped it. When a Wren saw me, however, she immediately called for an ambulance and rushed me to hospital. She was right. My arm and left shoulder had started to swell, and in the emergency ward I was diagnosed as having septicaemia. I was seriously ill for around ten days, drifting in and out of consciousness, until I awoke, very thin and weak, to observe a buxom matron with more medals on her chest than Montgomery standing next to me. I was extremely lucky to be alive, she told me, and I believed her. I think that my natural resistance to infection had been weakened by the inoculations I had been given at the start of my cruise on *Formidable*, and the stress and strains of the tour of duty had not helped, but to this day I still do not know why I became so ill without any warning.

On the day the matron said that I was fit enough to go for a walk, she told me to go to the hospital gates and turn right.

'Why right?' I asked.

'Because left is to the pub.'

I did as I was told (I must still have been extremely weak) and walked along a lovely stretch of road with the sea to one side. After a mile I came to the local churchyard, which was enclosed by an old stone wall. Quite prominent was a large, black gravestone with the frightening words engraved on it: HERE LIES JOHN MOFFAT. I could not bring myself to walk past it, and returned to the hospital.

After a period of sick leave, I had a medical examination and was told that I would not be recommended for carrier duties again. To my surprise, I found that I was not unduly upset. Something had gone out of me – whether it was the endless patrols over the Indian Ocean or the gradual weariness at friends and colleagues dying I don't know, but carrier operations no longer seemed so exciting. It was a truth that I had not admitted when I first heard I was to be sent to *Formidable*. I had done the best that I ever could in the *Ark*, and deep down I did not believe that anything could reach that pitch again. I needed something else.

I was posted to become officer in charge of flying at a satellite base in the south of England, Naval Air Station Cowdray Park, near Midhurst in Sussex. Here I was responsible for the preparation of aircraft to go into squadron service after they had been delivered from the manufacturer. Later, with D-Day approaching, I took on further responsibilities for organizing air transport around the country and communications to liberated areas of France. I became friendly with the CO of a Communications Squadron at Lee-on-Solent, Sir George Lewis, who, in civilian life, had been a well-known lawyer. Sadly, shortly after D-Day, he died in northern France when a Hudson aircraft crashed soon after take-off, killing everyone on board, including Admiral Ramsey, who had planned the amphibious operation of 6 June.

While I was stationed there I persuaded Marjorie to travel down to meet me and get married. At last she consented. The plan was that I would meet her in London and, because travel restrictions in the south of England were getting tighter and tighter as D-Day approached, I would be able to escort her to Midhurst. I had pursued my relationship with her whenever I had the opportunity. Naturally I had not seen her while I was in the *Ark* or *Formidable*, but my dogged approach had paid dividends. I had taken regular leaves in Scotland, and gradually she had come round. We had decided to get married some time before I went to Midhurst, but the question really was when. My father, when he heard the news, was outraged. It was utter foolishness to get married in wartime, according to him – but I had never listened.

So I went to London and stayed at the Russell Hotel in Russell Square in order to be able to get to Euston to meet Marjorie on the platform as her train from Glasgow came in. The next morning, as I was preparing to leave the hotel, there was an air-raid warning. This was not for the Luftwaffe flying overhead, but attacks from V1 flying bombs were now commonplace throughout the south of England. I heard one go over and crouched in the hotel lobby, thinking that I would be late. The all-clear still did not sound. I decided that I had to leave and started to walk north to the station. Suddenly I heard another V1 clattering overhead and then it cut out. I flung myself against a building and waited. The explosion was tremendous: the buzz bomb had landed in the next street. It was dreadful. A horrible stink of burned wood, rubble and brick dust got up my nostrils. Pieces of debris were flying everywhere, windows were shattered, and there was a deathly silence after the explosion before the ambulance bells started.

I lay on the pavement, unhurt, but a little frightened and covered in dust.

Eventually the all-clear went and I stood up and dusted myself down. I was nearly an hour late. Running to the station, I hoped Marjorie would still be there. Of course, sometimes the trains were very late. Sometimes they were stopped outside London during an air-raid alert, but I had no way of knowing. I rushed into the station and found it completely empty. All the trains had left, no doubt because of the raid. I went up to a porter and asked about the Glasgow train. Oh, that had been and gone, he said, forty-five minutes ago.

I didn't know what to do. I walked to the platform where the train should have been standing. At the far end I spotted a figure sitting on two large cases. I rushed down the platform and, sure enough, it was Marjorie. 'You knew I would come, didn't you?' I asked.

'I couldn't go anywhere,' she replied. 'These cases are full of champagne for the wedding. Go and fetch a porter's trolley.'

A few days later we were married, at a small church in Midhurst with a guard of honour from the ratings and petty officers at Cowdray Park. It was the best day's work I ever did in my life. Sadly, Marjorie died six years ago, suddenly, while we were on holiday in England. She was the most important influence in my life. Marrying her was the one thing that I can honestly say I have never ever regretted.

Conclusion
A Lifetime Later

I had one other accident in an aircraft shortly after the war had come to an end. I was flight testing an Albacore that had just been returned from engineering work at Lee on Solent and I was taking off from Cowdray Park in the direction of Midhurst. Everything seemed to be fine: lining up at the end of the runway, the engine was running smoothly and all the instruments looked good. I took off easily and started to climb out to 1,000 feet to go round for a few circuits. I had reached perhaps 600 feet when the engine, alarmingly, started to backfire and then cut out completely. It was standard procedure in this situation to attempt to crash straight ahead, but for some reason I decided to attempt a landing back at Cowdray Park.

I executed a quick turn and, sinking lower and lower, struggled to keep the Albacore on an even keel. There is always a point where you think that at last you have made a fatal mistake, although a crash from 600 feet would also probably have killed me. I managed, however, to coax the plane over the threshold and brought it thumping in to land.

I was commended for that action, with an entry in green ink in my logbook written and signed by my senior officer to commemorate it. That was my last flying accident until my crash in 2001.

Within a few months of the war ending I had said goodbye to the navy and started life on Civvy Street, right back in a sense to where I had been at the start of the war. I had some anxious months worrying what my future would be, but I eventually started work in the hotel industry and made a successful career out of it for the rest of my working life.

Over the years, working as a hotel manager, bringing up two lovely daughters, there has rarely been a day in the sixty-eight years since the events of 26 May 1941 when I have not remembered what it felt like to fly towards that great monster of a ship, the *Bismarck*, or what I saw the next morning as she toppled over into the sea. I kept those thoughts mostly to myself, and when I attended reunions of the Fleet Air Arm, or met some of my old colleagues from 818 Squadron in *Ark Royal* and *Formidable*, we would talk about the times we enjoyed in Gibraltar or the wardroom, or the marvellous hospitality we encountered in Cape Town or Mombasa. I was very fortunate to build friendships after the war with some of the officers from *Ark Royal*. I was to meet both Lt Commander Stringer and Commander Traill in peacetime, and we were able to enjoy each other's company over a meal and a drink. We did not dwell on the past, but occasionally we would talk about what had happened to so many of our former friends. Sadly, many of the pilots who took part in the *Bismarck* attack did not survive the war. It's worth observing that most of their deaths were caused by unexplained crashes or mechanical failures of some kind. This was a brutal fact of life in the Fleet Air Arm; it is one of the reasons why even operations that were apparently uneventful patrols over the ocean could ultimately become stressful.

The story of the sinking of the *Bismarck* eventually took on a life of its own. A few years after the end of the war there was a well-known feature film, *Sink the Bismarck!*, starring Jack Hawkins, and several books and articles were published. Most of them seemed to downplay the importance of the Fleet Air Arm, our fifteen Swordfish and the absolutely vital nature of our intervention in preventing *Bismarck* from reaching St-Nazaire.

In 1989 the man who found the wreck of *Titanic*, Bob Ballard, discovered the wreck of *Bismarck*, and this started a fresh wave of interest in the German warship. Since his discovery, several other expeditions have filmed the wreck or tried to investigate it by using research submarines. Some of these, and the TV documentaries that were made about them, have attempted to argue that *Bismarck* was not sunk, but was scuttled by her own crew.

In 2004 I heard that the wreck of *Ark Royal* had also been discovered, and a few months later I found myself on board a very large yacht, operating a remote underwater camera. I was allowed to manoeuvre this camera as though I were landing on the flight deck of *Ark Royal*, now lying 3,000 feet below the surface of the Mediterranean. It was a remarkable feeling – I never in all my life imagined that something like that would be possible, never mind that I would be the one so privileged to do it. From that same yacht I was able to look at many other pieces of the wreck, including the wreckage of a Swordfish aircraft that I think had fallen from the flight deck when the *Ark* was torpedoed six months after attacking *Bismarck*.

On the whole, I think knowledge of the events around the sinking of the *Bismarck* should be kept alive, if only to prevent anything like that happening again.

But a few years before I looked at *Ark Royal* once again, something else was brought to my attention: a report into the attack that was written with the assistance of the Fleet Air

Arm Museum in the Royal Naval Air Station at Yeovilton in Somerset. This report tried to answer the question, 'Whose torpedoes hit the *Bismarck*, and where?' I need to repeat that there was a great deal of confusion during the attack and it was almost impossible to tell what was happening. In the debriefing after we had landed on we tried to be as factual as we could, but drawing up an accurate picture was impossible. The atrocious gale, the bad visibility, *Bismarck* herself manoeuvring violently behind a wall of gunfire, all conspired to prevent any one person forming an accurate picture of their own role in the attack, let alone building up any sort of wider vision. In the immediate aftermath we didn't believe that we had caused any damage. It was not until reports from *Sheffield* and the reconnaissance Swordfish confirmed that *Bismarck* had radically altered her course and appeared to be out of control that some very tentative assessments by some of the pilots were suddenly transformed into firmer facts. I think this was natural. Many senior pilots had had the experience of reporting hits on warships to find that they were later mistaken. It was, though, still unclear whose torpedoes had actually hit the ship, let alone whose had been the one that damaged the rudder, and at the time it was not of great importance to us. Our main concern was getting some rest before we had to mount another attack in the morning.

I never claimed any result from my attack. As a junior sub-lieutenant in the Volunteer Reserve, I was not self-confident enough to make any claim before the likes of Tim Coode or the senior pilots of 810 and 820 Squadrons. But this new document, compiled by a young American researcher, Mark Horan, using action reports written at the time, came to the conclusion that out of the two pilots who could possibly claim to have dropped the torpedo that hit *Bismarck*'s stern, myself and Lieutenant Keane, I was the most probable candidate.

It is now so long after the event I think it is impossible to say anything with any certainty. If it was my torpedo, as the report suggests, that crippled the *Bismarck*, then I feel no personal pleasure in this, any more than I did at the time. I saw the result, which few others have had the misfortune to do, and no matter how pleased I might be to remove a threat to Britain and our convoys, I cannot take any satisfaction from the deaths of nearly two thousand sailors. Many people have said that we attacked *Bismarck* to seek revenge for the loss of *Hood*. Nothing could have been further from our minds. We did it because we were at war and it was our job. If we thought of anything – and we did – it was the threat that *Bismarck* presented to our ships, to our merchant fleet and to Britain's survival.

What I would say is that the forty-three crew members of the fifteen Swordfish that attacked *Bismarck*, and I was one of them, did what was demanded of us, and anyone in the wardroom who saw us afterwards would know what that effort cost us. If we hadn't decided that we could fly in such appalling conditions, if we hadn't pressed on against the gun-fire, if we had failed, then the *Bismarck* would have escaped to safety. That was something that the senior officers in the navy did not want to admit. We were in the Fleet Air Arm and, what's more, we were in Force H – a slightly irregular operation headed by a slightly irregular officer, Admiral Somerville, who barely six months previously had had to face allegations that he was not sufficiently aggressive in taking on the Italian fleet. Similarly, the investigations that purport to show that *Bismarck* was scuttled, that she was destroyed by her own crew, tend to write us and the whole of the Royal Navy out of the picture.

Whether or not it was my torpedo that hit the *Bismarck*'s stern and made her uncontrollable does not really matter to me. What is important is that I along with the rest of my colleagues did it. Flying back to *Ark Royal*, desperate to find the safety of the flight deck in a darkening night and a stormy sea, no one realized it then, but after our attack the end was inevitable. It was only a matter of time – the *Bismarck* was sunk.

Author's Note

I met John Moffat in February 2002 when I was producing a series about the history of the navy. Even then, I was surprised by his energy and his sense of humour. It hasn't diminished. We continued to meet, and when I heard that he was being pressed by his children to put on paper what he remembered of his early life, I suggested to him that there might be a book in it. He was hesitant at first, but after a few months I was allowed to look through the initial notes he had produced, and I managed to persuade him to continue. We met several times, and as we talked and discussed various drafts of the chapters, personalities and incidents arose fresh in his memory.

The story that John has to tell is unique because he was one of the very few pilots in the Fleet Air Arm who took part in the attack on the *Bismarck*, an action that required a great deal of courage, skill and luck, and which really did affect the course of the Second World War. John's account, however, is a deeply human one, and since I have known him he has never tried to hide how affected he was by what he saw when the *Bismarck* sank, or how he felt when so many of his friends were killed, or disappeared. These emotions are common to the great majority of people who lived through the war years of 1939–45, or indeed of those who took part in the wars that have happened since, and I think that it is for this reason that John's story deserves the widest possible audience. It is almost beyond imagination now to read or hear about what ordinary people were once called upon to do, and it should not be forgotten.

John and I checked a great deal of his story against documents in the National Archives and other records, but in the one or two instances where there seemed to be some discrepancy, I decided to rely on John's memory. I take full responsibility for this, because during my search for the wreck of the *Ark Royal*, I learnt that sometimes personal memories, if they are very strong, can be as accurate as the official account.

Mike Rossiter

Picture Acknowledgements

Where not credited, photographs were kindly supplied by John Moffat.

Page 2/3
Argus, c. 1928: © TopFoto; Swordfish brought up to the deck, *Argus*, c. 1935: © Hulton-Deutsch Collection/CORBIS; Skua and Swordfish on deck, *Ark Royal*: courtesy Percy North; extra pilots standing by, *Ark Royal*: IWM A3740.

Page 4/5
Scharnhorst, 1936–9: © ullsteinbild/TopFoto; Admiral Somerville: © Trinity Mirror/Mirrorpix; bombs miss the *Ark Royal* off Norway; view of bombing from *Ark Royal* and bombs dropping in the Mediterranean: all courtesy Percy North; battle of Oran, 1940: © Hulton-Deutsch Collection/ CORBIS; ships in Taranto harbour, 12 November 1940: © 2003 Topham Picturepoint; *Hood*, 24 May 1941: © Trinity Mirror/Mirrorpix/Alamy.

Page 6/7
Hitler inspects the *Bismarck*, 12 April 1941 – 2nd from left, Admiral Günther Lutjens, 3rd from left, General Field Marshall Wilhelm Keitel, next to Hitler, Captain Ernst

John Moffat

Lindemann: akg-images/ullsteinbild; the *Bismarck* seen from the deck of the *Prinz Eugen*: © 2000 Topham Picturepoint; the *Bismarck* firing at the *Prince of Wales*, 24 May 1941; survivors from the *Bismarck*, 27 May 1941: © Trinity Mirror/ Mirrorpix/Alamy; *Formidable* enters Sydney Harbour, spring 1945.

Index